# Nutshell Series
# Hornbook Series
and
# Black Letter Series
of
# WEST PUBLISHING COMPANY
P.O. Box 64526
St. Paul, Minnesota 55164–0526

---

## Accounting

FARIS' ACCOUNTING AND LAW IN A NUTSHELL, 377 pages, 1984. Softcover. (Text)

## Administrative Law

GELLHORN AND LEVIN'S ADMINISTRATIVE LAW AND PROCESS IN A NUTSHELL, Third Edition, 479 pages, 1990. Softcover. (Text)

## Admiralty

MARAIST'S ADMIRALTY IN A NUTSHELL, Second Edition, 379 pages, 1988. Softcover. (Text)

SCHOENBAUM'S HORNBOOK ON ADMIRALTY AND MARITIME LAW, Student Edition, 692 pages, 1987 with 1989 pocket part. (Text)

## Agency—Partnership

REUSCHLEIN AND GREGORY'S HORNBOOK ON THE LAW OF AGENCY AND PARTNERSHIP, Second Edition, 683 pages, 1990. (Text)

STEFFEN'S AGENCY-PARTNERSHIP IN A NUTSHELL, 364 pages, 1977. Softcover. (Text)

## American Indian Law

CANBY'S AMERICAN INDIAN LAW IN A NUTSHELL, Second Edition, 336 pages, 1988. Softcover. (Text)

## Antitrust—see also Regulated Industries, Trade Regulation

GELLHORN'S ANTITRUST LAW AND ECONOMICS IN A NUTSHELL, Third Edition, 472 pages,

**Antitrust—**Continued

1986. Softcover. (Text)

HOVENKAMP'S BLACK LETTER ON ANTITRUST, 323 pages, 1986. Softcover. (Review)

HOVENKAMP'S HORNBOOK ON ECONOMICS AND FEDERAL ANTITRUST LAW, Student Edition, 414 pages, 1985. (Text)

SULLIVAN'S HORNBOOK OF THE LAW OF ANTITRUST, 886 pages, 1977. (Text)

**Appellate Advocacy—**see Trial and Appellate Advocacy

**Art Law**

DUBOFF'S ART LAW IN A NUTSHELL, 335 pages, 1984. Softcover. (Text)

**Banking Law**

BANKING LAW: SELECTED STATUTES AND REGULATIONS. Softcover. 263 pages, 1991.

LOVETT'S BANKING AND FINANCIAL INSTITUTIONS LAW IN A NUTSHELL, Second Edition, 464 pages, 1988. Softcover. (Text)

**Civil Procedure—**see also Federal Jurisdiction and Procedure

CLERMONT'S BLACK LETTER ON CIVIL PROCEDURE, Second Edition, 332 pages, 1988. Softcover. (Review)

FRIEDENTHAL, KANE AND MILLER'S HORNBOOK ON CIVIL PROCEDURE, 876 pages, 1985. (Text)

KANE'S CIVIL PROCEDURE IN A NUTSHELL, Third Edition, 303 pages, 1991. Softcover. (Text)

KOFFLER AND REPPY'S HORNBOOK ON COMMON LAW PLEADING, 663 pages, 1969. (Text)

SIEGEL'S HORNBOOK ON NEW YORK PRACTICE, Second Edition, Student Edition, 1068 pages, 1991. Softcover. (Text)

**Commercial Law**

BAILEY AND HAGEDORN'S SECURED TRANSACTIONS IN A NUTSHELL, Third Edition, 390 pages, 1988. Softcover. (Text)

HENSON'S HORNBOOK ON SECURED TRANSACTIONS UNDER THE U.C.C., Second Edition, 504 pages, 1979, with 1979 pocket part. (Text)

NICKLES' BLACK LETTER ON COMMERCIAL PAPER, 450 pages, 1988. Softcover. (Review)

SPEIDEL'S BLACK LETTER ON SALES AND SALES FINANCING, 363 pages, 1984. Softcover. (Review)

STOCKTON'S SALES IN A NUT-

**Commercial Law**—Continued

SHELL, Second Edition, 370 pages, 1981. Softcover. (Text)

STONE'S UNIFORM COMMERCIAL CODE IN A NUTSHELL, Third Edition, 580 pages, 1989. Softcover. (Text)

WEBER AND SPEIDEL'S COMMERCIAL PAPER IN A NUTSHELL, Third Edition, 404 pages, 1982. Softcover. (Text)

WHITE AND SUMMERS' HORNBOOK ON THE UNIFORM COMMERCIAL CODE, Third Edition, Student Edition, 1386 pages, 1988. (Text)

**Community Property**

MENNELL AND BOYKOFF'S COMMUNITY PROPERTY IN A NUTSHELL, Second Edition, 432 pages, 1988. Softcover. (Text)

**Comparative Law**

GLENDON, GORDON AND OSAKWE'S COMPARATIVE LEGAL TRADITIONS IN A NUTSHELL. 402 pages, 1982. Softcover. (Text)

**Conflict of Laws**

HAY'S BLACK LETTER ON CONFLICT OF LAWS, 330 pages, 1989. Softcover. (Review)

SCOLES AND HAY'S HORNBOOK ON CONFLICT OF LAWS, Student Edition, approximately 1100 pages, November 1991 Pub. (Text)

SIEGEL'S CONFLICTS IN A NUTSHELL, 470 pages, 1982. Softcover. (Text)

**Constitutional Law—Civil Rights**

BARRON AND DIENES' BLACK LETTER ON CONSTITUTIONAL LAW, Third Edition, 440 pages, 1991. Softcover. (Review)

BARRON AND DIENES' CONSTITUTIONAL LAW IN A NUTSHELL, Second Edition, 483 pages, 1991. Softcover. (Text)

ENGDAHL'S CONSTITUTIONAL FEDERALISM IN A NUTSHELL, Second Edition, 411 pages, 1987. Softcover. (Text)

MARKS AND COOPER'S STATE CONSTITUTIONAL LAW IN A NUTSHELL, 329 pages, 1988. Softcover. (Text)

NOWAK AND ROTUNDA'S HORNBOOK ON CONSTITUTIONAL LAW, Fourth Edition, approximately 1275 pages, August, 1991 Pub. (Text)

VIEIRA'S CONSTITUTIONAL CIVIL RIGHTS IN A NUTSHELL, Second Edition, 322 pages, 1990. Softcover. (Text)

**Constitutional Law—Civil Rights**—Continued

WILLIAMS' CONSTITUTIONAL ANALYSIS IN A NUTSHELL, 388 pages, 1979. Softcover. (Text)

**Consumer Law**—see also Commercial Law

EPSTEIN AND NICKLES' CONSUMER LAW IN A NUTSHELL, Second Edition, 418 pages, 1981. Softcover. (Text)

**Contracts**

CALAMARI AND PERILLO'S BLACK LETTER ON CONTRACTS, Second Edition, 462 pages, 1990. Softcover. (Review)

CALAMARI AND PERILLO'S HORNBOOK ON CONTRACTS, Third Edition, 1049 pages, 1987. (Text)

CORBIN'S TEXT ON CONTRACTS, One Volume Student Edition, 1224 pages, 1952. (Text)

FRIEDMAN'S CONTRACT REMEDIES IN A NUTSHELL, 323 pages, 1981. Softcover. (Text)

KEYES' GOVERNMENT CONTRACTS IN A NUTSHELL, Second Edition, 557 pages, 1990. Softcover. (Text)

SCHABER AND ROHWER'S CONTRACTS IN A NUTSHELL, Third Edition, 457 pages, 1990. Softcover. (Text)

**Copyright**—see Patent and Copyright Law

**Corporations**

HAMILTON'S BLACK LETTER ON CORPORATIONS, Second Edition, 513 pages, 1986. Softcover. (Review)

HAMILTON'S THE LAW OF CORPORATIONS IN A NUTSHELL, Third Edition, 518 pages, 1991. Softcover. (Text)

HENN AND ALEXANDER'S HORNBOOK ON LAWS OF CORPORATIONS, Third Edition, Student Edition, 1371 pages, 1983, with 1986 pocket part. (Text)

**Corrections**

KRANTZ' THE LAW OF CORRECTIONS AND PRISONERS' RIGHTS IN A NUTSHELL, Third Edition, 407 pages, 1988. Softcover. (Text)

**Creditors' Rights**

EPSTEIN'S DEBTOR-CREDITOR LAW IN A NUTSHELL, Fourth Edition, 401 pages, 1991. Softcover. (Text)

NICKLES AND EPSTEIN'S BLACK LETTER ON CREDITORS' RIGHTS AND BANKRUPTCY, 576 pages, 1989. (Review)

**Criminal Law and Criminal Procedure**—see also Corrections, Juvenile Justice

ISRAEL AND LaFAVE'S CRIMINAL PROCEDURE—CONSTITUTIONAL LIMITATIONS IN A NUTSHELL, Fourth Edition, 461 pages, 1988. Softcover. (Text)

LaFAVE AND ISRAEL'S HORNBOOK ON CRIMINAL PROCEDURE, Second Edition, Student Edition, approximately 1200 pages, December, 1991 Pub. (Text)

LaFAVE AND SCOTT'S HORNBOOK ON CRIMINAL LAW, Second Edition, 918 pages, 1986. (Text)

LOEWY'S CRIMINAL LAW IN A NUTSHELL, Second Edition, 321 pages, 1987. Softcover. (Text)

LOW'S BLACK LETTER ON CRIMINAL LAW, Revised First Edition, 443 pages, 1990. Softcover. (Review)

**Domestic Relations**

CLARK'S HORNBOOK ON DOMESTIC RELATIONS, Second Edition, Student Edition, 1050 pages, 1988. (Text)

KRAUSE'S BLACK LETTER ON FAMILY LAW, 314 pages, 1988. Softcover. (Review)

KRAUSE'S FAMILY LAW IN A NUTSHELL, Second Edition, 444 pages, 1986. Softcover. (Text)

MALLOY'S LAW AND ECONOMICS: A COMPARATIVE APPROACH TO THEORY AND PRACTICE, 166 pages, 1990. Softcover. (Text)

**Education Law**

ALEXANDER AND ALEXANDER'S THE LAW OF SCHOOLS, STUDENTS AND TEACHERS IN A NUTSHELL, 409 pages, 1984. Softcover. (Text)

**Employment Discrimination**—see also Gender Discrimination

PLAYER'S FEDERAL LAW OF EMPLOYMENT DISCRIMINATION IN A NUTSHELL, Second Edition, 402 pages, 1981. Softcover. (Text)

PLAYER'S HORNBOOK ON EMPLOYMENT DISCRIMINATION LAW, Student Edition, 708 pages, 1988. (Text)

**Energy and Natural Resources Law**—see also Oil and Gas

**Environmental Law**—see also Energy and Natural Resources Law; Sea, Law of

FINDLEY AND FARBER'S ENVIRONMENTAL LAW IN A NUTSHELL, Second Edition, 367

**Environmental Law**—Continued
pages, 1988. Softcover. (Text)

RODGERS' HORNBOOK ON ENVIRONMENTAL LAW, 956 pages, 1977, with 1984 pocket part. (Text)

**Equity**—see Remedies

**Estate Planning**—see also Trusts and Estates; Taxation—Estate and Gift

LYNN'S AN INTRODUCTION TO ESTATE PLANNING IN A NUTSHELL, Third Edition, 370 pages, 1983. Softcover. (Text)

**Evidence**

BROUN AND BLAKEY'S BLACK LETTER ON EVIDENCE, 269 pages, 1984. Softcover. (Review)

GRAHAM'S FEDERAL RULES OF EVIDENCE IN A NUTSHELL, Second Edition, 473 pages, 1987. Softcover. (Text)

LILLY'S AN INTRODUCTION TO THE LAW OF EVIDENCE, Second Edition, 585 pages, 1987. (Text)

MCCORMICK'S HORNBOOK ON EVIDENCE, Fourth Edition, Student Edition, approximately 1200 pages, January 1992 Pub. (Text)

ROTHSTEIN'S EVIDENCE IN A NUTSHELL: STATE AND FEDERAL RULES, Second Edition, 514 pages, 1981. Softcover. (Text)

**Federal Jurisdiction and Procedure**

CURRIE'S FEDERAL JURISDICTION IN A NUTSHELL, Third Edition, 242 pages, 1990. Softcover. (Text)

REDISH'S BLACK LETTER ON FEDERAL JURISDICTION, Second Edition, 234 pages, 1991. Softcover. (Review)

WRIGHT'S HORNBOOK ON FEDERAL COURTS, Fourth Edition, Student Edition, 870 pages, 1983. (Text)

**First Amendment**

**Future Interests**—see Trusts and Estates

**Gender Discrimination**—see also Employment Discrimination

THOMAS' SEX DISCRIMINATION IN A NUTSHELL, Second Edition, approximately 400 pages, 1991. Softcover. (Text)

**Health Law**—see Medicine, Law and

**Human Rights**—see International Law

**Immigration Law**

WEISSBRODT'S IMMIGRATION LAW AND PROCEDURE IN A NUTSHELL, Second Edition, 438 pages, 1989, Softcover. (Text)

**Indian Law**—see American Indian Law

**Insurance Law**

DOBBYN'S INSURANCE LAW IN A NUTSHELL, Second Edition, 316 pages, 1989. Softcover. (Text)

KEETON AND WIDISS' INSURANCE LAW, Student Edition, 1359 pages, 1988. (Text)

**International Law**—see also Sea, Law of

BUERGENTHAL'S INTERNATIONAL HUMAN RIGHTS IN A NUTSHELL, 283 pages, 1988. Softcover. (Text)

BUERGENTHAL AND MAIER'S PUBLIC INTERNATIONAL LAW IN A NUTSHELL, Second Edition, 275 pages, 1990. Softcover. (Text)

FOLSOM, GORDON AND SPANOGLE'S INTERNATIONAL BUSINESS TRANSACTIONS IN A NUTSHELL, Third Edition, 509 pages, 1988. Softcover. (Text)

**Interviewing and Counseling**

SHAFFER AND ELKINS' LEGAL INTERVIEWING AND COUNSELING IN A NUTSHELL, Second Edition, 487 pages, 1987. Softcover. (Text)

**Introduction to Law**—see Legal Method and Legal System

**Introduction to Law Study**

HEGLAND'S INTRODUCTION TO THE STUDY AND PRACTICE OF LAW IN A NUTSHELL, 418 pages, 1983. Softcover. (Text)

KINYON'S INTRODUCTION TO LAW STUDY AND LAW EXAMINATIONS IN A NUTSHELL, 389 pages, 1971. Softcover. (Text)

**Judicial Process**—see Legal Method and Legal System

**Juvenile Justice**

FOX'S JUVENILE COURTS IN A NUTSHELL, Third Edition, 291 pages, 1984. Softcover. (Text)

**Labor and Employment Law**—see also Employment Discrimination, Workers' Compensation

LESLIE'S LABOR LAW IN A NUTSHELL, Second Edition, 397 pages, 1986. Softcover. (Text)

**Labor and Employment Law—Continued**

NOLAN'S LABOR ARBITRATION LAW AND PRACTICE IN A NUTSHELL, 358 pages, 1979. Softcover. (Text)

**Land Finance—Property Security**—see Real Estate Transactions

**Land Use**

HAGMAN AND JUERGENSMEYER'S HORNBOOK ON URBAN PLANNING AND LAND DEVELOPMENT CONTROL LAW, Second Edition, Student Edition, 680 pages, 1986. (Text)

WRIGHT AND WRIGHT'S LAND USE IN A NUTSHELL, Second Edition, 356 pages, 1985. Softcover. (Text)

**Legal Method and Legal System**—see also Legal Research, Legal Writing

KEMPIN'S HISTORICAL INTRODUCTION TO ANGLO-AMERICAN LAW IN A NUTSHELL, Third Edition, 323 pages, 1990. Softcover. (Text)

REYNOLDS' JUDICIAL PROCESS IN A NUTSHELL, Second Edition, approximately 310 pages, 1991. Softcover. (Text)

**Legal Research**

COHEN'S LEGAL RESEARCH IN A NUTSHELL, Fourth Edition, 452 pages, 1985. Softcover. (Text)

COHEN, BERRING AND OLSON'S HOW TO FIND THE LAW, Ninth Edition, 716 pages, 1989. (Text)

**Legal Writing and Drafting**

SQUIRES AND ROMBAUER'S LEGAL WRITING IN A NUTSHELL, 294 pages, 1982. Softcover. (Text)

**Legislation—see also Legal Writing and Drafting**

DAVIES' LEGISLATIVE LAW AND PROCESS IN A NUTSHELL, Second Edition, 346 pages, 1986. Softcover. (Text)

**Local Government**

MCCARTHY'S LOCAL GOVERNMENT LAW IN A NUTSHELL, Third Edition, 435 pages, 1990. Softcover. (Text)

REYNOLDS' HORNBOOK ON LOCAL GOVERNMENT LAW, 860 pages, 1982, with 1990 pocket part. (Text)

**Mass Communication Law**

ZUCKMAN, GAYNES, CARTER AND DEE'S MASS COMMUNICATIONS LAW IN A NUTSHELL, Third Edition, 538 pages, 1988. Softcover. (Text)

**Medicine, Law and**

HALL AND ELLMAN'S HEALTH CARE LAW AND ETHICS IN A NUTSHELL, 401 pages, 1990. Softcover (Text)

JARVIS, CLOSEN, HERMANN AND LEONARD'S AIDS LAW IN A NUTSHELL, 349 pages, 1991. Softcover. (Text)

KING'S THE LAW OF MEDICAL MALPRACTICE IN A NUTSHELL, Second Edition, 342 pages, 1986. Softcover. (Text)

**Military Law**

SHANOR AND TERRELL'S MILITARY LAW IN A NUTSHELL, 378 pages, 1980. Softcover. (Text)

**Mortgages**—see Real Estate Transactions

**Natural Resources Law**—see Energy and Natural Resources Law, Environmental Law

**Office Practice**—see also Computers and Law, Interviewing and Counseling, Negotiation

HEGLAND'S TRIAL AND PRACTICE SKILLS IN A NUTSHELL, 346 pages, 1978. Softcover (Text)

**Oil and Gas**—see also Energy and Natural Resources Law

HEMINGWAY'S HORNBOOK ON THE LAW OF OIL AND GAS, Third Edition, Student Edition, approximately 700 pages, Aug., 1991 Pub. (Text)

LOWE'S OIL AND GAS LAW IN A NUTSHELL, Second Edition, 465 pages, 1988. Softcover. (Text)

**Partnership**—see Agency— Partnership

**Patent and Copyright Law**

MILLER AND DAVIS' INTELLECTUAL PROPERTY—PATENTS, TRADEMARKS AND COPYRIGHT IN A NUTSHELL, Second Edition, 437 pages, 1990. Softcover. (Text)

**Products Liability**

PHILLIPS' PRODUCTS LIABILITY IN A NUTSHELL, Third Edition, 307 pages, 1988. Softcover. (Text)

**Professional Responsibility**

ARONSON AND WECKSTEIN'S PROFESSIONAL RESPONSIBILITY IN A NUTSHELL, Second Edition, approximately 500 pages, 1991. Softcover. (Text)

ROTUNDA'S BLACK LETTER ON PROFESSIONAL RESPONSIBILITY, Second Edition, 414 pages, 1988. Softcover. (Review)

WOLFRAM'S HORNBOOK ON

## Professional Responsibility— Continued

MODERN LEGAL ETHICS, Student Edition, 1120 pages, 1986. (Text)

## Property—see also Real Estate Transactions, Land Use, Trusts and Estates

BERNHARDT'S BLACK LETTER ON PROPERTY, Second Edition, approximately 375 pages, 1991. Softcover. (Review)

BERNHARDT'S REAL PROPERTY IN A NUTSHELL, Second Edition, 448 pages, 1981. Softcover. (Text)

BURKE'S PERSONAL PROPERTY IN A NUTSHELL, 322 pages, 1983. Softcover. (Text)

CUNNINGHAM, STOEBUCK AND WHITMAN'S HORNBOOK ON THE LAW OF PROPERTY, Student Edition, 916 pages, 1984, with 1987 pocket part. (Text)

HILL'S LANDLORD AND TENANT LAW IN A NUTSHELL, Second Edition, 311 pages, 1986. Softcover. (Text)

## Real Estate Transactions

BRUCE'S REAL ESTATE FINANCE IN A NUTSHELL, Third Edition, approximately 270 pages, 1991. Softcover. (Text)

NELSON AND WHITMAN'S BLACK LETTER ON LAND TRANSACTIONS AND FINANCE, Second Edition, 466 pages, 1988. Softcover. (Review)

NELSON AND WHITMAN'S HORNBOOK ON REAL ESTATE FINANCE LAW, Second Edition, 941 pages, 1985 with 1989 pocket part. (Text)

## Regulated Industries—see also Mass Communication Law, Banking Law

GELLHORN AND PIERCE'S REGULATED INDUSTRIES IN A NUTSHELL, Second Edition, 389 pages, 1987. Softcover. (Text)

## Remedies

DOBBS' HORNBOOK ON REMEDIES, 1067 pages, 1973. (Text)

DOBBYN'S INJUNCTIONS IN A NUTSHELL, 264 pages, 1974. Softcover. (Text)

FRIEDMAN'S CONTRACT REMEDIES IN A NUTSHELL, 323 pages, 1981. Softcover. (Text)

O'CONNELL'S REMEDIES IN A NUTSHELL, Second Edition, 320 pages, 1985. Softcover. (Text)

## Sea, Law of

SOHN AND GUSTAFSON'S THE LAW OF THE SEA IN A NUTSHELL, 264 pages, 1984. Softcover. (Text)

**Securities Regulation**

HAZEN'S HORNBOOK ON THE LAW OF SECURITIES REGULATION, Second Edition, Student Edition, 1082 pages, 1990. (Text)

RATNER'S SECURITIES REGULATION IN A NUTSHELL, Third Edition, 316 pages, 1988. Softcover. (Text)

SECURITIES REGULATION, SELECTED STATUTES, RULES, AND FORMS. Softcover. 1331 pages, 1991.

**Sports Law**

SCHUBERT, SMITH AND TRENTADUE'S SPORTS LAW, 395 pages, 1986. (Text)

**Tax Practice and Procedure**

MORGAN'S TAX PROCEDURE AND TAX FRAUD IN A NUTSHELL, 400 pages, 1990. Softcover. (Text)

**Taxation—Corporate**

SCHWARZ AND LATHROPE'S BLACK LETTER ON CORPORATE AND PARTNERSHIP TAXATION, Approximately 500 pages, September, 1991 Pub. Softcover. (Review)

WEIDENBRUCH AND BURKE'S FEDERAL INCOME TAXATION OF CORPORATIONS AND STOCKHOLDERS IN A NUTSHELL, Third Edition, 309 pages, 1989. Softcover. (Text)

**Taxation—Estate & Gift**—see also Estate Planning, Trusts and Estates

MCNULTY'S FEDERAL ESTATE AND GIFT TAXATION IN A NUTSHELL, Fourth Edition, 496 pages, 1989. Softcover. (Text)

**Taxation—Individual**

HUDSON AND LIND'S BLACK LETTER ON FEDERAL INCOME TAXATION, Third Edition, 406 pages, 1990. Softcover. (Review)

MCNULTY'S FEDERAL INCOME TAXATION OF INDIVIDUALS IN A NUTSHELL, Fourth Edition, 503 pages, 1988. Softcover. (Text)

POSIN'S HORNBOOK ON FEDERAL INCOME TAXATION, Student Edition, 491 pages, 1983, with 1989 pocket part. (Text)

ROSE AND CHOMMIE'S HORNBOOK ON FEDERAL INCOME TAXATION, Third Edition, 923 pages, 1988, with 1989 pocket part. (Text)

**Taxation—International**

DOERNBERG'S INTERNATIONAL TAXATION IN A NUTSHELL, 325 pages, 1989. Softcover. (Text)

BISHOP AND BROOKS' FEDERAL

# WATER LAW
## IN A NUTSHELL

### SECOND EDITION

By

### DAVID H. GETCHES
**Professor of Law, University of Colorado**
**Boulder, Colorado**

**ST. PAUL, MINN.**
**WEST PUBLISHING CO.**
**1990**

**Library of Congress Cataloging-in-Publication Data**

Getches, David H.
    Water law in a nutshell / by David H. Getches.
        p.    cm. — (Nutshell series)
    Includes index.
    ISBN 0–314–73779–0
    1. Water—Law and legislation—United States.  I. Title.
II. Series.
KF5569.3.G48  1990
346.7304'691—dc20
[347.3064691]
                                         90–36566
                                            CIP

**ISBN** 0–314–73779–0

Getches, Water Law, 2d  NS
1st Reprint—1991

# FOREWORD TO THE SECOND EDITION

Water law has been an especially active field since the first edition of *Water Law in a Nutshell*. There have been court decisions in hundreds of cases and statutory changes in several states. In addition, scholarship in the field has been expanding. There are now three water law casebooks in use in law schools and a new treatise entitled *Law of Water Rights and Resources* by Professor A. Dan Tarlock. More law review articles are being written than ever before in water law.

This second edition represents a revision of the first in light of changes in the law through late 1989. Citations appear at relevant places to nearly all of the principal cases appearing in Meyers, Tarlock, Corbridge, and Getches, *Water Resource Management* (Third Edition, 1988), Trelease and Gould, *Water Law* (4th Edition, 1986), Sax and Abrams, *Legal Control of Water Resources* (1986). And a new chapter has been added on surface use of waters in light of the increased importance of public recreational water uses. Throughout this edition, wherever appropriate, information has been expanded on instream flow protection, water quality and public interest concerns in water use and water allocation. This reflects the growing interest in those matters throughout the country. For thorough treatment of water pollution control, however, readers are urged to look to other sources, including *Environmental Law in a Nutshell.*

I am indebted to research assistants from the University of Colorado School of Law for their work in making this edition possible. Ellen Ostheimer Creagar and Michael James Grode spent many hours to ensure the accuracy and currency of this edition and edited the manuscript with care. I am also grateful to Elizabeth Thomas and John S. Hajdik for their assistance earlier in the project.

DHG

Escazu, Costa Rica
April, 1990

# FOREWORD TO THE FIRST EDITION

In spite of all its interesting issues and its great practical importance, water law is a field in which there is a dearth of supplemental sources that are useful to students. A few voluminous treatises are available to aid the practitioner in finding answers to difficult questions. But there is no basic source. This book is a modest effort at providing a supplemental source for the student of water law. It also should serve as an orientation device for lawyers who do not regularly practice in the field and for non-lawyers who need a background in the subject.

The study of water is complicated by the widely differing systems that exist in the several states. No attempt is made here to draw together and explicate the complete law of any particular state. This book states the general rules that apply within major systems of water law and attempts to give examples of special rules applicable in particular states. Generally, the statutory and case law of the states is current through 1982, and relevant United States Supreme Court cases is current through July, 1983.

This book owes its existence to many people. A number of student research assistants at the University of Colorado School of Law worked on its preparation. Mark Cohen, Esq. worked diligently and made an important imprint on Chapters Two and Four. Richard Cauble, Esq. devoted many hours and made a fine, professional contribution to Chapters Five, Six, Eight, and Nine. George Jent, Esq., Stephen Ellis, Esq., Sharon Nelson, Esq. and Dary James all assisted with parts of Chapter Three.

The author is greatly indebted to Ann Amundson, Esq. for her splendid editorial assistance with the manuscript. My colleagues Professor Charles Wilkinson and Professor James Corbridge were kind enough to review portions of the draft manuscript and made important suggestions on how to improve it. I am very grateful to Anne Guthrie who typed and retyped successive drafts of the manuscript. Finally, I thank my wife Ann and my children on whose time this book was written.

DHG

Boulder, Colorado
February, 1984

# OUTLINE

## CHAPTER ONE. OVERVIEW AND INTRODUCTION TO WATER LAW

# CHAPTER TWO. RIPARIAN RIGHTS

Page

## CHAPTER THREE. PRIOR APPROPRIATION

# OUTLINE

XXVI

## CHAPTER FOUR. HYBRID SYSTEMS AND OTHER VARIATIONS

## CHAPTER FIVE.  RIGHTS TO USE THE SURFACE OF WATERWAYS

## CHAPTER SIX.  GROUNDWATER

**CHAPTER SEVEN.  DIFFUSED
SURFACE WATERS**

## CHAPTER EIGHT. FEDERAL AND INDIAN RESERVED RIGHTS

## CHAPTER NINE. FEDERAL POWER OVER WATER DEVELOPMENT

## CHAPTER TEN. INTERSTATE ALLOCATION

# TABLE OF CASES

**References are to Pages**

XLI

# TABLE OF CASES

## TABLE OF CASES

*

# WATER LAW
## IN A NUTSHELL
### SECOND EDITION

*

# CHAPTER ONE

# OVERVIEW AND INTRODUCTION TO WATER LAW

## I. THE STUDY OF WATER LAW

It is unusual for an area of law to be defined by a particular resource. But water is unique in the diversity and importance of needs it fills. It quenches our thirst, gives life to essential food crops, furnishes habitat to fish resources, satisfies recreational and aesthetic needs and purifies the air. Water is necessary to survival. It is one of the most plentiful substances, yet it is often considered precious because there is not always enough water of the right quality in the right place at the right time. This has sparked keen competition among water users.

The same stream may be sought by a farmer for irrigation, a municipality for domestic use, a factory for carrying away waste, a power plant for cooling, a coal company for mixing with coal dust to be transported as slurry, boaters and fishers for recreation, environmentalists for preservation of the stream in its natural state. Single choices from among the array of possible uses can have far-reaching impacts. For instance, a decision to transport water from a rural area across a moun-

1

tain range to a city may: force a decline in agricultural productivity and the farming community built on it; facilitate more rapid growth in the importing area; prevent future development of the exporting area; curtail recreational opportunities; make sewage treatment more difficult as diluting stream flows are diminished; deprive the exporting area of groundwater recharge; and cause ecological changes in both areas.

The role of law is particularly important when so many varied needs must be recognized. An absence of order—of clearly defined rights and rules of liability—can be dangerous. Lives have literally been lost over water disputes in the western states.

The study of water law is, at one level, the study of property concepts. The fact that water is a moving resource necessarily limits the appropriateness of traditional concepts of ownership. Although water laws differ widely, notions of substantial public rights in the resource cut across allocation regimes. One result is that lawmakers have superimposed administrative systems to enforce and regulate private water rights based on perceptions of a broader public interest.

The field of water law is implicitly a study of the legal process. In many areas the law is well-developed and changes only slowly and at the periphery, but water law is a comparatively young and dynamic field. It illustrates how courts and legislatures create and alter law according to societal stimuli: one set of historical conditions drove the initial development of water law while different modern circumstances coax further changes.

Three central tasks of legal study are: the comparison of established legal systems; the critical evaluation of the law's performance; and the search for solutions to unresolved problems. Success in meeting society's needs is measured by the weight one gives to considerations such as stability, efficiency, productivity, fairness and environmental integrity. As an evolving field replete with conflicts over a critical resource possessing various tangible and intangible values, water law presents unparalleled opportunities for analysis and creativity.

## II.  LEGAL SYSTEMS FOR WATER ALLOCATION

American jurisdictions can be grouped roughly into three doctrines of water law: riparian, prior appropriation and hybrid states. This book treats the systems separately, so that readers may concentrate attention on issues within the system of particular interest. The systems, however, overlap and borrow from one another so that it is useful to compare the regimes.

### A.  Riparian Rights

Landowners bordering a waterway are considered riparians. Their location gives them certain appurtenant rights under the laws of most states. A riparian location has special value because it enables the owner to operate water-driven mills and to have access to the water surface for boating, hunting, and fishing, and to consume reasonable quantities of water.

In states classified as "riparian" landowners have special rights to make use of water in a waterway adjoining their property. If the waterway is considered navigable, certain surface uses by members of the public must be tolerated by riparians.

Many American jurisdictions originally adopted a "natural flow" rule that gave every riparian owner the right to have water flow past undiminished in quantity or quality. Although exceptions for domestic uses were made, the doctrine seemed to bar almost any consumption of water and thus it was highly impractical. Later, riparian doctrine states (mostly located in the eastern United States) permitted riparians to use water in a way that is "reasonable" relative to all other users. If there is insufficient water to satisfy the reasonable needs of all riparians, all must reduce usage of water in proportion to their rights, usually based on the amount of land they own. There is generally no right to use water on non-riparian land; such uses are considered unreasonable per se. Because riparian rights inhere in land ownership, they need not be exercised to be kept alive. Thus, a landowner may begin using water at will.

Riparian rules have been altered by statute and case law so that today there are no pure riparian doctrine states. The most common alteration requires riparians to obtain permits from a state agency in order to use water. Permits may also be available to non-riparians.

The riparian doctrine which is covered in Chapter Two still applies in one form or another in twenty-nine states:

| | |
|---|---|
| Alabama | Missouri |
| Arkansas | New Hampshire |
| Connecticut | New Jersey |
| Delaware | New York |
| Florida | North Carolina |
| Georgia | Ohio |
| Illinois | Pennsylvania |
| Indiana | Rhode Island |
| Iowa | South Carolina |
| Kentucky | Tennessee |
| Maine | Vermont |
| Maryland | Virginia |
| Massachusetts | West Virginia |
| Michigan | Wisconsin |
| Minnesota | |

The doctrine also has some viability in the hybrid states listed in section C.

## B.  Prior Appropriation

In the arid west, where waterbodies are generally fewer, smaller and less dependable than in the east, riparian rights did not fit local needs. Mines and farms needing water could not always be located on riparian lands. Further, development would have been frustrated if scarce water resources were left unused until a riparian owner decided to put them to some use. The prior appropriation doctrine responded to early western needs by basing water rights on the "first in time, first in right" principle. Early court decisions in the West recognized rights in anyone who put water to use anywhere (on riparian or non-riparian land), with superiority over anyone who later began using water. Rights, then, depend on usage and not on land ownership. Once a person puts water to a beneficial use and complies with any statutory requirements, a water right is perfected and remains valid so long as it continues to be used.

Appropriative water rights can be transferred if it is shown that the ability of others to exercise vested rights is not impaired. The prior appropriation doctrine is the basis of water rights in nine states:

| | |
|---|---|
| Alaska | Nevada |
| Arizona | New Mexico |
| Colorado | Utah |
| Idaho | Wyoming |
| Montana | |

All "pure" appropriation states (except Colorado) presently impose administrative requirements and require permits to appropriate water. In the process, public interest concerns are weighed by the agency. Prior appropriation is the subject of Chapter Three.

## C. Hybrid Systems

The hybrid doctrine (sometimes called the "California doctrine") states originally recognized riparian rights but later converted to a system of appropriation while preserving existing riparian rights. The hybrid states are:

| | |
|---|---|
| California | Oklahoma |
| Kansas | Oregon |
| Mississippi | South Dakota |
| Nebraska | Texas |
| North Dakota | Washington |

Hawaii's system is a combination of rights established under laws of the ancient Hawaiian Kingdom and recent statutes. Louisiana's water law is adapted from the French Civil Code. Water laws of Hawaii and Louisiana are discussed along with hybrid systems in Chapter Four.

## III.  SPECIAL TYPES OF WATER

Most water available for use is subject to one of the three water allocation schemes listed above, but certain waters fall outside those systems.

### A.  Groundwater

Water law is most in flux concerning groundwater. Vast underground resources supply much of the nation's needs. The recent attention to groundwater is due in part to concern for the future of what is, in many cases, a depletable resource. It also reflects an increased understanding of the dynamics of groundwater occurrence and movement. For some time groundwater was not managed or allocated by state law simply because so little was known about it. Overlying owners could do as they pleased with water drawn from under their land.

Even when water beneath the surface of land was connected with a stream or lake, the law treated groundwater separately. More enlightened legal approaches now integrate groundwater and surface water management. For example, when pumping from a well would affect the rights of a person using stream water (or vice-versa) extraction of the water is administered and regulated as a part of the stream system. Some jurisdictions, however, continue to subject all groundwater, even water that is hydrologically connected with a surface source, to a separate set of rules designed for groundwater without such a connection (i.e., non-tributary, connate or isolated groundwater).

Special rules are needed for groundwater management because waters may be withdrawn at a faster rate than they are replenished. Another problem is that a new well may endanger existing wells. Some theories for allocating rights in groundwater are analogous to riparian rights (absolute ownership of water underlying land) and prior appropriation (groundwater is subject to appropriation, with older wells protected against harm from newer pumpers). But these systems do not adequately prevent overpumping or protect existing well owners against newcomers. Consequently special rules have been developed to balance competing interests of new and old well users and overlying owners, and to fulfill the state's obligation to prolong the life of the resource while allowing efficient usage. Many jurisdictions base rules of liability between pumpers and criteria for granting permits for new wells on a reasonable use standard, requiring that the utility of relative uses and equities of the parties be weighed. Groundwater laws are discussed in Chapter Six.

## B.  Diffused Surface Water

Obviously not all water on earth is capable of management by governments. Thus water rights systems exclude from their coverage water in the oceans, water in the process of evaporation or transpiration, and precipitation. For some time groundwater was not under any legal system because of the technical difficulty in tracing its movement and understanding where and how much was available.

Water that is on the surface of land because of rain, melting snow or floods is called diffused surface water and generally is not subject to water allocation rules. Nearly all states allow diffused surface waters to be captured and used by a landowner without regulation or limitation. Such waters are simply outside the realm of state control. Ordinarily only waters in natural streams are considered subject to state control.

The special rules concerning diffused surface waters are treated in Chapter Seven. They were developed primarily to determine liability when someone attempts to avoid such waters. A majority of states allow landowners to divert or channel floodwaters away from their lands if reasonable under the circumstances.

## IV. PUBLIC RIGHTS

Water is legally and historically a public resource. Although private property rights can be perfected in the use of water, it remains essentially public; private rights are always incomplete and subject to the public's common needs. The earliest expression of these needs, still viable, was for navigation. Navigable waters remain subject to public use and access for uses such as boating, bathing, fishing, hunting and, more recently, recreational and aesthetic interests. Throughout the study of water law it is evident that private activity affecting the quantity and quality of water cannot lawfully interfere with the overriding public interest.

Chapter Five deals with the special public rights that exist in the use of the surface of waterways. These rights may turn on the definition of navigability, which is also the point of reference for ownership of the beds of waterways. Public rights to use the surface of non-navigable waters have also been recognized based on their capacity to support recreational uses, the public trust doctrine and various state statutes. Access to and from waterbodies where public surface rights exist, including oceans, have been implied by courts based on several theories.

## V.  INTERGOVERNMENTAL PROBLEMS

Although creation and regulation of rights to use water is primarily a state affair, there are important spheres of federal ownership and control. Chapter Eight is concerned with waters that the federal govenment and Indian tribes hold for use on their lands and Chapter Nine deals with exercises of congressional power that may affect the operation of state water laws.  The difficult interjurisdictional problems of adjusting rights of states whose inhabitants are competing for use of water from a common source are treated in Chapter Ten.

### A.  Reserved Rights

When the United States sets aside some of its lands for a special use such as a park, a military base, or a national forest, or when an Indian reservation is established, it has been held that sufficient water is reserved to fulfill the purposes of the reservation.  Reserved water rights have a priority as of the date the reservation was established, whether or not water has ever been used.  In a system in which water rights are based on prior use, assertions of reserved water rights can cause dislocations among those whose water rights have a priority date later than the establishment of the reservation.  To temper the effects of the reserved rights doctrine, Congress and the courts have narrowly construed the extent of rights reserved and

have allowed reserved rights to be quantified in
state courts in general stream adjudications.

## B.  Federal Actions Affecting State Water Rights

The United States is involved in activities that
sometimes affect, and because of federal supremacy, may preempt state water law.  The government
has built dams, assured the ability to navigate,
licensed power projects and regulated water quality.  Each of these functions is within powers granted to Congress by the Constitution.  Each is important to a significant part of the public.  When they
conflict with state water rights, however, serious
federalism issues arise and courts must resolve
close questions of whether Congress intended to
override state law.

## C.  Interstate Problems

Tensions frequently exist among states that
share access to rivers, lakes and groundwater
sources.  Allocations among states can be made by
compact—a negotiated interstate agreement made
with the consent of Congress—or by adjudication
in a judicial proceeding.  In one instance Congress
passed legislation effectively allocating waters of
the Colorado River among the abutting states, suggesting a third means for interstate allocation.

In attempting to protect their water resources,
states may not improperly inhibit interstate commerce by placing limits on exports.  Water is considered an article of commerce and, as such, trade

in it must not be restricted by regulations that discriminate against interstate commerce.

## VI.  WATER INSTITUTIONS

The final chapter describes a number of types of organizations formed to develop and distribute water.  They are the operating entities that deliver most of the water in the country.

# CHAPTER TWO

# RIPARIAN RIGHTS

Twenty-nine states have systems rooted in the riparian doctrine. Nine others have a system based on some combination of riparian and prior appropriation doctrines. See Chapter Four. The states that fall into each classification of water law are listed on pages 5–7.

The fundamental principle of the riparian doctrine is that the owner of land bordering a waterbody acquires certain rights to use the water. Each landowner bordering on a waterbody may make reasonable use of the water on the same land if the use does not interfere with reasonable uses of other riparians. Today statutory systems have largely replaced pure riparianism in virtually all jurisdictions though these systems usually apply some elements of the doctrine in allocating rights.

## I. HISTORY OF THE RIPARIAN DOCTRINE

### A. European Precedents

Scholars differ on the origin of the riparian doctrine. Some believe it is a product of the civil law; others maintain it has its roots in the English Common Law. Elements of the doctrine can be traced to precedents from both France and England but it is essentially an American doctrine.

Prior to the 18th century, most water cases involved rights of navigation and fishing. The dawn of the Industrial Revolution and the consequent increase in water-driven mills created a need for uniform principles of law that could be applied in the growing number of water disputes concerned with access to the flow of the stream. The law's response was the development of the riparian doctrine.

## 1. France

The Institutes of Justinian, published in 533–34 A.D., held that running water was a part of the "negative community" of things that could not be owned, along with air, seas and wildlife. At the same time, it was recognized that things in the negative community could be used and that the "usufruct," or right to use the advantages of the resource, must be regulated to provide order and prevent over-exploitation. The Institutes declared that the right to use water belonged only to those who had access to the water by virtue of their ownership of riparian land. Others could not gain access without committing a trespass, unless the stream was on the public domain.

Doctrine was formalized in 1804 with the promulgation of the French Civil Code. The Code allowed a riparian landowner to use water from an abutting stream for irrigation if the water was returned to its ordinary course before it left the land. Two facets of the modern riparian doctrine are present in the Code: the limitation confining water rights to riparian landowners, and the requirement that the water be restored to its ordinary course. The Code also provided that in disputes between riparian landowners the courts should reconcile the interests of agriculture with property rights (for example, the right of a nonagricultural riparian to have a continued flow of water past the property). This provision is a forerunner of the reasonable use theory that was eventually incorporated into the American riparian law.

## 2. *England*

England developed a regular system of courts and lawyers only after the Norman Conquest. Prior to 1066, English society was largely decentralized, and disputes concerning water were apparently settled locally.

The early English law of water rights resembled the modern prior appropriation system. One who had made use of a stream from time immemorial was entitled to continue making that use even if the use deprived others of the natural flow of the stream. In the Eighteenth Century, the English courts modified this doctrine of "ancient use" and substituted a test of "prior use". Under this test, one could not use or divert water if the effect would be to deprive a prior user of water. The principle protected earlier mills from interference with their water supplies by newer mills. E.g., Bealey v. Shaw (1805).

The prior use test was short-lived. In the 1820's the English courts began to accept a "natural flow" theory under which every riparian landowner had an equal right to use water in the stream and a duty not to diminish the quantity of water otherwise flowing to proprietors lower on the stream. Wright v. Howard (1823). This remained the law in England for a few decades until the English judges, borrowing from the American opinions of Story and Kent, incorporated the "reasonable use" theory into English riparian doctrine. Mason v. Hill (1833). Application of reasonable use principles modified the natural flow theory by allowing each riparian the right to make all reasonable uses of the waters so long as those uses did not interfere with the reasonable uses of other riparians.

## B. Early Development in the Eastern United States

After the Revolutionary War each state began developing its own case law. The sparse population of the United States lived mostly on the eastern seaboard, a rainy area with abundant brooks, streams, and rivers. Some states, including Connecticut and Massachusetts, had few restrictions on the use of streams, and allowed diversions of water if the surplus was returned to the stream. Other states, such as New Jersey, adopted a type of natural flow rule that allowed a riparian landowner to make use of the stream in its natural state but prohibited any diversion that might reduce the flow to another.

The same industrial revolution that modernized Europe occurred in America. Large mills required reservoirs for storage and irrigation and industry spread away from the stream banks. The notion of preserving the natural flow of the stream was rendered obsolete by the need to alter the stream to maximize water uses. Against this backdrop the famous case of Tyler v. Wilkinson (1827), was decided. The plaintiffs in *Tyler* were riparian proprietors with mills just below a small dam used to retain the water so that it would flow faster past their mills. The defendants constructed an upstream dam and diverted water into a trench that began just above plaintiffs' mills. The defendants' water use deprived plaintiffs of the flow of the lower dam. Justice Story held that the defendants were entitled only to the quantity of water that was accustomed to flow in the trench during the twenty years before the initiation of the suit (the passage of time giving rise to a conclusive presumption that they had a right to water). In setting forth the principles of law applicable to watercourses in general, Justice Story stated that all riparians had an equal right to the use of the balance of the water flowing in the stream, but rejected the natural flow doctrine, holding that each riparian was entitled to make a reasonable use of the waters. That use could not interfere with the reasonable use of any other riparian land-owner.

In 1828, less than one year after Story's decision in Tyler v. Wilkinson, Chancellor Kent discussed the law of water rights in his *Commentaries*. He embraced the reasonable use doctrine and specifically cited Story's opinion along with numerous civil law authorities (mostly dealing with diffused surface waters). Many courts in the United States and England relied on Kent's *Commentaries* and Story's decision in Tyler v. Wilkinson. The importance of the natural flow theory gradually diminished.

Today all riparian states have adopted some form of the reasonable use doctrine; nearly all of them have statutory permit schemes, further departing from early riparian doctrine. Though some courts continue to use "natural flow" language, most actually apply some variant of the reasonable use doctrine.

## C. Repudiation and Recognition in the American West

The westward expansion of the United States was the product of a variety of factors. Acquisition of lands from foreign powers and the subjugation of American Indians paved the way for large numbers of people to settle in the West. The discovery of areas rich in timber, furs and minerals, and vast land areas thought suitable for farming provided powerful incentives for westward movement.

The riparian doctrine was thought to be impractical for the arid region beyond the one-hundredth meridian (a line running south through the middle of North Dakota into Texas). A system that limited rights to owners of land bordering a stream and water use to the watershed of origin would have stifled development. Almost all western land was owned by the federal government, yet homesteaders and miners were encouraged to settle there. The early miners and homesteaders were essentially trespassers on the public domain; thus they could have no riparian rights. The most promising mineral deposits were often far from any stream; without water many mines, particularly placer mines, could not operate. Besides denying waters to any but property owners, the doctrine required water to be used only on lands abutting a stream. Often the dry lands settled by farmers were far from any stream, making importation of water necessary.

By its silence the federal government acquiesced in the settlers' trespasses and use of water. The miners developed their own customary "law." They rejected the riparian doctrine and allowed people to divert quantities of water from a stream, transport it many miles—usually via ditch—and put it to use for mining or irrigation. This right to "appropriate" a quantity of water was available on a first come-first served basis. Anyone could make a diversion that did not deprive "prior appropriators" of the quantity of water already being diverted by them. Prior appropriation was gradually adopted by state courts and incorporated into state statutes. The federal government also recognized the validity of the doctrine in early mining acts and in the Desert Land Act of 1877. See Chapter Three.

## D. Riparian Law Today

Increased population and development of the United States caused most eastern riparian states to adopt statutory permit systems for some or all water uses. See Section V of this chapter. Early statutory and case law defining reasonable use is reflected in the permit system. In addition, common law disputes between individuals may be resolved by reference to riparian principles. Riparian rights are still recognized in the "hybrid" states and therefore courts still refer to riparian law in cases arising there.

Riparian rights include a right to have water remain unpolluted (the right of purity), and rights to fish, to have access to the stream, and to protect the banks of a stream from erosion. These rights all have been upheld to some extent in the appropriation states as well as in riparian states.

## II. RIPARIAN LANDS

Only the owner of riparian land acquires any rights to make use of the adjacent watercourse.

This section defines what constitutes riparian land
and the types of waterbodies in which the owner of
adjacent land may hold rights. The status of riparian rights if riparian land is divided into smaller
parcels is then discussed.

## A. Contiguity to Source

All land masses are surrounded by bodies of
water and in that sense all land could be called
riparian. The law distinguishes between riparian
land and non-riparian land through the somewhat
artificial concept of ownership. Only the owner of
a parcel of land touching the watercourse has
riparian rights; but it is no longer required that
the landowner own a portion of the bed of a watercourse. See Restatement (Second) of Torts § 843.
Riparian rights to use water attach only to riparian land and do not extend to any portion of the
tract that is outside the immediate watershed of
the waterbody.

## B. Types of Watercourses

To have riparian rights a landowner must own
property adjacent to a waterbody that fits the
definition of a "watercourse." No rights attach,
for instance, to diffused surface waters.

### 1. Streams

The term "watercourse" means a natural stream
flowing constantly or recurrently on the surface of
the earth in a reasonably definite natural channel.
The term may also include springs, lakes or mar-

shes in which a stream originates or through which it flows.

In the eastern states the courts generally require that a stream flow all year to constitute a watercourse. In the arid West natural streams may be dry for much of the year, coming to life only during the rainy season, and may still be included within the definition of a watercourse.

In contrast to a watercourse, diffused surface water usually comes from the runoff of rains or melting snow, and generally flows intermittently without a defined channel. It is not subject to riparian rights until it enters a watercourse. The special rules applicable to diffused surface water are covered in Chapter Seven.

## 2. Lakes and Ponds

A lake also is a watercourse subject to riparian rights. A lake is defined as a reasonably permanent body of water substantially at rest in a depression in the surface of the earth, if both the depression and the body of water are of natural origin or part of a watercourse. Smaller bodies of water, particularly ones with an abundance of aquatic life, are sometimes called ponds, but no legal distinction exists. In some eastern states bodies of water known as "great ponds" are considerably larger than many lakes.

A person who owns land bordering on a lake or pond is technically referred to as a "littoral" landowner, but it is common to call such owners ripari-

ans.  Some argue that littoral landowners actually
own the water in the lake rather than simply
possessing certain rights to make use of it, since
water in a lake is stationary rather than flowing.
This ignores a reality of the hydrologic cycle:
water is constantly evaporating from lakes and
being replaced with water from other sources such
as streams, springs, surface runoff and rainfall.  It
is now settled that the same riparian rights to use
water attach to land abutting on a natural lake or
pond as attach to land bordering on a flowing
stream.

The rights of littoral landowners to use the surface of a lake for such purposes as fishing and
boating usually depend on whether the lake is
"navigable" or "non-navigable."  Those rights are
discussed in Section III B of this chapter.  Generally, any person, whether or not a littoral owner,
may make use of the surface of a navigable lake.
Each state may adopt its own definition of navigability for this purpose.  If the lake is non-navigable
all littoral landowners own the surface rights in
common and each may make use of the entire
surface provided the use does not unreasonably
interfere with the exercise of similar rights by
other littoral landowners.  Some states follow this
rule even if one person owns the bed of the entire
lake.  Other states hold that use of the surface of a
non-navigable lake above that portion of the bed
owned by another constitutes a trespass.

### 3. *Springs and Other Natural Water Bodies*

A spring is a concentrated surface flow of water coming from under the ground due to natural causes. Whether the owner of land with a spring on it has riparian rights depends upon the source of the spring. The riparian doctrine usually applies to springs emanating from definite underground watercourses, landowners being entitled only to make reasonable use of the waters from such springs. In the absence of evidence as to the source of a spring, it is presumed that the spring was formed and fed by percolating groundwater and the law of groundwater treated in Chapter Six applies.

A spring will be treated as diffused surface water if its flow dissipates before reaching a watercourse or before leaving the boundary of the land on which it is located. See Chapter Seven. The owner of the land owns the spring and may use all the water from it. Sometimes courts treat springs as watercourses, however, even if the water from them does not flow off the owner's land in a regular, well-defined channel.

### 4. *Underground Watercourses*

The owner of land above an underground stream has all rights of a riparian landowner. The course and the channel of the stream, however, must be definitely ascertained. An underground watercourse connecting two aquifers is usually treated as part of the groundwater system and not as an underground stream. In most states there is a presumption that groundwater is not in an underground stream. Evidence of an underground stream is provided by soil composition, growth of vegetation in dry seasons, and by comparing amounts withdrawn from wells during certain periods with measurements of nearby surface water levels during the same periods.

A riparian landowner who believes that a neighbor's wells are affecting the use of the surface waterbody must prove that the waters are interconnected to establish liability. This may require the testimony of engineers. There is a presumption that underground water is groundwater and not subject to surface water (riparian) principles. Courts may not apply the presumption, though, if wells are very close to surface watercourses.

## 5. Foreign Waters

Foreign waters are waters transported from one watershed into another by human effort. Use of water outside its watershed is often held to be unreasonable per se. But once water is nevertheless exported, the exporter may obtain rights to it by prescription. Ownership of land bordering on a stream or ditch carrying foreign waters does not usually give the landowner riparian rights to the water.

## 6. Artificially Created Watercourses

Sometimes a canal is built, a stream re-channelled, or a lake created through human effort.

The new waterbody may be an important source of
water for those adjoining it. Yet the general rule
is that riparian rights attach only to natural watercourses and lakes. Thus, the rights of owners of
land riparian to an artificial stream or lake are not
controlled by riparian doctrine. Artificial watercourses that are maintained long enough, however,
may be treated by courts as natural watercourses.
In Bollinger v. Henry (1964) the court treated a
century-old millrace as if it were a watercourse.

If an artificial lake is created by building a dam
and the lake borders on the property of others,
those others may acquire certain rights in the lake
based on theories of estoppel, reliance or reciprocal
easements. In the leading case of Kray v. Muggli
(1901) a dam impounded water to form a lake.
After forty years the defendants wanted to remove
the dam. The court enjoined the defendant because the plaintiff had made improvements such as
docks relying on the level of the lake. The court
noted that defendants had acquired a prescriptive
right (flowage easement) to flood plaintiffs uplands,
and therefore plaintiff acquired a reciprocal prescriptive right to the artificial water level.

A case more typical of modern trends is Kiwanis
Club Found. v. Yost (1966). That case held that
existence of a man-made dam put the upper landowner, who had built a boys camp on the shore, on
notice that the water level was artificial. No
rights were created to maintain the lake, and the
lower landowner was allowed to alter the level at

will. A different result was reached in Greisinger v. Klinhardt (1928), in which a country club sold lakefront lots on an artificial lake to the plaintiffs thereby inducing them to make substantial improvements based on the understanding that the lake was to be permanent.

In upholding rights of plaintiffs in artificial watercourses the courts in *Kray* and *Greisinger* did not say that riparian rights existed in artificial waters. Instead, they held that the defendants were estopped from denying plaintiffs' rights or found that the waterway had become effectively a natural watercourse.

## C. Extent

Two limitations exist on land to which riparian rights can attach. First, no rights attach to lands outside the watershed. Second, rights once attached to a parcel may be extinguished by conveyance of a portion of the land without any frontage on the waterway.

## 1. Watershed Limitation

Riparian rights attach only to an owner's land within the watershed. This is true whether a parcel is non-contiguous or part of a tract that fronts on a stream. A riparian landowner still may be able to use water for land outside the watershed, however. Although some jurisdictions bar all use of water outside the watershed, others permit it subject to the reasonable use restriction. Most jurisdictions consider use outside the watershed of origin to be unreasonable per se, although many will not prevent it unless a riparian is actually harmed. Long-standing non-watershed use may ripen into a prescriptive right. Several exceptions to the watershed limitation have developed. See Section IV B 3 of this chapter.

## 2. Divisions of Riparian Land

A conveyance of riparian land carries with it all of the appurtenant riparian rights unless there has been a severance of those rights. The extent to which rights can be reserved by a grantor or conveyed to a grantee are discussed in Section VI of this chapter. Riparian rights attach only to waterfront land; consequently, when a riparian owner conveys a parcel of land that is not on the water riparian rights no longer attach to the conveyed parcel. If the parcels are reunited under common ownership, the parcel of land that is not on the water may remain without riparian rights, depending on which of the following rules prevails in the jurisdiction.

### a. Source of Title Rule

Under the source of title rule (also called the smallest tract rule), riparian rights attach only to the smallest subdivision of waterfront land in the chain of title leading to the present owner. Thus, even if the original riparian owner later reacquires the tract, only the smallest parcel with frontage on the waterway has riparian rights; any land ever severed from contact with the waterway by conveyance can never regain riparian rights. Under this rule the amount of riparian land shrinks as conveyances sever waterfront lands from uplands. An exception to the rule is that partition of riparian lands among tenants in common does not deprive non-waterfront parcels of riparian rights.

The source of title rule is applied in western states with a hybrid system of water law. The apparent harshness of reducing the amount of land subject to riparian rights is tempered by the fact that water rights may be acquired for the severed parcels by appropriation. The rule furthers the policy, typical in hybrid jurisdictions, of minimizing the reach of riparian rights and building a reliable system based on prior appropriation. Hybrid systems are discussed in Chapter Four.

Example: In Figure 1 Jones conveys the north portion of a tract of riparian land—the part bordering the stream—to Smith. No riparian rights remain with the south plot. If Smith later reconveys the north plot back to Jones riparian rights will not reattach to the south plot.

### b. *Unity of Title Rule*

Under the unity of title rule an entire tract of land fronting on a waterway held by a single owner is entitled to riparian rights. It does not matter that the land earlier had been divided into several parcels some of which did not front on the waterway. Thus all land contiguous to a riparian parcel that is held by the same riparian landowner

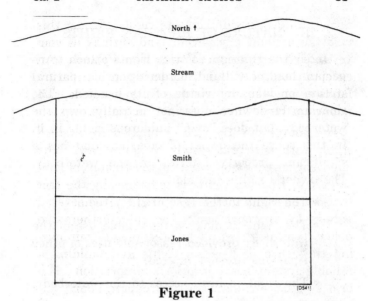

**Figure 1**

has riparian rights regardless of when or from whom the contiguous lands were conveyed. Most riparian states follow this rule.

Example: In Figure 1 Jones severs riparian land and conveys the north plot to Smith. Only Smith has the riparian rights. Under the unity of title rule, if Smith later reconveys the north plot back to Jones, the entire tract (both plots) would again have riparian rights. Similarly, if Smith conveyed the south plot, kept the north plot, then later reacquired the south plot, riparian rights would attach to the entire tract.

## III.  NATURE OF RIPARIAN RIGHTS

Under the riparian doctrine rights attach to riparian land, i.e., land bordering on a natural stream or lake, by virtue of its location.  The riparian landowner does not actually own the waterbody, but does "own" numerous rights in it. In this sense the owner of riparian land has a significant property interest in the waterbody. The owner's rights include:

- The right to the flow of the stream;

- The right to make a reasonable use of the waterbody provided reasonable uses of other riparians are not injured;

- The right to have access to the waterbody;

- The right to fish;

- The right to wharf out;

- The right to prevent erosion of the banks;

- The right to purity of the water;

- The right to claim title to the beds of non-navigable lakes and streams.

The ownership of riparian land not only creates rights, it also creates duties.  Each riparian landowner has a duty to refrain from interfering with the rights of fellow riparians.  Riparian rights are further limited by "public rights" to use the surface of certain water ways.  At common law all persons had the right to navigate on any navigable river (including the associated right to hunt and fish along the river).  Today public uses include not only navigation but recreational uses and they have been extended to non-navigable waters in many states.  Public surface use rights are covered in Chapter Five.

Use of water in place—instream uses—by the general public for navigation, recreation, and even aesthetics have substantial modern importance and may be recognized by statute or court decision in non-riparian jurisdictions.

## A.  Rights of Riparian Proprietors

### 1.  *Preference for "Natural" Uses*

Riparian law distinguishes between "natural" or "domestic" uses and "artificial" uses.  Natural uses include those that meet the domestic needs of the riparian landowner, such as drinking, washing, and watering small gardens or a few livestock. Under the natural flow rule a riparian could use water for natural or domestic purposes even if it diminished the flow to the harm of lower riparians. Natural uses were the only consumptive uses allowed.

The reasonable use doctrine also reflects a preference for natural uses.  E.g., Prather v. Hoberg (1944). In most jurisdictions today any riparian can make natural uses of the water in the adjacent stream regardless of consequences to lower riparians, while artificial uses such as irrigation and industry are subject to reasonableness restrictions.

There are practical reasons for the preference for natural or domestic uses. First, such uses are unlikely to consume enough water to injure lower riparians. Second, enforcement of any restriction on domestic uses is difficult. Finally, such uses as are necessary to sustain life are bound to be "reasonable."

## 2. *Irrigation, Industrial and Mining Uses*

At common law any significant irrigation was an "artificial" use of water, and no irrigation was allowed other than for small household gardens. The reasonable use rule permits "reasonable" irrigation under the rules discussed in Section IV. Some riparian states have enacted laws that prefer certain agricultural uses, manifesting a public policy to encourage agriculture. For example, in Kentucky permits required for other riparian uses are not required for agricultural uses. Other states single out specific crops for preferential treatment (e.g., Wisconsin allows cranberry growers to divert water to irrigate their crops). Agriculture also may get preferential treatment through statutes exempting farm ponds from regulations governing construction of dams.

Manufacturing and industrial uses of water are, like agricultural uses, artificial uses. Today those uses are subject to the reasonable use rule.

Mining often requires substantial amounts of water and is also considered an artificial use. Several riparian states, however, have declared mining to be in the public interest (e.g., Michigan and Wisconsin) thus giving the courts another factor to consider when determining reasonableness of a mining use. Some permit states (e.g., Minnesota) require a finding that a particular mining operation is in the public interest before a permit will be issued. Other states have statutes stating that miners have a right of access to the waters, implying that miners have a right to use those waters (e.g., Georgia, Maine, North Carolina).

Industrial and mining uses may come into conflict with the rights of downstream riparians to pure water. The reasonable use rule requires a balancing test that may allow some pollution, similar to the approach used in actions for private nuisance or public nuisance brought by private litigants. Reasonableness may be measured by standards in state and federal legislation enacted to deal with water pollution (e.g., federal Clean Water Act). In riparian permit states, pollution is a factor to be weighed in issuing permits to take water.

## 3. Municipal Uses

When the United States was predominantly rural, local streams or individual wells provided most of the water needed for domestic uses but the dramatic population explosion of the last century has urbanized America. Cities need water for municipal uses including supplying for domestic needs, fighting fires and for watering public parks. Since few residents of cities are riparian landowners, cities require centralized water supply systems. The riparian doctrine has met these social needs by exceptions allowing municipal uses.

### a. Common Law

Generally, a city whose boundaries include or abut a stream or lake does not actually own land on the watercourse and therefore has no right to take water for a public water supply. If a city does own a tract of riparian land, then it is a riparian landowner entitled to make reasonable use of the waters in the adjacent water body just like any other riparian landowner. E.g., Botton v. State (1966). But the city would have to own substantial riparian land to justify as "reasonable" the heavy burdens imposed by drawing enough water to supply its inhabitants.

The power of eminent domain allows municipalities to condemn private riparian water rights for a public purpose if just compensation is paid. Dimmock v. New London (1968); Town of Purcellville v. Potts (1942). Eminent domain can be very expensive, particularly under the natural flow rule, which requires compensation even in the absence of present harm. The usual measure of compensation for condemnation of riparian rights is the diminution in the value of affected riparian land. If a city takes water without condemning the riparian right, injured riparians may bring an action for inverse condemnation, in effect forcing the city to condemn the riparian rights and compensate for the loss.

### b. *Statutory and Charter Provisions*

Individual cities were originally given powers to procure water supplies for such purposes as firefighting, watering public parks, supplying public buildings, and for meeting the domestic needs of their residents in the charters incorporating them, or in special legislative acts. The trend today is to grant such powers in general statutes applicable to all municipalities.

Some municipalities are not granted powers to supply water for the domestic needs of their residents. Instead powers are vested in public water supply companies regulated as public utilities. Such companies often are set up by special statute.

### 4. *Storage Rights*

Sometimes a riparian owner needs to build a dam to impound water during wet seasons and store it for use during dry seasons. A few courts have held storage to be unreasonable per se. See Evans v. Merriweather (1842). But with the demise of the natural flow rule most courts have been convinced that storage ought to be governed by the general rule of reasonableness.

Under the reasonable use rule a riparian can impound water so long as the reasonable uses of others are not impaired. Heise v. Schulz (1949). It has also been held that a riparian may not unreasonably alter the flow when releasing water from the storage facility. In Moore v. California Oregon Power Co. (1943), plaintiffs owned land riparian to the Klamath River. The defendant operated a dam above the plaintiffs' lands that generated electricity for a power plant. The defendant released water from the dam at intervals to satisfy its need to supply peak loads of electricity. This caused the flow in the stream below the dam to fluctuate greatly, repeatedly washing away the plaintiffs' diversion works. The Supreme Court of California held for the plaintiffs on the ground that storage in one season for use in another deprived lower riparians of the natural flow of the stream. Even under a theory of reasonable use the outcome probably would have been the same because of the unreasonable nature of the defendant's storage and release methods.

Despite recognition that storage can be beneficial and ought to be subject to the rule of reasonableness, the majority of states still follow the rule of Rylands v. Fletcher (1868), that a riparian who stores water is absolutely liable for any damage caused to another's property by escaping water. Liability can also be based on negligent construction or maintenance of storage dams.

## 5. Water Power

Harnessing the flow of a stream to generate power is one of the oldest uses of water. Water power uses range from the earliest waterwheels to the construction of the large hydroelectric dams.

### a. *Waterwheels, Mills, etc.*

Early in the nation's history, small waterwheels and mills adorned numerous streams, providing a cheap and accessible source of power. Eventually larger mills were needed for manufacturing. As bigger waterwheels were needed dams were often constructed upstream from the mills, creating storage pools from which releases could be made to provide a stronger current for some but deepening and slowing the water for others. Some state legislatures enacted mill dam acts to allow storage dams provided they did not injure existing mills. Thus an element of priority was built into the riparian system by assuring protection to the earliest uses, but protecting the flow of the stream, not the consumptive use of water.

### b. *Hydroelectric Generation*

Generation of electrical power is an important riparian use. Under the reasonable use rule operators of a hydroelectric dam may not unreasonably store or release water to the detriment of other riparians. Factors weighed in determining the reasonableness of dam operators' storage and release methods include the stream size, the state of technology and uses of the stream by other riparians. Hazard Powder Co. v. Somersville Mfg. Co., (1905). Although the riparian doctrine usually allows water to be used only on riparian land, electricity generated from hydroelectric dams may be transmitted to and used by owners of non-riparian land.

The public also may be concerned with hydroelectric dams since such structures can interfere with use of the surface of navigable rivers. Pursuant to its power under the commerce clause, Congress has dictated in the Federal Power Act that no hydroelectric dam may be built on any navigable river unless first licensed by the Federal Energy Regulatory Commission (formerly the Federal Power Commission). Before it issues a license, the Commission must find that the proposed project is in the public interest. See Chapter Nine, Section III.

## 6. Recovery of Gravel

The natural flow rule, giving each riparian the right to have the stream flow undiminished in quantity or quality, protects a riparian owner who took and sold gravel washed onto the land by the stream's flow. The reasonable use doctrine would balance the utility of using the waters to transport gravel against competing uses.

A riparian's right to recover sand and gravel was the issue in Joslin v. Marin Mun. Water Dist. (1967). In that case the plaintiffs owned lands riparian to a stream that deposited sand and gravel on plaintiffs' lands enabling them to run a profitable sand and gravel business. The defendant water district built a dam upstream from the plaintiffs that caused the flow of suspended sand and gravel to cease, but still allowed water to flow past the plaintiffs' lands. The plaintiffs brought suit alleging that their land had diminished in value because they had been deprived of $25,000 worth of sand and gravel annually. Relief was denied. The court recognized that the public interest was served by the dam, but saw no comparable benefit to the public from operation of the sand and gravel business. It held that use of a stream to transport suspended sand and gravel was unreasonable as a matter of law. The result is odd in that both parties operated businesses that supplied products needed by the public. To hold that the plaintiffs' use was unreasonable as a matter of law forsakes the balancing approach that should be used under the reasonable use rule. Presumably, however, the problem in *Joslin* could be solved by economic adjustments (payments) between the parties.

## 7. *Discharge of Waste*

Although the doctrine originally gave riparians the right, and reciprocal duty, to prevent any deterioration of water quality, this absolute prohibition has given way to the reasonable use principles. Almost every use of water necessarily alters the chemistry or temperature of a stream or lake either because it discharges some waste back into the stream or because the removal of water makes the stream less capable of diluting other contaminants. Consequently, it has always been a question of fact whether or not the amount of change renders a water use unreasonable. Snow v. Parsons (1856) (remanded to determine if tannery discharging waste into stream was a reasonable use).

Even where the primary "use" of the waterway is to discharge waste, it is not necessarily unreasonable per se. Borough of Westville v. Whitney Home Builders (1956). The beneficial use of the discharger must be balanced against the beneficial uses of other riparians according to the same criteria and standards that are applied when the dispute is over the quantity of water that is being taken by one riparian relative to another. Where a city discharging waste is a non-riparian the same issues arise as in the case of a city diverting water for use on non-riparian land.

A riparian also has a remedy in tort for pollution of a waterway by another. Causes of action exist in trespass (for negligent or intentional interference with the possession of riparian rights), and in nuisance (for interference with the use and enjoyment of land). The doctrine of reasonable use does away with technical violations of rights so a court is likely to consider essentially the same factors whether the plaintiff sues in nuisance or for a violation (trespass) to riparian rights. To find nuisance under Restatement (Second) of Torts § 826, a court uses a balancing test to decide if defendant's conduct was unreasonable by asking whether: "(a) the gravity of the harm outweighs the utility of the actor's conduct, or (b) the harm caused by the conduct is serious and the financial burden of compensating . . . would not make continuation of the conduct not feasible."

Today most water pollution is regulated by statutes under which specific effluent limitations are applied to virtually every major discharger through a permitting system. See description of federal Clean Water Act, Chapter Nine, Section V A. Violation of such limitations may show that a use is unreasonable in an action for violation of riparian rights. Arguably, the satisfaction of statutory standards should not excuse the defendant's behavior in a nuisance suit. But courts have been reluctant to impose burdens on dischargers going beyond statutory limitations.

There are many discharges, including those from agricultural irrigation, that are exempt from the Clean Water Act's permit system. They could potentially be controlled through common law action; however, there is a dearth of cases. It is likely that the problems of proof and multiple parties have made it not worthwhile for riparians to pursue such cases.

One who discharges sewage into a municipal sewer is usually immune from civil liability. However, in Springer v. Joseph Schlitz Brewing Co. (1975) the court refused to give immunity to a discharger where it knew that the city could not treat the sewage adequately and did not give the city accurate information but nevertheless used the sewer for waste disposal. The court applied a negligence theory.

## B. Rights in the Surface of Waterways

### 1. Reciprocal Rights Among Riparians

The property rights of riparians in waters overlying privately owned beds are qualified by the common right of other riparians to use all of the water surface for transportation, fishing and other purposes. Ownership of beds of navigable waterways is discussed in Chapter Five, Section I A 3.

Some courts have begun to recognize a riparian's right to make recreational uses of an adjoining waterway and to enjoy its scenic beauty. In Collens v. New Canaan Water Co. (1967), plaintiffs were awarded compensatory damages and injunctive relief because defendant's pumping of river water for municipal purposes had an adverse effect upon "the recreational and scenic advantages of the plaintiffs' [river-front] property." In an action to condemn the rights of riparian owners surrounding famous Mono Lake in northern California so that the lake could be drawn down for Los Angeles's water supply, the court awarded damages to owners based on scenic and recreational values. Because of the poor quality of the water, which could not be used for irrigation or domestic purposes, the city argued that no compensation for water rights was due. But the court found that "use of the lake in its natural condition is reasonably beneficial to their land, and the littoral rights thereof may therefore not be appropriated, even for a higher or more beneficial use for public welfare, without just compensation therefor." City of Los Angeles v. Aitken (1935).

## 2. Rights of the Public

### a. Navigable Waters

The rights of riparians whose lands border navigable waters are limited to the extent that public rights exist in such waters. The English common law rule allowed any person to navigate on navigable waters and to make uses incident to navigation such as hunting and fishing. This rule has been universally accepted in the United States, although the definition of "navigable waters" has varied.

The public right to navigate on a navigable river or lake clearly includes the right to use it for transportation. To accommodate increased public demand for water-related recreational opportunities, some state legislatures and courts have broadened the scope of permissible uses of navigable waters. The property rights of riparians are qualified to the extent necessary to allow these public use rights.

Riparian landowners on navigable waterways acquire certain rights that members of the public do not have. Chief among these is the right to "wharf out." This allows a riparian to build a wharf for private use if the structure does not impede navigation, although any obstruction which is a purpresture (an enclosure of what belongs to the public) is not allowed at common law. If the public right to navigation is injured, the obstruction can be removed as a nuisance. Courts ordinarily apply a balancing test. Most Eastern and Midwestern states recognize a right to wharf out; Pacific Coast states do not, except by statute. Similarly, in Michigan, state permission is required for any dock, for private use. The riparian landowner also usually has a right to erect structures to prevent bank erosion.

### b. Other Waterways

A riparian's ownership of lakebeds and streambeds may be further qualified by state laws recognizing public rights in waterways over private lands.

Wisconsin considers title to beds of non-navigable streams to have passed to riparians subject to public rights. Since colonial times in what is now Maine, Massachusetts and New Hampshire, large, freshwater lakes known as "great ponds" (having a surface area over ten acres), although non-navigable, have been considered open to public use with limited right of public access across private lands to reach the ponds. A Minnesota statute declares certain defined waters that are managed or accessible for public purposes to be public waters.

State law, legislatures and judiciary dictate the degree of public use allowed on waterways, whether navigable or not. Thus, public rights in waters overlying private beds may limit riparian rights. See Chapter Five for a fuller discussion of public rights.

## IV.  LIMITS ON RIPARIAN RIGHTS

### A.  Reasonable Use Limitation

All riparian states follow some variant of the reasonable use doctrine. Under the short-lived rule of natural flow each riparian had the right to have the stream flow undiminished in quality or quantity and the right to make only limited uses of the water as it flowed past. The rule was impractical because a riparian landowner could obtain an injunction against any person who depleted the water flowing past the land, even if the landowner was not injured. Thus, reasonable use principles prevailed.

Some courts still use natural flow language, particularly in disputes between riparians and nonriparians, but they do not actually apply natural flow principles. E.g., Pyle v. Gilbert (1980) (rule of natural flow applies but is "modified by the right of the upper riparian to make a reasonable use of the water").

The reasonable use rule allows riparian landowners to use adjacent waters if the use does not interfere with the reasonable uses of other riparians. Reasonableness thus is determined in comparison with the uses of other riparians. Other less universal rules have been implemented in some riparian states to deal with specific problems. They include rules specifying preferences for some types of uses over others and those governing municipal uses. See Section III of this chapter.

Most riparian states have adopted statutory schemes requiring permits for certain uses in a number of situations. See Section V of this chapter. Relative rights of riparians are determined by permit-granting authorities by reference to reasonable use criteria. Courts also apply the criteria in disputes between permittees over limited water. Unlike permit systems in the prior appropriation states, in the riparian states the holder of an earlier permit has no absolute preference over the holder of a later permit.

The reasonableness of a riparian use is determined by comparing it with the reasonableness of the uses of other riparians. The Restatement (Second) of Torts contains two sections applicable to riparian disputes that provide an analytical framework often used by the courts:

## § 850. Harm by One Riparian Proprietor to Another

A riparian proprietor is subject to liability for making an unreasonable use of the water of a watercourse or lake that causes harm to another riparian proprietor's reasonable use of the water or his land.

## § 850A. Reasonableness of the Use of Water

The determination of the reasonableness of a use of water depends upon a consideration of the interests of the riparian proprietor making the use, of any riparian proprietor harmed by it and of society as a whole. Factors that affect the determination include the following:

(a) the purpose of the use,

(b) the suitability of the use to the watercourse or lake,

(c) the economic value of the use,

(d) the social value of the use,

(e) the extent and amount of the harm it causes,

(f) the practicality of avoiding the harm by adjusting the use or method of use of one proprietor or the other,

(g) the practicality of adjusting the quantity of water used by each proprietor,

(h) the protection of existing values of water uses, land, investments and enterprises, and

(i) the justice of requiring the user causing harm to bear the loss.

The Restatement incorporates the common law notion that reasonableness is relative. In suits between riparian landowners the reasonableness of both uses is in issue. In proving that rights have been infringed, the plaintiff's own use of the water must be shown to be reasonable. This usually calls for application of factors (a)–(d). The same analysis is used to determine reasonableness of the defendant's use.

A dispute often involves riparians who are each putting the water to good use by suitable means, producing socially and economically desirable results. But the uses are inconsistent and the court must test the reasonableness of each use by considering additional factors (e)–(i). Factor (e) requires in effect that insubstantial, or de minimis, harms be borne by the complaining party. Factors (f) and (g) require the court to determine if the dispute can be settled by making adjustments. In times of drought it is reasonable to require both the water and the harm to be shared.

Factors (h) and (i) generally are applied if the defendant's reasonable use causes serious harm that cannot be avoided by adjustments. For instance, a court might require that the parties use the stream at different times. E.g., Harris v. Harrison (1892). Factor (h) is a recognition that, other things being equal, it is usually unreasonable for a new use to destroy an existing use. Factor (i) allows courts to deal with situations in which the defendant's use is of greater utility but fairness requires that the defendant pay for the harm he has caused.

In Bollinger v. Henry (1964) the court applied the § 850A factors. The dispute involved a millrace that flowed through the defendant's land and then past the plaintiffs' land. Plaintiffs had a mill on their land and used the flow of the millrace to power a mill used once a week to grind corn. The defendant diverted water from the millrace during the summer months to irrigate land. The court denied plaintiff's request for an injunction preventing the defendant from using the millrace. Although both uses appeared to be reasonable the harm suffered by the plaintiffs was minimal in that the defendant diverted water only a few months out of the year.

## B. Non-riparian Uses

Common law rules restricted use of water to "riparian land." As explained in Section II of this chapter, riparian lands are only those on a watercourse lying within the same watershed.

### 1. Use Limited to Riparian Land

Early cases enjoined water use on parcels not touching the waterbody, even those owned by a riparian within the watershed, regardless of actual harm to the plaintiff. Reasonable use jurisdictions generally require proof of actual harm from a riparian's use of water on non-riparian land within the watershed.

### 2. Use Limited to Watershed

At common law, any use of water on land outside the watershed (the area draining into the waterbody) of the source of supply was unreasonable per se and actionable even if it caused no injury. The philosophical premise of the rule is that watercourses and lakes exist primarily to benefit the lands through which they flow, rather than for the benefit of riparian landowners. Thus it

applied even to the parts of otherwise riparian
tracts that lay outside the watershed. Despite
adoption of a reasonable use theory, the majority
of states continue to apply the watershed limitation. Strict application of the watershed limitation has been the subject of much criticism and
was rejected in the Restatement (Second) of Torts
§ 855. Several exceptions have evolved.

## 3.   *Limitations on Rules Preventing Non-riparian Use*

### a.   *Restatement Rule*

The Restatement (Second) of Torts § 855 rejects
the absolute prohibition of non-riparian uses. It
says that reasonableness of a water use by a riparian proprietor is not controlled by classification of
the use as riparian or non-riparian. Thus use on
unconnected land or land outside the watershed
may be reasonable.

The Restatement rule evaluates the reasonableness of non-riparian uses relative to riparian uses,
but only if the user of the water on non-riparian
land also owns riparian land. Expansion of the
reasonable use approach to non-riparian uses recognizes that the best economic use of water may be
for agriculture, mining, manufacturing or other
purposes on land apart from the waterbody. The
Restatement rule retains the somewhat artificial
requirement that one must own riparian land.
The formality of owning a square foot of riparian
land may satisfy doctrinal purists because the

right to use water on non-riparian land is at least limited to people who are riparian landowners. It also may provide an argument that the extent of riparian land owned should be a factor in determining reasonableness.

The Restatement rule has been embraced in a number of states including Georgia, Kansas, Massachusetts, New Hampshire, New York, North Carolina, Oklahoma, Texas and Vermont. The majority of riparian states continue to apply the common law rule limiting uses to riparian lands.

### b. Requirement of Actual Harm

Some courts allow uses on non-riparian land or on land outside the watershed in the absence of harm to another riparian. In Stratton v. Mt. Hermon Boys' School (1913) the plaintiff was a riparian who owned a mill on a small stream. The defendant was a school that owned a tract of riparian land upstream from the plaintiff, but the actual campus was on a non-contiguous tract of land about one mile from the riparian land and in a different watershed. The school transported water from the stream to its campus. The diversion lowered the volume of water in the stream available to power the plaintiff's mill, but the plaintiff did not show this would actually injure present or future reasonable uses. The court held that riparian rights extended only to reasonable uses connected with riparian land and within the watershed, but said that actual injury had to be shown before the plaintiff could recover.

The rule requiring actual injury remains a minority rule; most states allow recovery against any person using water on unconnected land or outside the watershed even in the absence of actual harm to the complaining party. See Anaheim Union Water Co. v. Fuller (1907) (out of watershed use on non-riparian land).

New York has a "harmless use law" that allows a non-riparian to divert water if no riparian is harmed. The statute protects riparians by providing that the non-riparian cannot begin to acquire a prescriptive right until the use causes unreasonable harm to riparians.

### c. Permit and Hybrid States

The harshness of the watershed limitation is tempered by permit systems and in hybrid states. Permits may be issued for water use outside the watershed of origin. The permittee need not be a riparian landowner. In hybrid states water rights for non-riparian lands may be established by appropriation if sufficient water is available.

### d. Prescription

Because non-riparian uses are unreasonable per se, they are adverse to other riparians. Thus non-riparian uses can ripen into prescriptive rights they continue for the statutory period. If the jurisdiction requires actual harm before a remedy will be granted, prescriptive rights arise only if the party against whom the right is asserted has been harmed. But in states where actual harm is not necessary, a non-riparian use can ripen into a prescriptive right because a riparian could have interrupted it by seeking a judicial remedy. Prescriptive rights are more fully discussed in Section VII C of this chapter.

### e. Economic Solutions

A non-riparian use that is relatively more valuable than riparian uses presumably should be allowed. The requirement that one must show actual harm to get judicial relief from non-riparian uses reflects this policy. But courts generally do not balance relative harm in deciding whether to allow a remedy to a complaining riparian; any substantial harm will suffice. Balancing harm would amount to an application of the Restatement approach between riparians and non-riparians.

Transfers of water rights are restricted in most riparian states. See Section VI of this chapter. But if state law allows non-riparians to purchase water rights from riparians, or allows non-riparian use with the consent of a riparian, the new uses must be reasonable in relation to riparian uses by others.

An alternative to transfer of riparian rights is to purchase riparian land. Purchasers acquire riparian rights, at least on parcels bordering the stream. Where the Restatement rule applies, riparian land ownership allows the owner's use on non-riparian land if it is reasonable.

## V.  PERMIT SYSTEMS

The system of riparian rights was an acceptable way of allocating water in most of the eastern states because there was an ample water supply. When increased demands due to urban and industrial growth coincided with dry years in the middle of this century, several states adopted statutory permit systems. They were designed to protect the public's interest in sustaining a reliable supply of water. The legal requirement to obtain a permit before using water effectively limits rights inherent in riparian property ownership. Consequently, many permit requirements were challenged, although unsuccessfully.

The following states now have permit statutes: Arkansas, Delaware, Florida, Georgia, Illinois, Indiana, Iowa, Kentucky, Maryland, Massachusetts, Minnesota, New Jersey, New York, North Carolina, Pennsylvania, South Carolina and Wisconsin.

## A.  Applicability of Permit Requirements

Typically, permit statutes require anyone wanting to divert or impound water to obtain a permit from a state administrative agency. Several also require permits for use of groundwater. Use of diffused surface water is exempt in all states except Delaware, Florida, Maryland, Minnesota and New Jersey. A number of states exempt springs, farm ponds, water used for domestic purposes, and other uses having minor effect on streamflows and supplies needed by others. Even agricultural irrigation is exempt from the permit requirement in Kentucky and Maryland (up to 10,000 gal./day); Georgia grants agricultural permits for pre July, 1988 uses as a matter of course. Permits are required only for water use in "critical areas" in Indiana, North Carolina and South Carolina.

## B. Permit Criteria

Administrative officials charged with issuing permits must make tough choices among competing users. They decide the quantity one may divert and set the terms and conditions. They determine how much water should remain in a stream at a particular point in order to sustain minimum stream flows needed for maintenance of fish and wildlife and other public purposes.

All permit legislation (except New Jersey's) establishes criteria to be considered by the permitting agency. Criteria may relate to the type of watercourse, the probable impacts of the diversion and use (both negative and beneficial), and the effects on the public. Some states set forth detailed factors to be considered. Georgia and North Carolina list factors quite similar to those contained in Restatement (Second) of Torts § 850A. See Section IV A of this chapter.

Arkansas, Illinois, Iowa, Kentucky, Maryland and Minnesota have statutes setting priorities for allocation of water resources when there is not enough water for all applicants. Domestic uses rank highest. No state awards any priority to an applicant based on seniority of the applicant's use.

## C. Permit Provisions

About half the permit states grant perpetual permits. In the others, a permit is for a fixed term ranging from ten to fifty years. Renewal of fixed term permits is not automatic, but in Florida, Georgia and Iowa renewal applications are favored.

A permit is specific as to the location, volume and rate of diversion and the location and nature of the permitted use. Some permit statutes allow use of water on non-riparian land and out of the watershed that ordinarily would be restricted by riparian doctrine. Generally permittees are required to monitor and report on their diversions.

Permits may be forfeited if their use does not commence soon after they are granted or if use is interrupted for a statutorily fixed time. See VII D 2 of this chapter.

Iowa and Kentucky provide that permits may be modified to deal with shortages or otherwise to accommodate the public interest or property rights of others. Seniority gives no priority in times of shortage.

## VI. TRANSFERS OF RIPARIAN RIGHTS

## A. Appurtenance

Riparian rights are property rights that may be held only by owners of riparian land. A riparian landowner ordinarily transfers riparian water rights in a sale of the land. Because parties generally intend to transfer water rights along with the land, the courts have held that a conveyance of riparian land carries with it all of the riparian rights appurtenant to that land even if not expressly conveyed by the deed. The presumption that a conveyance of riparian land conveys the appurtenant riparian rights is rebuttable. To avoid disputes, parties generally express their intent in the deed.

Riparian rights may be reserved from the conveyance of land and conveyed to others. Riparian rights are interests in real property as opposed to personalty. Consequently, any grant of riparian rights apart from land must be made in writing to satisfy the applicable statute of frauds.

## B. Grants and Reservations

Although riparian rights attach only to riparian land, the right to use the water may be expressly reserved by a riparian landowner in conveying part of a riparian parcel to another. Such grants are sometimes held to be binding only as between the parties.

Reservations typically arise in two settings. In the first, a landowner divides a riparian parcel, expressly reserving the water rights that had attached to the parcel. The grantor may later convey to some other person the retained portion of the riparian parcel, granting along with it the

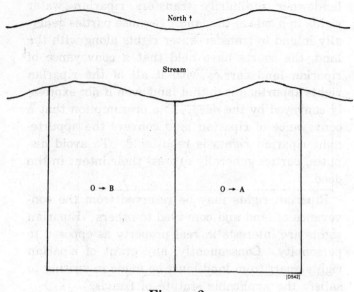

**Figure 2**

riparian rights expressly reserved from the first conveyance. As a practical matter, the grantor who reserves water rights in such a situation will usually allow the grantee at least sufficient water to satisfy the grantee's domestic needs.

In Figure 2 O owns a tract of riparian land. O conveys the eastern half of the tract to A, but expressly reserves all riparian rights. Subsequently O conveys the western half of the tract to B, granting B all riparian rights. B has a parcel of land with riparian rights and A has no riparian rights, although both border the stream. Note that O could have conveyed the western

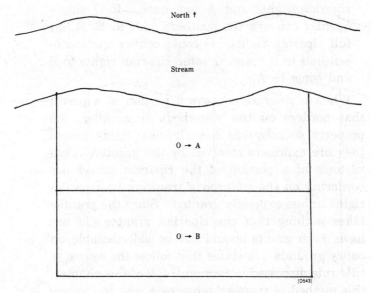

**Figure 3**

parcel to B and separately granted the previously reserved riparian rights to A in which case both A and B would have riparian rights.

The second situation in which reservations are commonly used arises when a riparian landowner retains a portion of the original riparian tract that does not border on the waterbody and conveys the abutting riparian portion to another, reserving some or all riparian rights.

In Figure 3 O owns a tract of riparian land. O conveys the northern half to A, but retains the southern half reserving for the retained parcel all water rights from the entire tract. O has full riparian rights and A has none. If O subsequently conveys the southern half to B, B has full riparian rights. O could convey the southern half to B granting some riparian rights to B and some to A.

When a riparian conveys a portion of a parcel that borders on the waterbody to another, the property so conveyed has riparian rights unless they are expressly reserved by the grantor. Conveyance of a portion of the riparian parcel not bordering on the waterbody transfers no riparian rights unless expressly granted. Since the grantee takes nothing that the riparian grantor did not have, such grants should not be objectionable on policy grounds. In states that follow the source of title rule discussed in Section II C 2 of this chapter, this method of transfer provides a way to circumvent the rule.

In Figure 3, assume that O conveys the southern half of the parcel to B, granting B a proportionate share of riparian rights, then the remainder of the land and water rights to A. Both A and B have riparian rights even if the tract is in a source of title state.

A different situation arises if a riparian landowner seeks to grant riparian rights to a nonriparian without conveying a portion of the riparian parcel. The validity of such grants is in doubt.

The general rule is that a conveyance of riparian rights by a riparian landowner to a grantee is binding. By making a grant the riparian owner gives up the right to divert or use any water to the detriment of the grantee. In effect the grantor waives all claims based upon the doctrine of riparian rights and the waiver binds successors in interest. Obviously, a riparian who grants away all riparian rights cannot convey those rights with the remaining riparian land.

Although grants are valid as between the parties, a majority of states hold that grants of riparian rights separate from the grant of any portion of riparian land held by the grantor are invalid as to other riparians. Duckworth v. Watsonville Water and Light Co. (1910). Thus a non-riparian grantee of riparian water rights cannot object to a riparian's conduct even if the conduct would have been unreasonable as to the original riparian grantor. However, a minority of jurisdictions allow the grantee any reasonable use that the grantor could have made. In other words, if challenged by a riparian, the non-riparian grantee's use will be judged by the reasonable use rule just as if the riparian grantor were making a non-riparian use of water (See Section IV B of this chapter). Lawrie v. Silsby (1904); State v. Apfelbacher (1918).

The watershed limitation, discussed in Section IV B 2 of this chapter, limits a riparian's ability to grant riparian rights. In states that hold use of water outside the watershed to be unreasonable per se, the riparian who owns a contiguous parcel (part of which is outside the watershed) and who transfers a non-abutting portion including the por-

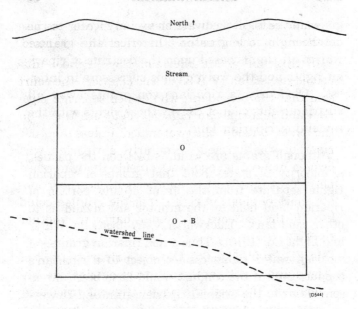

**Figure 4**

tion outside the watershed, cannot grant the purchaser any right to use water outside the watershed; however, many jurisdictions will not bar the non-riparian use unless others are harmed.

In Figure 4 O owns a riparian tract of land. O conveys the southern half, part of which is outside the watershed, to B, granting half the riparian rights. In states that allow water to be used outside the watershed so long as no riparian is actually harmed, O can grant B the right to use water outside the watershed and B can exercise the right so long as no other riparian is harmed.

In Stratton v. Mt. Hermon Boys' School (discussed in Section IV B 3b of this chapter), the court said that the defendant, who owned separate riparian and non-riparian parcels, could use water on the tract outside the watershed unless another riparian was harmed. Similarly, a riparian who owns a non-contiguous tract outside the watershed may grant that tract to another with a proportionate share of riparian rights that the grantee could use in the absence of actual harm to another riparian.

In Figure 5 (page 66), O owns a riparian tract of land and a non-contiguous tract outside the watershed. O grants the non-contiguous tract to A with some riparian rights. In states that allow use outside the watershed in the absence of actual harm to other riparians, A can make a reasonable use of the water.

## VII. LOSS OF RIPARIAN RIGHTS

Riparian rights, like other property rights, can be terminated or "lost" in a number of ways. The general rule is that riparian rights cannot be lost by non-use. The rule, however, is not absolute. Riparian rights may be extinguished by prescription, avulsion, and under permit systems. In most states with hybrid systems, statutes limit the right of a riparian to initiate new uses and may even declare vested riparian rights to be forfeited by

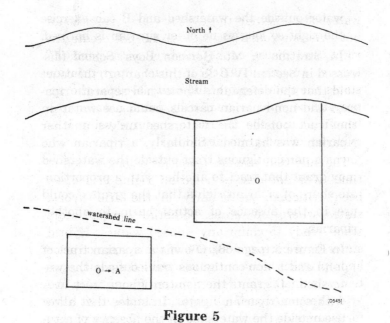

**Figure 5**

non-use over a statutorily prescribed period. Statutory permit schemes that require a riparian to obtain a permit before initiating new uses effectively limit common law riparian rights. Riparian rights also may be lost by eminent domain, typically used when a city seeks to secure a water supply.

## A.  Effect of Non-Use

Ordinarily, riparian rights are not lost by non-use. Because riparian rights attach only to riparian land, it follows that the owner of a riparian parcel also "owns" riparian rights in the adjacent waterbody whether those rights are exercised or not. As one court put it, "use did not create the right, and disuse cannot destroy or suspend it." Lux v. Haggin (1886). In prior appropriation states the rule is quite different; because the appropriative right is created by putting water to a beneficial use, the failure to continue using it is evidence of intent to abandon it.

The rule that non-use (even for a long period of time) will not destroy riparian rights has often been criticized, particularly in the arid hybrid states where numerous potential appropriators stand ready to claim any unused water. Hybrid states have borrowed aspects of the system of prior appropriation because the unmodified riparian system was unable to allocate water efficiently in the arid West. Almost all hybrid states now have forfeiture statutes that limit the ability of riparian landowners to initiate new riparian uses after a certain date, although in most, vested riparian rights still cannot be lost simply by non-use.

Although there is a dearth of cases, riparian rights arguably could be abandoned. Under the common law doctrine of abandonment, a property right is considered abandoned if its owner does not use it and manifests an intent to abandon it.

## B. Avulsion and Accretion

Avulsion occurs when a stream suddenly changes its channel. If avulsion moves a stream away from a landowner's property, the property boundary line remains where it was before the stream left its channel. Avulsion can effectively transform riparian land into non-riparian, thereby depriving the unfortunate owner of riparian rights. Conversely, a non-riparian landowner may suddenly gain riparian rights as a result of avulsion.

When a stream changes course over a period of many years, accretion and reliction may result. Accretion is the gradual addition of sediment to one bank along the waterline. Reliction occurs when water gradually withdraws from one side of the stream. If accretion and reliction occur, rather than avulsion, the rule is that the property boundary line shifts with the waterline so that a riparian adjacent to added land will gain title to the new land, keeping riparian rights. See Burkart v. City of Fort Lauderdale (1964). A riparian whose land is carried away loses title to that land but retains appurtenant riparian rights so long as the stream remains adjacent to the land.

The distinction between avulsion and accretion is not clear. Most courts have held that a change in stream course constitutes avulsion only if it is considerable, violent, and abrupt.

## C. Prescription

Typical adverse possession laws provide that the open and notorious, hostile, exclusive, actual and continuous possession of property for a prescribed number of years vests title in the adverse possessor. Like other property rights, riparian rights can be lost by adverse possession. Obtaining a prescriptive right in riparian law turns on two factors: whether the person against whom the prescriptive right is sought is: (1) a riparian or a non-riparian; and (2) upstream or downstream from the riparian plaintiff.

The natural flow theory gave each riparian the right to have the stream flow past the land undiminished in quantity or quality, subject only to the right of other riparians to limited domestic use of the water. Under this theory the prescriptive period would start to run as soon as an upstream riparian began to take more water than needed for domestic purposes; this was true even if the downstream riparian plaintiff were not actually harmed.

Prescription has always been an important way to obtain exclusive rights to use water which are not otherwise recognized in riparian jurisdictions. Tyler v. Wilkinson (1827), considered the foundation case in American riparian law, stated that while "mere priority of appropriation of running water . . . confers no exclusive right . . . by our law, upon principles of public convenience, the term of twenty years of exclusive uninterrupted enjoyment has been held a conclusive presumption of a grant or right." The equities of longstanding users are thus protected in a system where prior use as such does not give rise to any rights. Of course any water use for less than the prescriptive period gives one no rights. Martin v. Bigelow (1827).

All states now follow some form of the reasonable use rule. When a prescription conflict is between two riparians—an upstream defendant and a down-stream plaintiff—the rule is that an upper ripari-an's use is not adverse unless it unreasonably interferes with the rights of lower riparians. Pabst v. Finmand (1922). This rule is sensible because all riparians are entitled to make reasonable use of the water.

If a prescription conflict is between an upstream non-riparian defendant and a downstream riparian plaintiff, the reasonable use states have followed two different rules. Some courts have held that, under the reasonable use theory, if the non-riparian use does not unreasonably interfere with reasonable uses of downstream riparians, the non-riparian use cannot ripen into a prescriptive right. Other courts have held that a non-riparian use by an upstream defendant that does not unreasonably interfere with uses of lower riparians is nevertheless unlawful and can become a prescriptive right. Consequently the downstream riparian must seek injunctive relief, even in the absence of harm.

The courts have long held that a downstream user (riparian or non-riparian) cannot acquire prescrip-tive rights against upstream riparians. The rule is sometimes stated as "prescription does not run upstream." Its rationale is that since a downstream use cannot adversely affect an upstream riparian use, the downstream use is not hostile and cannot be the basis of a prescriptive right. For an interesting exception see Dontanello v. Gust (1915) (lower riparian acquired prescriptive right by building diversion mechanism on upper riparian's land).

To the extent prescriptive rights have been perfected on a waterway, the rights of riparians are diminished. Typically, courts (e.g., California) have granted the adverse user a specific quantity of water based on the amount used in acquiring the prescriptive right. The right so acquired is similar to an appropriative right in that it is not diminished in times of shortage. However, some courts (e.g., Washington) have measured the prescriptive right as the proportion of the adverse use to the total flow of the river. Under this rule the adverse user would be required to reduce usage pro rata with other riparians in times of shortage.

Generally, the rules governing prescription in riparian states also apply in the hybrid states, at least as between riparian landowners. As between a riparian and a non-riparian the rules may differ because, under most appropriation systems, new (non-riparian) uses must be acquired by making an appropriation pursuant to statutory requirements. Prescription in hybrid states is discussed in Chapter Four, Section III C.

## D. Legislation

### 1. *Statutes Modifying Water Rights*

#### a. *Permit Systems*

As population increased and new cities grew up far from the great eastern rivers, riparian states began to enact statutory schemes designed to promote efficient allocation of water. The most common statutory modification was adoption of permit systems. Some states required permits not only for new riparian uses but also for existing uses. A few required that unused riparian rights be claimed and recognized to be valid in the future.

### b. Hybrid Systems

The common law riparian doctrine was unsuited to much of the American West because many mines and farm lands needing water were located miles from streams. Early miners on the public domain were moved to adopt the rule that a prior appropriator acquires a right superior to those all subsequent appropriators. This system worked relatively well during settlement of the public domain. Other states recognized both the prior appropriation and riparian doctrines. Because California was the first to announce its recognition of both types of rights, the hybrid approach is sometimes called the "California Doctrine." It is not truly a "doctrine," however, since important differences exist between systems developed by different states. Chapter Four discusses the development of hybrid systems. Constitutional challenges to statutory modifications of riparian rights in favor of the appropriation doctrine are discussed in Chapter Four, Section II C.

### 2. Forfeiture Statutes

Forfeiture is a statutory concept dictating that non-use for a specified period of time automatically terminates property rights regardless of the owner's intent. Many permit statutes in riparian states and in most hybrid states have provisions requiring forfeiture of riparian rights in certain circumstances. Typically one must begin using a permit within a reasonable time or forfeit it. Forfeiture may also occur if water use under a permit is discontinued for two or three years.

Conversion to statutory permit systems or to hybrid systems was intended in part to remedy the uncertainty and insecurity of the riparian system. A riparian's ability to commence any reasonable uses in the future, as well as to continue existing uses, allows great and unanticipated increases in water use. Forfeiture statutes cutting off or limiting riparian rights not exercised within a certain period of time diminish the problem. In the hybrid states of Kansas and Washington, even vested riparian rights—those the riparian has historically exercised—can be lost by a period of non-use under statutory forfeiture provisions. Some forfeiture statutes have been challenged on the ground that they violate the Fifth and Fourteenth Amendments to the United States Constitution by permitting states to take water rights without compensation. Constitutional challenges have been largely unsuccessful.

# CHAPTER THREE

# PRIOR APPROPRIATION

## I. GENERAL DESCRIPTION

The prior appropriation doctrine was developed to meet the unique needs of nineteenth century water users in the western United States. It originated in the customs of miners on the public lands who accorded the best rights to those who first used water. It was later extended to farmers and other users, even on private lands. Where it applies, water rights are granted according to when a person applies a particular quantity of water to a beneficial use. Those rights continue so long as the beneficial use is maintained.

The appropriation doctrine has developed into complex statutory schemes in nineteen states. Ten of those states have "hybrid" systems that employ elements of the riparian doctrine as well as the appropriation doctrine. Hybrid systems and other doctrinal variants are discussed in Chapter Four. Although prior appropriation is used to allocate rights to divert and consume water, several forms of riparian rights relating principally to use of the surface of waterways apply in prior appropriation states. See Chapter Two, Section III.

Most appropriation jurisdictions consider water to be a public resource owned by no one. The right

74

of individuals to use water under the prior appropriation system is based on application of a quantity of water to beneficial use.

The traditional elements of a valid appropriation are:

- *Intent* to apply water to a beneficial use;

- An actual *diversion* of water from a natural source;

- Application of the water to a *beneficial use* within a reasonable time.

When all requirements are met and any other procedures specified by state law (e.g., posting, filing) have been followed, the appropriation is complete. A permit or decree must usually be obtained from an administrative agency or court before the right is fully perfected.

The date of the appropriation determines the user's priority to use water, with the earliest user having the superior right. If water is insufficient to meet all needs, those early in time of appropriation (senior appropriators) will obtain all of their allotted water; those who appropriated later (junior appropriators) may receive only some, or none, of the water to which they have rights. Thus the "first in time, first in right" concept contrasts sharply with the riparian tradition of prorating the entitlement to water among all users during times of scarcity.

A beneficial use that will support an appropriation must have a specific, stated purpose. The property where water is applied to a beneficial use does not have to be adjacent to the source, and usually does not even need to be within the source's watershed. Most states allow the transfer of water away from the property to which the rights have attached if the rights of other appropriators are not harmed.

In general, water may be appropriated for any use the state deems beneficial. More economically or socially useful purposes ordinarily will not be preferred over less useful ones. Priority depends on which use was commenced earlier in time. Some state statutes or constitutions express preferences for certain uses, but they do not alter the basic principle of priority based on first use. Preferences may be used administratively in determining which potential users will be granted appropriation permits; more commonly they are applied to allow holders of rights for more preferred uses to condemn less preferred uses upon payment of compensation.

The measure of an appropriative right is the quantity that can be put to a beneficial use within a reasonable time, using reasonable diligence. The right to use water does not include the right to waste it. Diverting more water than is reasonably necessary is wasteful, deprives other users, and theoretically should not be considered a beneficial use.

Long term failure to use appropriated water can result in loss of the right. If disuse is intentional it may be construed as abandonment; unintended disuse results in forfeiture in some states.

Statutes charge administrative agencies in most states with assuring that the appropriation is in the public interest, resulting in denial of permits to early appropriators and choices among competing appropriators based on whether the public interest will be served. Some state courts have held that states have a "public trust" obligation not to allow water to be used inconsistently with public purposes. The public trust doctrine may negate even existing appropriations that are contrary to the public interest.

## II.  DEVELOPMENT OF PRIOR APPROPRIATION DOCTRINE

The doctrine of prior appropriation that evolved into modern statutory systems can be traced to local customs and regulations developed during the nation's rapid western expansion, particularly after the discovery of gold in California in 1848. Available water sources were limited, and mining (especially placer mining) demanded large quantities of water. Agriculture to support a growing population also required water.

The common law riparian system did not meet the miners' needs because it restricted rights to those owning land bordering often scarce streams and barred use of water on other lands or outside the watershed. Most lands were owned by the United States and water users were essentially trespassers who assumed that they could use the public land.

Rules were developed in the mining camps for the allocation of water rights. The rules were similar to those adopted for the establishment and protection of mining claims on public lands: first in time, first in right. Essentially, the first to use water from a specific source held a prior right that would be protected against the claims of others. This system was applied to agricultural lands as homesteaders moved west.

The United States disposed of its lands through a variety of public land laws. The territory it had acquired from foreign nations and Indian nations included nearly all the West. The government could have decided to convey the land and (riparian) water rights together. Instead it acquiesced in the establishment of private water rights on public lands under local customs, including rights to divert water across public land to distant mining claims and irrigated tracts. Lands were then conveyed separately from these water rights and subject to them.

## A. Federal Statutes

### 1. 1866 Mining Act

Shortly after the Civil War, proposals were made in Congress to withdraw mines from the public domain and operate or sell them to pay war debts. Western legislators in whose states private mineral exploration was rampant opposed this suggestion, resulting in enactment of the 1866 Mining Act, codified as amended at 30 U.S.C.A. § 51 and 43 U.S.C.A. § 661. A portion of the Act is quoted in Chapter Four, Section I B. The Act expressly confirmed the rights of miners and appropriators of water. It formally sanctioned appropriations of water on the public lands, made before or after passage of the Act, including rights of way for carrying the water to the land on which it was used. The Act failed to define any method of acquiring water rights from the federal government, thus deferring to established local customs, state or territorial laws, or court rulings. The law recognized a federal obligation to respect rights developed with its tacit approval.

## 2. *1870 Amendment to Mining Act*

Even after the 1866 Act, it was not clear if riparian landowners who obtained grants of land from the United States held riparian water rights superior or subject to claims of prior appropriators. The 1870 Amendment to the Mining Act clarified that issue in favor of prior appropriators. It stipulated that anyone who acquired title to public lands through federal patents, homestead rights, or rights of preemption took title subject to any water rights, easements for water rights, or rights of way acquired by others while lands were in public ownership. These rights were good against the United States and its grantees.

## 3. 1877 Desert Land Act

The Desert Land Act, codified at 43 U.S.C.A. §§ 321–329, provided that water from non-navigable sources on the public lands was available for appropriation for irrigation, mining and manufacturing purposes subject to existing rights. It applied specifically to arid lands within Arizona, California, Idaho, Montana, Nevada, New Mexico, North Dakota, Oregon, South Dakota, Utah, Washington and Wyoming. Colorado was added by amendment in 1891.

Until 1935, western states were divided concerning whether the Desert Land Act applied only to desert lands. In that year the Supreme Court decided that the appropriation doctrine applied to all public domain in the named states and territories. California Oregon Power Co. v. Beaver Portland Cement Co. (1935). The decision also said that the Desert Land Act severed the water from public lands, so that only water rights established under local law passed with a patent. Thus, all unappropriated waters of non-navigable sources remained open to appropriation and use according to state law. The Act is excerpted in Chapter Four, Section I B.

## B. Development of Modern Systems

The appropriation system was an expedient means to encourage development of the arid West, where much of the land is distant from streams, and water is limited. It rewarded those who first risked their effort and money. Many feared that adoption of the riparian doctrine in this situation would allow a few landowners to monopolize water supplies.

The eight most arid states (Arizona, Colorado, Idaho, Montana, Nevada, New Mexico, Utah and Wyoming) constitutionally or statutorily repudiated riparian rights very early and adopted prior appropriation as the sole method of acquiring rights to the use of water for all beneficial purposes. In these states statutory systems have evolved to provide for initiation of appropriations, establishment and enforcement of priorities, and water distribution.

Early in Alaska's development some riparian uses for mining purposes were allowed, but in 1966 its legislature enacted the Water Use Act, converting all riparian rights into rights of prior appropriation. This conversion of existing riparian rights is more ambitious than the approach taken by several other western states in which existing riparian rights were preserved to some extent after adoption of the appropriation doctrine.

Some degree of riparian common law continues to exist side-by-side with the statutory provisions of prior appropriation in California, Kansas, Mississippi, Nebraska, North Dakota, Oklahoma, Oregon, South Dakota, Texas and Washington. Hybrid states generally recognized riparian rights but limited their expansion and recognized new rights only by prior appropriation. Hybrid systems are discussed in Chapter Four.

## III.  APPROPRIATIVE WATER RIGHTS AS PROPERTY

### A.  No Individual Ownership of Flowing Water

As a general rule, private persons do not "own" water in its natural state. Water, like fish and game, ordinarily is a public resource. A government uses its police power to allocate rights to use the water and to conserve and regulate the resource in the interest of the public.

The prior appropriation states have all constitutionally or statutorily asserted their prerogative to administer use of their waters for the benefit of their citizens. Most declare that water belongs to the public or claim ownership of water to be in the state. These provisions assert sovereign, rather than proprietary interests; they establish a state's power and duty to regulate appropriation of water by individuals under the rubric of state "ownership."

The nature of the private property interest in the right to use water varies from state to state. One who lawfully diverts water for some useful purpose ordinarily is to be the lawful custodian of water, and has certain rights and duties with respect to other users and the state. Water thus should not be considered personal property while it is in canals, conduits, reservoirs and the like.

When put into containers or held in swimming pools after being delivered to consumers, however, water may properly be treated as personal property. Some states go farther and treat all water in the hands of a beneficial user as personal property that can be bought and sold, stolen and in some circumstances subject to taxation.

In appropriation states the property interest in water is limited to a right to divert and use a certain quantity. The right to divert water and to use it beneficially is called a "usufructuary" right, as opposed to a "possessory" right. As property, the right to appropriate water has certain standard characteristics throughout the West. Generally, the appropriative right can be used on a particular parcel of land. In most states the holder of the right can, without loss of priority, transfer it to be used on another parcel of land or may sell the right to another party who will do so if other appropriators will not be injured. See Section IX of this chapter.

Water rights usually can be assigned and mortgaged, and cannot be taken from an appropriator by the state or federal government without just compensation. The Supreme Court has ruled that a water right is an article of commerce; thus states are forbidden to restrict unreasonably interstate commerce in such rights and Congress may legislate concerning it. The fact that the state retains an interest in the water is relevant to the question of whether state restrictions are reasonable under the Commerce Clause. Sporhase v. Nebraska *ex rel.* Douglas (1982).

Generally, it is held that an appropriator has an easement for the flow of water in the bed of the stream from which water is diverted and in the tributaries above the point of diversion. The appropriator may have legal and equitable remedies for diminution of quantity or quality of the available water.

The extent of regulation further defines the property interest in water rights. States require that appropriated water continue to be used for the purpose for which it was originally taken. This purpose is determined when the priority date is established, as are the quantity, rate of flow, point of diversion and times when water may be taken from the stream. Other regulations may concern the degree of efficiency required and restrict the pollution of the water source.

Once water has been used for its stated beneficial purpose, a portion of the water remaining unconsumed ordinarily leaves the land by seepage, drainage ditches, sewer pipes or the like, eventually returning to the stream from which it was diverted. At the point it leaves the control of the holder of the water right and use ceases, any private property interest in the water ends.

## B. State Constitutional and Statutory Provisions

The nineteen appropriation and hybrid states have constitutional or statutory provisions that set out policies of state control and define public rights in the resource. The provisions assume that water in its natural state belongs to no person or entity, but rather is a common resource to be administered for the benefit of society. Most also provide that private rights may be allocated in the resource pursuant to the law of prior appropriation.

State control of water resources may be expressed in a constitutional or statutory provision stating that water "belong[s] to the public" (Arizona, Nevada, New Mexico, Oregon), is "property of the state" (Idaho, Montana, North Dakota, Texas, Wyoming), is "property of the people of the state" (California, Colorado, South Dakota), is "property of the public" (Nebraska, Utah) or similar language. Although state authority is typically expressed in ownership terms the effect is essentially to assert broad police power over the resource while allowing private rights to be created in its use.

## C. Statutes Limiting Riparian Rights

Statutes and constitutional provisions in nearly all prior appropriation states abrogate or limit the scope of any formerly recognized riparian rights. Ten states have instituted permit systems or imposed prior appropriation systems to replace or modify riparian rights. Riparian rights not related to diversion and consumptive use of water (e.g., right of access, right to wharf out) are usually not affected. See Chapter Two, Section III. The states generally restrict or abolish riparian rights to the reasonable use of water that were unused at the time of enactment. Compliance with statutory provisions for appropriation then becomes the sole method of acquiring water rights. States in which some riparian rights continue to coexist with rights by appropriation have "hybrid systems." See Chapter Four.

In rejecting the riparian system a common pattern has been to declare riparian rights "vested," and to fit them into the prior appropriation system according to the date of original acquisition of the riparian land from the government. Because riparian uses can later arise or expand, uncertainty as to how much water has been allocated is built into the combined riparian and appropriation systems. Many states have responded by recognizing riparian rights to extend only to the amount of water applied to a beneficial purpose within a designated time and by barring subsequent exercise of unused riparian rights. Such declarations obviously diminish the property right of riparian proprietors, and have been challenged as unconstitutional takings without just compensation.

Constitutional attacks on statutes limiting riparian rights have failed in most states because the provision was read as not applying to vested rights, because unused riparian rights had not actually vested, or simply because the ability to diminish or modify water rights was within the state's police power. In Baeth v. Hoisveen (1968) the North Dakota Supreme Court treated riparian water rights as inchoate until exercised, holding that no taking occurred when the right to expand reasonable use in the future was statutorily destroyed.

The Kansas Supreme Court upheld legislation reducing the scope of riparian rights in order to achieve the goals of preventing (1) underdevelopment due to holding water in perpetuity for common law owners who may never use it, and (2) the resultant injury to established users. It grounded broad legislative authority in the state's police power. F. Arthur Stone & Sons v. Gibson (1981).

The South Dakota court upheld a legislative modification of a riparian owner's "vested right" that limited it to "water having been applied to any beneficial use on March 2, 1955 or within three years immediately prior thereto to the extent of the existing beneficial use made thereof." Belle Fourche Irrigation Dist. v. Smiley (1970).

California's statutory adjudication procedure empowering the Water Resources Control Board to determine water rights in an entire stream system has been held not to extinguish a riparian owner's claim to future use of waters in a stream system. Yet the state Supreme Court held constitutional legislation authorizing the Board to define and limit the riparian owner's future right to use water in a stream system adjudication. This forces riparians to participate in proceedings to assert rights to future use of water. *In re* Waters of Long Valley Creek (1979).

Riparian rights in Texas have been limited to the maximum amount used in any year from 1963–1967 by the Water Rights Adjudication Act of 1967. The Texas Supreme Court upheld the constitutionality of the provision, rejecting claims that early land grants carried vested riparian rights that are property rights not to be taken without compensation. *In re* Adjudication of Water Rights of Upper Guadalupe Segment of the Guadalupe River Basin (1982).

## IV. ELEMENTS OF APPROPRIATION

It is unreliable to generalize about the appropriation doctrine in all jurisdictions, but three elements are important in finding that a valid appropriation has been made. Generally, water must be *diverted* with an *intent* to appropriate it for a *beneficial use.*

At first the appropriation system was encumbered by few procedures and legal requirements. One who needed water usually had only to begin using it. But in order to perfect a legal right in the water the user had to show that the use amounted to an appropriation. The three elements were designed to prevent fraud and to provide some order in an otherwise unstructured system. Additionally, states have a special interest in assuring that the resource is devoted to purposes consistent with the public good. Hence a requirement that water be applied to a beneficial use.

Historically, it was necessary for an appropriator to be able to prove that all three elements were satisfied. Now their importance is largely theoretical, since they have become incorporated into modern state water allocation statutes. Permit systems and administrative agencies that review the sufficiency of applications for water rights include requirements and criteria that achieve the purposes of the common law elements of appropriation.

## A. Intent

An appropriation is not valid unless the appropriator intends to divert water and apply it to a beneficial use. Thus, one who diverts water away from its normal flow pattern in order to prevent flood damage is not an appropriator. But such a diverter who later perceives a beneficial use for the water as channeled may become an appropriator as of the time intent is manifested.

The problem of proving intent arises most frequently when one seeks to secure a priority that predates the first appropriation. The doctrine of relation back allows an appropriator to perfect a water right with a priority date as of the time an intent to appropriate was first formed. Evidence must be presented to prove that one had such intent and that work was proceeding toward an actual diversion of water (not just speculation) as of the priority date.

In states where a permit is required for a valid appropriation, application for a permit is objective evidence of intent. However, one may not apply for a water right and then seek a place to use it as that would constitute speculation. Lemmon v. Hardy (1974). Early statutory systems gave appropriators the option of actual diversion or applying for a permit. A person could choose to divert without a permit and still relate back the appropriation to the time work on the diversion facilities began. Sand Point Water & Light Co. v. Panhandle Dev. (1905).

Where permits are not required for a valid appropriation, primarily in Colorado, proof of intent retains some importance. To establish the priority of an appropriation, an applicant must make a clear decision to use water and make an "open, physical demonstration of that intent." Historically the physical act requirement was also a means of giving notice to others that one intended to appropriate water before there was actual diversion.

Colorado law provides for conditional decrees to hold rights to a particular quantity of water for a specific future use. Thus, anyone seriously pursuing a project requiring water seeks a conditional decree early in the planning. In order to get a conditional decree one must demonstrate present intent to put the water to a beneficial use and proceed with due diligence to divert the water. The applicant must describe with particularity the amount of water to be appropriated and the construction plans. Those opposing the proposed conditional decree can file objections, and the application is adjudicated with respect to the rights of all parties in the stream system.

The Colorado Supreme Court has held that plans, but no firm contracts, to sell water to cities that will grow and have future needs are not sufficient to show an intent to appropriate, but constitute only speculation. Colorado River Water Conservation Dist. v. Vidler Tunnel Water Co. (1979); Rocky Mountain Power Co. v. Colorado River Water Conservation Dist. (1982).

The physical act requirement in Colorado has become something of a formality to obtain a conditional decree, with little pretense that it puts others on notice. Although the court has held that the physical act be on the land where water will be diverted and that engineering work done in the office is not adequate, a cursory survey on the ground (that almost certainly would give no indication of the nature of one's intent) will suffice. Elk-Rifle Water Co. v. Templeton (1971).

The Colorado courts examine other relevant evidence besides the first open physical act in setting a priority date to determine whether the requisite intent was present. Thus a survey not accompanied by a clear decision to undertake the project may not be sufficient. Colorado River Water Conservation Dist. v. Rocky Mountain Power Co. (1971), *cert. denied* (1972) (water right dates from

1961 when final decision to build project was made, not from 1954 when survey was made). The priority date of an appropriation can be no earlier than the time an intent to divert water to put it to a beneficial use was formulated. But as the *Rocky Mountain Power* case shows, it is possible for intent to be formed after the physical act, in which case priority is based on the later of the two events. See Harvey Land & Cattle Co. v. Southeastern Colo. Water Conservancy Dist. (1981) (drilling wells with capacity greater than old right constituted "physical act" for new water right but appropriation related back only to time, years after wells were drilled, when intent to use for larger quantity was later formed). The right may also have a priority predating the conditional decree if it is based on evidence of earlier events showing intent.

## B. Diversion

Some jurisdictions require that water be physically diverted from a stream in order to effect a valid appropriation. Others consider various uses that do not depend on structures or human acts, and even some instream uses, to be appropriations.

The diversion requirement provides notice to present and prospective appropriators that water has been appropriated, and gives authorities and courts a concrete basis to determine an appropriator's priority date. The capacity of diversion works can be used to define the quantity of water one has appropriated. These functions of the requirement are not important where there is a permit requirement. An appropriation cannot be complete without some use of water, however, and the diversion requirement is often the last ingredient necessary to perfect a water right. In some jurisdictions it need not be satisfied by removal of the water from the stream.

## 1. Types of Diversions

A diversion is an alteration of part or all of a stream's flow away from its natural course. A common method of diversion is to build a dam across a stream to channel water into a canal or ditch. Water may be channeled further into smaller ditches, each with a "headgate" that controls when and how much water is used in each of several parcels of land, often by several appropriators. Other methods of diverting water include reservoirs, flumes, pipes, pumps and even water wheels.

Traditionally, a diversion had to be man-made, but courts have forged numerous exceptions as discussed below. Even in states adhering to a strict physical diversion requirement (e.g., California, Montana, New Mexico) exceptions are allowed for various water uses.

## 2. Due Diligence Requirement and Conditional Rights

In states that require a permit to appropriate water, the priority date may relate back to the date the application was filed. In order to keep that priority date and to perfect a water right, the appropriator must complete construction with due diligence and actually use the water within the time specified in the permit or statute.

The time period in which an applicant for a water right must complete construction of diversion facilities and actually use the water may be set by statute, fixed by regulation, or based on a finding of an administrative agency, an official or a court charged with determining whether the applicant's acts constitute due diligence. The finding involves consideration of the difficulty and expense of the work required to complete construction.

Some state statutes set maximum time periods for construction of facilities and application of water to beneficial use, often five years, subject to extension for good cause (e.g., Arizona, Idaho, Nevada, Oregon, Wyoming; New Mexico allows four additional years after construction to apply water). A few require actual construction to begin within a certain time, ranging from six months to two years after approval of the application (Arizona, two years; Nebraska, six months; Oklahoma, two years; Oregon, one year; Texas, two years). Some states allow time extensions readily upon a showing that the applicant has proceeded with due diligence; others grant extensions only in narrowly defined or extraordinary circumstances. Idaho, for example, allows extensions after its five year limit only if the applicant is prevented from continuing by delays in necessary federal approvals or the completion of litigation, or if the project is extremely large.

In Colorado, which does not have a permit system, an appropriator's priority date is generally the date of the first open, physical act toward appropriating water such as the date construction of diversion facilities commenced. City and County of Denver v. Sheriff (1939). An early priority date will be lost, however, unless the prospective appropriator completes construction with due diligence within a reasonable time.

Colorado's procedure for protecting unused rights by obtaining a conditional decree is discussed in the preceding subsection. If a conditional decree is granted, the prospective user must proceed with due diligence in constructing the waterworks or risk forfeiture of the conditional right. The decree holder must obtain a finding of due diligence by a water court referee every four years. Failure to do so will result in cancellation of the conditionally decreed water rights. Town of DeBeque v. Enewold (1980). Once the diversion takes place an absolute decree can be obtained that is senior to all appropriators who commenced their appropriations after the initiation of the conditional decree.

## 3.  *Exceptions to the Diversion Requirement*

Several states no longer require an actual, physical diversion from the stream; exceptions have been fashioned to meet particular policy considerations. A physical diversion from a stream may not be required if intent to appropriate to a beneficial use, notice to others, and actual application to a beneficial use are clearly established. For example, courts in Montana and Oregon have held that farm land can be irrigated naturally, with the help of existing channels and depressions, if it would be a waste of money to require a system of artificial ditches. California, Colorado, Idaho and Nevada law consider it to be an appropriation when ranchers allow livestock to drink water from ponds, marshes or directly from a stream. One court even said that mist from a waterfall that nourished vegetation might constitute an appropriation. Empire Water & Power Co. v. Cascade Town Co. (1913).

Several states have embraced a trend allowing instream (in situ) appropriations of water. An instream appropriation right generally requires that an amount of water be allowed to flow through the stream at particular places in order to protect fish and wildlife, scenic beauty or waterborne recreation. States have recognized that water can be put to beneficial use while flowing in the stream itself, for recreation, hydropower, aesthetics, navigation or simply to protect the surrounding ecosystem. See Dept. of Parks v. Idaho Dept. of Water Administration (1974) (upholding a statute declaring preservation of waters in Malad Canyon for scenic and recreational purpose to be a beneficial use).

Instream flows generally may be appropriated or reserved only by a state agency, although the agency may be able to act upon requests of private individuals, other state and local agencies or the federal government. The following states have legislation allowing instream uses of water: Alaska, California, Colorado, Hawaii, Idaho, Kansas, Montana, Oklahoma, Oregon, Nebraska, Utah, Washington and Wyoming. The Colorado Supreme Court upheld legislation allowing a state agency to appropriate instream flows over an argument that it was inconsistent with the "right to divert" water in the state constitution. Colorado River Water Conservation Dist. v. Colorado Water Conservation Board (1979).

## C.  Beneficial Use

The last and most important step in perfecting an appropriation is application of the water to beneficial use. All prior appropriation states that follow appropriation law consider domestic, municipal, agricultural and industrial uses to be beneficial uses. Beneficial use is defined specifically in most state statutes (see Table A).

Domestic use generally includes household uses such as eating, drinking, laundering, washing and watering a small garden. In rural areas domestic use also includes water for raising animals on a small scale, such as keeping a few dairy cows or chickens. Municipal use includes domestic use

## BENEFICIAL USES SPECIFIED BY STATE LAW

| Use: | Domestic | Municipal | Irrigation or agricultural | Industrial | Stock-watering | Power | Mining | Recreation | Fish & wildlife | Other |
|---|---|---|---|---|---|---|---|---|---|---|
| Alaska | X | X | X | X | | X | X | X | X | maintenance of water quality |
| Arizona | X | X | X | | X | X | X | X | X | groundwater recharge; water quality |
| California | X | X | X | X | | X | X | X | X | |
| Colorado | X | X | X | X | | X | | X | | aesthetics |
| Idaho * | X | X | X | X | X | X | X | X | | |
| Kansas | X | X | X | X | | X | | X | | |
| Montana | X | X | X | X | X | X | | X | | |
| Nebraska * | X | X | X | | | X | | X | | |
| Nevada | X | X | X | | X | X | | X | X | state conservation purposes |
| New Mexico ** | | X | X | | X | | | | | |
| North Dakota | X | | | X | X | | | X | X | |
| Oklahoma * | X | | | | | | | | | |
| Oregon | X | X | X | X | | X | X | X | X | pollution abatement, navigation |
| South Dakota *** | X | | | | | | | | | |
| Texas | X | X | X | X | X | X | X | X | X | |
| Utah * | X | X | X | X | X | X | X | X | X | |
| Washington | X | X | X | X | | X | X | X | X | |
| Wyoming * | X | X | X | X | | X | X | X | X | |

\*   No comprehensive definition furnished by statute or case law.

\*\*   Case law defines beneficial use as "the use of such water as may be necessary for some useful and beneficial purpose in connection with the land from which it is taken." Erickson v. McLean, 62 N.M. 264, 308 P.2d 983, 988 (1957).

\*\*\*   Statute defines beneficial use as " . . . any use of water that is reasonable and useful and beneficial to the appropriator, and at the same time is consistent with the interests of the public in the best utilization of water supplies." S.D.Cod.Laws § 46-1-6.

and water used in operation of public buildings and even irrigation of city parks.

Initially the range of beneficial uses was very limited, including only domestic, irrigation, stock and mining uses. In Empire Water & Power Co. v. Cascade Town Co. (1913), a federal appeals court refused to consider recreation a beneficial use. The court would not allow the resort town of Cascade, Colorado to assert the right to keep the town's major attraction, a waterfall, flowing merely to retain its scenic beauty. However, the court seemed willing to allow the waterfall to continue flowing if the town could assert an agricultural use, such as misting the vegetation growing on the banks of Cascade Falls. Most states now have accepted recreation as a beneficial use. Some even specify that scenic or aesthetic uses are beneficial.

Once an appropriator puts water to a use considered beneficial by state law, the right is perfected. The right becomes absolute and its priority in times of shortage will not be defeated even by more socially important, economically more valuable or more efficient uses by a junior appropriator. Thus, a senior user applying vast quantities of water to the unprofitable production of rice in the desert might prevent a city with a junior right from receiving desperately needed water for domestic purposes, or a highly profitable industry from taking the water it requires to function. Some jurisdictions have preference statutes creating a hierarchy of rights that allows persons seeking certain uses, primarily municipalities, to condemn rights that are being put to a less beneficial use. See Section V D of this chapter. Furthermore, modern interpretations of beneficial use require that water not be wasted by inefficient diversion works and excessive applications (e.g., more water than the crops need). These limitations are embodied in statutes and administrative regulations on the manner and quantity of water that may be put to a particular beneficial use. Section VII B of this chapter. When a change in use or transfer of right is sought by an appropriator, courts and agencies have limited the quantity of one's water rights that will be recognized to that which is necessary to the former uses using reasonably efficient methods.

Some states permit municipal water agencies to perfect rights in water they do not yet need and then sell the rights to others. This is allowed so that municipalities may justify investments in diversion facilities that may be needed to accommodate future growth. In City and County of Denver v. Sheriff (1939), the Court recognized the validity of an appropriation for municipal purposes although the city leased a large quantity of water to irrigators until it was needed for municipal uses, in compliance with Colorado statutes. Most states allow municipal users to appropriate excess water for anticipated future uses without requiring that the unneeded water be used in the interim.

## V.  PRIORITY: LINCHPIN OF THE APPROPRIATIVE RIGHT

### A.  Priority

Priority is the essential feature of the doctrine of prior appropriation.  It holds that a person whose appropriation is first in time (the prior appropriator) has the highest priority and hence a right to make beneficial use of water superior to all others.

All water rights holders are ranked according to the date of their appropriations.  As discussed in the preceding section, the priority date may relate back to an earlier date when one first formulated the intent to appropriate or received a permit or decree for a planned future use.  An appropriator with an earlier priority date is known as the senior appropriator when compared to a later appropriator, who is junior.  When there is not enough water for both senior and junior appropriators, the doctrine of priority allows the full senior right to be exercised before the junior can use any water.  The first user to be limited is the most junior on the list of priorities; juniors must abate their use until everyone senior to them has been served.

The appropriation doctrine protects priorities of early appropriators, providing an incentive for senior water users to invest in expensive diversion works by assuring them of a water supply in times of shortage.  But the doctrine as applied may have adverse economic consequences in its application.  First, appropriators may build diversion works prematurely or unnecessarily in order to protect their early priority. Second, the appropriation doctrine often frustrates transfers of water to higher economic uses. For example, a senior appropriator may hold a very reliable water right, used to irrigate crops of comparatively low value, while a nearby municipal or industrial user may wish to use that water in a higher-value use. Theoretically, the potential user need only "buy out" the senior's water right, but in practice the transfer of water rights may be legally prohibited or at least inhibited by transaction costs. "Transaction costs" arise because transfers of water are permitted only if a transferee can show other appropriators will not be injured. Legal challenges may generate such high costs that the transfer is rendered impractical, and the water rights "frozen" into a low-value use.

## B. Qualifications of the Senior's Right

A senior appropriator's right is subject to some qualifications.

The senior must appropriate water in such a way as to ensure a junior the same stream conditions that existed at the time of the junior's priority date. A leading case discussing this qualification is Farmers Highline Canal & Reservoir Co. v. City of Golden (1954). That case held that the senior cannot change the place water is taken out of the stream ("point of diversion") if that change adversely affects a junior. Nor may the senior transfer the right to another or change the place or purpose of the use if it will adversely affect the junior. Similarly, an appropriator may not change the time of use to the detriment of another. If, for example, an appropriator has only used water during a specific growing season the right may be limited to that season. See Section IX D 3 of this chapter.

A senior cannot waste water. Water in a stream belongs to the public, and appropriators have rights only to the water they can use beneficially. As a practical matter, however, one who holds a right to a specific quantity of water is rarely restricted from diverting the full quantity so long as it is not applied to different lands or different uses than those for which the right was recognized. States are beginning to be more rigorous in imposing regulations that prevent polluting, wasteful, inefficient uses. Many states also limit the amount of water that one can transfer to another to the quantity that is actually needed, regardless of whether one holds greater rights. See Section IX D 4 of this chapter.

## C. Enforcement of Priorities

Senior appropriators have rights to enforce claims against junior appropriators to prevent interference with their beneficial uses. Thus, juniors can be enjoined from depriving the seniors of water in quantities, at times, at places or of a quality that is necessary to support the seniors' use. That enforcement privilege does not mean a senior can force the junior to stop taking water out of turn under all circumstances. A senior cannot enforce a water right if a junior can prove that the water would not be put to a beneficial use by the senior or that water would not reach the senior in usable quantities.

In Colorado when a senior appropriator complains that a junior is taking water and the senior has unsatisfied rights, the senior "calls the river." The state engineer is asked to prevent the junior from taking any more water. If shutting down the junior will not actually result in water being delivered to the senior, however, the senior is said to have made a "futile call" and it will not be enforced by the state engineer.

Waste may be produced by strict enforcement of priorities. This possibility is graphically illustrated by State *ex rel.* Cary v. Cochran (1940). In *Cary* senior appropriators downstream on the Platte River sued to compel the state engineer to prevent upstream junior appropriators from interfering with their rights. Because of seepage and evaporation along the lengthy stretch of river between the juniors and seniors the juniors had to let 700 c.f.s. of water go by in order for the 162 c.f.s. needed to satsify the seniors' rights to reach them. The court enforced the seniors' right to shut off the juniors but only so long as any usable quantity would reach the seniors. Although some water was required to be deliverable before the seniors' call would be heeded, the juniors gave up far more water than the seniors gained.

## D. Preferences

Many states have statutes or constitutional provisions that express a preference for certain types of water use over others. Typically they rank various types of uses according to the prevailing view of the relative importance of various water uses at the time the preferences were established. Almost all reserve the highest use for domestic or municipal purposes. Although there are many variations, most put agricultural use second and industrial and mining third.

Preference laws in most states appear to require that in times of shortage those with rights for the most preferred uses receive water before those with rights for less preferred uses, but they are rarely so interpreted. Such an application of preferences would upset the system of priorities which is based on who appropriated water first. This has led some courts to refuse to apply preference statutes if to do so would conflict with prior rights. E.g., Phillips v. Gardner (1970) (legislature intended statutory adoption of prior appropriation to supersede earlier enacted preference statute). Other courts have said that application of preferences over prior rights is a taking of property requiring compensation.

All western states allow condemnation of water rights for municipal uses. Some statutes or constitutional provisions require condemnation and compensation as the means of effectuating preferred uses—more preferred users must condemn rights of less preferred users. E.g., Nebraska, Idaho, Wyoming. In other states, courts have given the same effect to preference laws that appear to require preference among users in times of shortage. E.g., Town of Sterling v. Pawnee Ditch Extension Co. (1908). A few state preference laws are stated or interpreted essentially as mandates for agencies to give preference to applicants for higher water uses over those whose applications for less preferred uses are simultaneously pending. E.g., Arizona, California, Texas. See East Bay Municipal Utility Dist. v. Department of Public Works (1934) (upholding preference to applicant for future preferred use over applicant for present lower uses).

## VI.  WATERS SUBJECT TO APPROPRIATION

Private rights to use water cannot be acquired in all types of water. As one would expect, a state's laws governing appropriation apply only to waters within the jurisdiction of the state. Further, a state's constitution or statutes may define waters subject to appropriation in a way that excludes certain waters within the state from state control. As discussed in Section III of this chapter, such constitutional or statutory provisions may describe waters of a "natural stream" as being "public property" or subject to appropriation, or they may exclude certain types of waters (such as runoff or seasonal floods) from the reach of state water law. State law may also recognize greater or lesser private property rights in various types of water (e.g., groundwater) and define the extent to which waters are subject to public use. Private rights to use water are subject to state police power regulation of how they may be perfected and the manner in which they are administered.

## A. Watercourses

Once water joins a watercourse it becomes subject to state control; in appropriation states it becomes available for members of the public to take and use according to state law.

As explained in Chapter Seven, Section I A, a watercourse could be defined to include not only rivers and lakes, but every tiny brook flowing into them, all the gullies through which water flows to the brooks, the snowpack and rainfall that feed them, and the evaporating or transpiring water in the process of forming clouds. But we need not require scientists to trace water to such remote sources because it would be beyond the ability of governments to regulate these sources anyway. Legal definitions are intended to define a point beyond which a state does not regulate water use. Usually that point is when water is not in a "natural stream."

Diffused surface water ordinarily may be freely taken and used by landowners without state regulation. Alaska, Montana, Nevada, Oregon, Texas and Utah specifically claim broader control of waters within their states. Only Utah construes this authority to extend beyond natural watercourses as does Colorado which has judicially interpreted statutes to allow state control (and appropriation) of virtually all surface water in the state, even out of watercourses, and which has a statute claiming control of precipitation. Asserting control beyond watercourses recognizes that if waters otherwise contributing to streamflow are intercepted, streamflow may be affected.

A "watercourse" is often defined by courts as a body of water flowing in a defined channel with a bed and banks. Generally the waterbody must have some permanence. A variety of other tests are sometimes used. Disputes are often resolved by a rule of reason.

## 1. Streams

Although requirements of a definite bed, bank and channel are universal, resort to them rarely resolves hard cases. For example, freshets (flows due to runoff from rainfall or melting snow) may appear to be streams at least part of the year, cutting draws or ravines as waters flow toward rivers and their tributaries. They may have a rocky bottom evidencing regular flows. But a court may require in addition that it have a continuous flow to be a natural stream. It has been held that to be a "watercourse" a stream must do more than conduct seasonal runoffs of precipitation. Yet some indisputable "watercourses" flow only intermittently and are made up solely of snowmelt and rainwater. This is especially true in the high mountains of the West where streams dry up in summer months after snows have melted. Further, some genuine streams simply do not run in great enough volume or speed to carve out banks or scour a bed. In flat areas a river may spread out and avoid cutting a defined channel, or it may meander through different routes each season.

In addition to considering the geographic characteristics discussed above, some courts resort to a functional test. In Texas the courts have asked whether the volume and regularity make it practicable to use the stream for irrigation. Hoefs v. Short (1925). This seems to be a pragmatic way to distinguish waters subject to appropriation and those that are not, but presumably a contest would exist only if someone considered the water valuable enough to put it to some use.

Because the courts apply a legal, not a scientific, definition to determine whether a watercourse exists, the lack of precision should not be surprising. The purpose, after all, is to identify waters intended to be within state control by the legislature or framers of the state constitution. Hence, courts tend to rest their decisions on factual determinations that escape easy classification. In State v. Hiber (1935) the state sought to enjoin the defendant from impounding waters that flowed down a swale or draw behind a small dam because it allegedly interfered with the flow of a natural stream. The court reviewed decisions in various states that distinguished between watercourses and diffused surface water. It found some attributes of a watercourse present, some lacking. Concluding that it was not a watercourse, the court leaned heavily on the peculiar characteristics of the water flow in question, stating "[j]udging from the testimony, no one would instantaneously perceive that it is a watercourse."

This perception test ("I know a stream when I see it") may seem unworkable, but in difficult cases determining the appropriate limits of state authority, the outcome may be dictated by the practicality and utility of state regulation of the water. Presumably, the more arid the area, the more important a small flow will be and the greater the likelihood it will be found to be a watercourse in a close case.

### 2. Lakes and Ponds

The water of natural lakes and ponds is often made subject to appropriation by state law. If not expressly mentioned in state constitution or statutes they may be treated as parts of watercourses that feed or are fed by them. The right to appropriate water from such sources may be qualified by riparian rights recognized in littoral (lakeshore) landowners. These are not riparian rights to consume water but rather other rights appurtenant to riparian land, even in prior appropriation states. See Chapter Two, Section III. For instance, an appropriator may be precluded from drawing water from a lake if it would substantially lower water level. See *In re* Martha Lake Water Co. (1929).

## 3. *Springs*

The treatment of spring water varies with the state in question and with the type of spring. The laws of some states (e.g., Oklahoma) consider a spring subject to appropriation only if its flow forms a stream. Others (e.g., Arizona and Utah) make spring water subject to appropriation even if the water would remain entirely on private property. A few states regulate springs as part of the groundwater system.

## B. Waters Made Available by Human Effort

Sometimes water is in a natural stream at times and places and in quantities other than would occur in nature. This may be simply because irrigation return flows delay the seasonal decline in natural streamflow, or it may be the result of massive diversions from one watershed to another. The general rule is that water that would never be available in the stream except for human efforts can be used without restriction by the person responsible for its being there, and it is not subject to appropriation until that person abandons it.

## 1. *Foreign Water*

Foreign water is that which would not have been in a stream without human effort. It includes imported water brought to the stream from another watershed by tunnels, canals, pumps and other such facilities. It also includes developed water such as groundwater pumped from an aquifer not hydrologically connected with the stream or trapped water recovered from a mine. If groundwater is hydrologically connected with the stream it is subject to appropriation as part of the stream in many states. The rainfall from artificially-induced precipitation, i.e., "rain-making" by seeding clouds, is considered developed water in some states but not others. It may be sound policy to reward such private efforts, but there would be considerable difficulty differentiating natural precipitation in the watershed from the results of cloud seeding.

One who introduces foreign water to a stream can use or reuse it at will. Unlike water subject to appropriation, foreign water is not subject to restrictions on when and how an importer can make a new or different use. See Section IX of this chapter. One may not use appropriated water for any different purpose or in any different place without permission from a court or state agency. The rule's purpose is to maintain the conditions upon which other appropriators have relied. Western irrigation practices involve repeated diversion, application and return flow of waters as they move downstream. Thus, successive irrigators, often relying on return flows from upstream irrigators, depend upon waters being used in essentially the same manner year after year. The reliance factor is not present, however, if water is not naturally in the stream. Imported water therefore can be treated differently; it is not part of the stream and thus not subject to appropriation. City and County of Denver v. Fulton Irrigating Ditch Co. (1972).

Thanks to importers, appropriators may have supplies available to them at times when they otherwise would have insufficient water. For instance, in a year of low natural flow juniors below the point where a large importer ceases using water may, in effect, be using almost entirely imported water. Although such water users may benefit incidentally, they can have no appropriative right in the imported water.

An importer, of course, can stop importing water at any time. Similarly an importer can decide to reuse the water, remove it from the stream at a different location, or sell it to others, without legal restraint. Typically the water has been obtained from another watershed pursuant to a water right in that watershed. The right is, as to the original watershed, 100% consumptive. Streams in the new watershed are used only to transport the water; it never becomes a part of the "natural stream." An exception arises if both the importing and exporting watersheds are part of the same larger watershed. In that case the water remaining in the stream below the confluence of the two sub-watersheds would belong to the stream and again be subject to appropriation.

Once an importer ceases using imported waters, they are similar to abandoned personalty. See

Elgin v. Weatherstone (1923). They can be taken and used by others, but no right in them can arise under the prior appropriation system because they are not technically subject to appropriation. In a heavily appropriated stream the "abandoned" waters will be consumed by junior appropriators who otherwise would not have the water available to them.

## 2. Salvaged Water

The general rule is that one may recapture and reuse seepage and "waste" water so long as it is recaptured and reused within the original land and for the original purpose of the right. See Cleaver v. Judd (1964). As soon as the water leaves the appropriator's land and is in or destined for a natural stream it becomes subject to appropriation by others. Fuss v. Franks (1980). Oregon further qualifies the rule by requiring that the appropriator intend to recapture the water at the time of the original appropriation and that the recapture be within a reasonable time or else the water will be considered abandoned to the stream. Jones v. Warm Springs Irrigation Dist. (1939).

The rule allowing recapture and reuse of salvaged water on the original land can result in more water being consumed. For instance, if a water user is consuming less than the permitted amount of water and plants a more water-intensive crop or puts in a more efficient irrigation system, most or all of the water that had previously been returned to the stream might be consumed. This can deprive other appropriators of water on which they depend but it is allowed since it is technically within the terms of the original appropriation.

Water that is salvaged by using less water-intensive crops or more efficient irrigation systems may not be used on other than the original land or for new purposes (e.g., industrial instead of agricultural) without permission. This is true notwithstanding the fact that the salvager may not be using the full quantity of water allowed under the original appropriation. These types of salvage are considered changes of use and are subject to the no harm rule discussed in Section IX D 1 of this chapter. The rule disallows changes that deprive juniors of a senior's return flows which supply their appropriations. E.g., Comstock v. Ramsey (1913). The amount of water that may be put to a changed use is limited to the quantity of water one historically used, even if there was a paper right to use more. This protects other appropriators' expectations. Procedures for making such changes may be burdensome. To encourage more efficient water use some states (e.g., California and Oregon) have passed laws facilitating the use of salvaged water on other land or for new purposes.

## C. Withdrawals From Appropriation

Water in natural watercourses can be removed from availability for some or all forms of appropriation by state action to preserve it for some future use or for present instream uses. Some state legislation withdraws specific rivers from appropriation, or allows administrative designation, to preserve them for scenic or recreational uses. The federal Wild and Scenic Rivers Act protects certain rivers designated by Congress or by the state.

Montana has allowed state and local government entities to reserve minimum flows from appropriation for future uses, either to protect instream values or for projected consumptive needs. The federal governments' reserved water rights may also effectively remove significant amounts of water from appropriation for the future needs of federal lands and Indian reservations. See Chapter Eight.

## 1. *Maintenance of Instream Flows*

Protection of streamflows or lake levels for fish and wildlife, recreation, water quality and scenic beauty is accomplished in two ways. The waters can be "appropriated" for instream uses or can be considered withdrawn from appropriation so that the instream flows are preserved from depletion by private appropriators. The first approach initially encountered the fundamental requirements of the appropriation doctrine that water be diverted and put to a beneficial use. Uses in the stream—those not effected by diverting water—originally were not considered "appropriations." Besides not complying with the diversion requirement, the uses supported by instream flows were not beneficial uses in many states. Now several states have expressly relaxed diversion requirements, and most now consider recreation and wildlife protection to be beneficial uses.

The other method of preserving instream flows—withdrawing water from appropriation—was pursued as a way of avoiding the obstacles that prevented appropriations for instream flows. It remains an important and viable means of assuring protection to the waters in streams and lakes. Laws were passed in Oregon and Idaho early in the century that removed certain rivers and lakes from appropriation and protected them from damage by state or private projects. More recent state laws identify rivers or lakes to be protected, for example, as "scenic river areas," "wild rivers," or "free-flowing rivers" (e.g., Oklahoma and California). Utah allows its state engineer to deny appropriation rights if they would be inimical to recreation or the natural stream environment. Arizona has no specific provision but statute and case law have recognized state power to maintain water flows. The state engineer of North Dakota has power to reserve water for maintaining aquatic life, recreation or other beneficial uses in the future.

Washington allows administrative withdrawal of certain amounts of water from important rivers or lakes. Montana enacted the most sweeping law of this type in 1973. State, municipal and federal agencies were given the right to apply for the reservation of waters for instream flows for fish and wildlife, recreation and water quality. Such reservations may not exceed 50% of the average annual flow. Montana law also allows for reservations of water for future uses, as discussed in the next subsection.

Instream flows have protection under the federal Wild and Scenic Rivers Act, 16 U.S.C.A. §§ 1271–87. The Act effectively reserves federal water rights that limit future development. See Chapter Nine, Section V C. Congress, or state legislatures with the Secretary of Interior's approval, may designate certain rivers that contain "remarkable scenic, recreational, geologic, fish and wildlife, historic, cultural or other similar values." Once a river is designated, projects that affect its flow are restricted. But if the United States wants to protect the flow from existing appropriations it must purchase rights or exercise its power of eminent domain to purchase the rights of existing appropriators.

Statutes that remove waters from appropriation usually preserve all appropriations existing on the date of enactment. Whether police power regulations could restrict the use of existing appropriations to preserve instream flows would depend on the degree of interference. Extinguishing private rights would amount to a taking of private property for a public use and would require just compensation.

The doctrine of federal reserved water rights (see Chapter Eight) may also be applied to preserve instream flows. If the federal government reserves the public land for particular uses that require maintenance of instream flows (e.g., enough water to sustain aquatic life in a wildlife refuge or natural conditions in a park), the courts have held that the government has impliedly reserved the land.

The Supreme Court has held, however, that for water rights to be reserved, it must be essential to an original purpose of the reservation. United States v. New Mexico (1978) (water was not reserved for instream flows in national forest because fish and wildlife maintenance was not among the original purposes of the national forest reservation). Thus each reservation must be examined to determine whether reserved instream flows were essential to its purposes. It has been held that Congress intends to reserve rights for instream flows when it designates wilderness areas. Sierra Club v. Block (1985). Reserved rights for many Indian reservations include enough water for new population growth and new industrial endeavors as well as instream flows needed for continuing ability to hunt and fish.

## 2. *Reservations for Future Uses*

It is reasonable to anticipate that water will be needed in the future for particular purposes. One of the most commonly anticipated uses is municipal supplies for growing cities. A number of states have provided by statute (Arizona, California, Nevada, Oklahoma, Oregon, Washington) or by judicial decision (Idaho, Wyoming), or both (Colorado), that municipalities can appropriate water for reasonably anticipated needs. In most states the water need not be put to a beneficial use in the meantime. Colorado and California require that a beneficial use be made, but this can be satisfied by leasing the water for other purposes. Kansas provides for reservation of water storage rights in federal reservoirs by application to the responsible federal agency.

The 1973 Montana Water Use Act allowed all levels of government to apply for water rights for any future beneficial use (including irrigation). To accommodate agency planning for these future uses the legislature declared a three-year moratorium on all new appropriations in the Yellowstone River basin where applications were being made for massive appropriations for energy-related developments. No other western state has so qualified the scope of the right to appropriate water for present needs in order to protect future public needs.

Federal and Indian reserved water rights extend to enough water for future uses within the original purposes.

## VII.   EXTENT OF THE APPROPRIATIVE RIGHT

The quantity of water to which one is entitled under the prior appropriation doctrine is theoretically the amount of water continuously taken and benefically used each year beginning with the initial appropriation. The quantities stated in many old permits or decrees manifesting rights of appropriators, however, are much larger than the amounts actually diverted or needed for the appropriator's purposes. This is because old paper rights often were based only on declarations of the appropriators or the capacity of the diversion works. Overstating rights is less widespread today, largely because state appropriative water rights systems are administered by professional engineers who verify claims before rights are granted.

The right also extends to a sufficient quality of water to allow a continuation of beneficial uses. Early cases prevented upstream miners from polluting water to the detriment of downstream seniors. Application of rights under the appropriation doctrine has not been used extensively to prevent water pollution; however, a number of administrative procedures are designed to prevent appropriation, use or transfer of excessive amounts of water.

All modern appropriation systems provide that persons may object to the granting or recognition of a new right by an administrative agency or court on the ground that the right is excessive for the purposes claimed. See Section VIII of this chapter. If one seeks to challenge the manner, place or purpose of the water use, or the point of diversion, or to transfer the rights to another, the rights may be limited to the amount of water historically put to a beneficial use. This is to avoid prejudicing other users.

Finally, junior appropriators may challenge water rights of a senior, claiming that some portion of the rights has been abandoned by lengthy non-use. A state legislature or court presumably could declare that rights in excess of reasonable needs for beneficial uses were not properly granted since private rights depend on water being put to a beneficial use.

## A. Measure of the Right

To establish a right by prior appropriation water must be applied to a beneficial use. Beneficial use is the measure, the basis and the limit of the appropriator's right to use water. This principle is rooted in the constitutions, statutes or case law of all western states.

Before development of modern administrative systems, an appropriator claimed a right to use a certain quantity of water. Usually the only limit on the claim was the capacity of the diversion facilities. See Fort Morgan Land & Canal Co. v. South Platte Ditch Co. (1892). This was based on the reasonable assumption that one would not go to the expense of building ditches with a capacity far greater than was necessary. In fact, it sanctioned excessive claims because most appropriators built oversized ditches to be certain they had sufficient capacity. Further, they did not use the ditches continuously during the irrigation season although they claimed rights to do so. Challenges to an appropriator's claim were rare. Most over-claimed and sometimes the claims on a stream amounted to many times its total flow. Only in extreme cases did a court find that an appropriator's right exceeded beneficial use. E.g., State *ex rel.* Erickson v. McLean (1957) (uncontrolled flooding of grazing lands for 24 hours a day is not a beneficial use).

Now the statutory systems of all states include administrative mechanisms for verifying amounts of water that are to be put to a beneficial use before rights are embodied in a permit or decree. Many systems provided for review of old rights and required persons claiming water rights to justify their claims before recognizing the rights in a new permit or decree. This usually was not a rigorous process demanding exacting proof, but it caught some flagrant abuses. Montana has the most recently enacted statute requiring adjudication of existing rights. It involves presentation of evidence of existing uses and application of standards intended to check inefficient use. All competing users may participate before the responsible agency or court and object to appropriations of excessive quantities of water.

A water right once manifested in a permit or decree is rarely disturbed. Change of place or purpose of use or of point of diversion requires permission by an agency or court. No change in use may be made if it results in harm to other appropriators. In assessing harm, the agency or court may deny the application if the change will result in an increase in the amount of water that has historically been put to a beneficial use. Thus, the quantity of the right may be reduced to less than the amount of the original appropriation. The same process is followed when one appropriator seeks to transfer a water right to another. Historical use may be limited to the amount of water actually required for optimum beneficial uses of the kind made. The historical use approach could be equally useful in showing that one has abandoned the unused portion of a water right. In fact there are few reported cases in which a court or administrative body has found partial abandonment on this basis.

## B. Limits on the Right

Because appropriative rights extend only to water that is beneficially used, they do not extend to water that is wastefully (or inefficiently) used. Standards for efficiency change as the demand for scarce western water grows and conservation technology improves.

States have begun to make efforts to force more efficient use of water. One is the imposition of absolute limits on the amount or rate of irrigation diversions for certain land areas. Another is the requirement that appropriators divert, transport and use water reasonably. States are also requiring the use of water conserving devices (such as low-flush toilets).

## 1. *"Duty of Water" Limitations*

Irrigation uses account for 90% of all water withdrawals in the West. Water is frequently applied to land far in excess of what crops can use; thus an early approach was to limit the amount or rate of water use on an acre of land based on a presumption of the maximum quantity required in the area. This limit is called the "duty of water." South Dakota, Wyoming and Nebraska, for example, allow an appropriator to apply water at a rate of no more than one cubic foot per second (c.f.s.) for every seventy acres irrigated. Idaho allows appropriations of 1 c.f.s. for every fifty acres, and North Dakota allows 1 c.f.s. for eighty acres. In addition North Dakota, South Dakota and Nebraska allow no more than three acre feet of water to be used each year for each acre of land. New Mexico requires the amount of water appropriated for irrigation to be consistent with good agricultural practices. Rates or amounts are determined according to informed judgments of the maximum amounts of water needed for agriculture in the area and the maximum rate at which it could be applied without waste considering soil conditions, climate, crops and other relevant factors into account.

Duty of water considerations are taken into account by most state engineers and courts when they review applications for new appropriations or changes in use. In most states they do not impose absolute limits but are among factors considered when water needs on the specific lands to be served are examined.

If a user can show that particular circumstances make possible a beneficial use of more water than allowed by a duty of water statute, the law may be found to constitute an impermissible interference with vested water rights.   In Enterprise Irrigation Dist. v. Willis (1939), the Nebraska Supreme Court enjoined enforcement of a state law limiting irrigation appropriations to 1 c.f.s. per 70 acres of land and 3 acre feet per acre per year against an appropriator who had perfected greater rights before passage of the act.   There was evidence that enforcement of the limitation would result in some loss of crop returns.   Indeed, sound public policy arguably could require that a duty of water be set allowing a crop yield that is less than the maximum.   That is, if three acre feet produces $1000 worth of crops but five acre feet will produce $1100, the use perhaps should be limited to the lower quantity.   But duty of water restrictions are applied as if they granted a right to use water up to the statutory maximum.

## 2.  *Reasonably Efficient Means of Diversion*

Inherent in the beneficial use doctrine is the principle that water cannot be used wastefully. Blatant waste was always precluded by the beneficial use requirement.   Early cases involved inefficient diversion facilities and stream pollution.   As competition for limited water increases modern courts and administrative agencies must struggle

with what level of inefficiency constitutes wasteful
(and therefore non-beneficial) use.

Today, the most difficult issue is what degree of
efficiency should be required for a water use to be
"beneficial." This involves assessing available
technology, economic analysis and, ultimately,
comparing relative efficiencies of competing users.
Use of the doctrine to force efficient water use
remains in its infancy but it is bound to be an area
of considerable activity. Junior water users will
challenge wasteful (including relatively unproduc-
tive) senior uses. Recreationists may seek to inval-
idate excessive diversions to maintain more water
for streamflows. And water administrators are
already under greater public pressure to insist on
efficient use through their regulations and administration of water laws.

Many cases hold that facilities for diversion and
transportation of water must be reasonably efficient. Easy cases concern facilities that are absolutely wasteful. For instance where ⁵⁄₆ths of the
water diverted by an appropriator was lost to evaporation, evapotranspiration and seepage by a 2.5
mile open ditch the court said it was an unreasonable waste. Erickson v. Queen Valley Ranch Co.
(1971). More difficult cases involve facilities and
uses that are inefficient compared to those of other
appropriators.

In an early case the Supreme Court refused
relief to a party whose waterwheel, used to remove
water from the Snake River to irrigate 429 acres,

was inundated by the defendant's downstream dam which was part of a project to irrigate some 300,000 acres. Schodde v. Twin Falls Land & Water Co. (1912). One of the Court's alternate holdings was that an unreasonable and inefficient means of diversion could not interfere with the reasonable use of water by others.

*Schodde* suggests a balancing of the utility of each appropriator's use. State courts generally insist only that a senior have a reasonably efficient means of diversion, judged by standards of "reasonableness" applicable when the diversion works were built. Thus in State *ex rel.* Crowley v. District Court (1939), the court upheld the right of a downstream senior appropriator to insist that upstream juniors leave sufficient water in the stream to reach the senior's rudimentary, turn-of-the-century wing dam. Water in the stream was adequate, but to divert it would have required modification of the senior's diversion dam. A few states, such as Oregon, take the approach that diversion facilities efficient enough to support a water right at the time they are built may still have to be made more efficient as conditions and technology change. E.g., *In re* Willow Creek (1914), *modified on other grounds* (1915).

Economic theory indicates that water use will become efficient whether the burden of efficiency is placed on the senior or junior. Under the *Crowley* rule, if greater efficiency by the senior would benefit the junior appropriators, the juniors would

pay the senior to make the needed improvements
or buy out the senior's rights. If the Oregon rule
applied and the senior had to bear the burden of
upgrading the diversion facilities to modern standards, the senior would either make the expendi-
ture or buy out the juniors. If it was not to the
senior's advantage to do so, the senior would sell to
the juniors. In practice, transaction costs may be
barriers to moving water to efficient use in these
ways. Other factors may also influence actions.
Devotion to a lifestyle or a location, stubbornness,
immobility, disparity in size of use and other
causes of resistance may prevent sound economic
decisions. Thus legislatures and courts are seeking rules that maximize efficiency.

The statutes of some states (e.g., Alaska, Colorado, Idaho, Oregon, South Dakota) require water
facilities to be reasonably efficient. Decisions of
most courts confronting the issue also support the
requirement of reasonable efficiency. For instance, the Idaho court has refused to apply the
rule applicable in some states (e.g., California) that
the quantity one is entitled to appropriate is measured at the place of use. Instead, it held that
public policy dictates that one's entitlement should
be measured at the point of diversion. Glenn Dale
Ranches, Inc. v. Shaub (1972). In this way losses
from inefficient facilities are borne by the diverter.
If the loss through diversion facilities (by evaporation, leaky ditches, weeds and trees, and so on) is

great enough the appropriator will find it economical to repair and improve the ditches.

A novel case illustrates the modern thinking concerning the need for more efficient facilities and use. In A–B Cattle Co. v. United States (1978), the Colorado Supreme Court refused to recognize the right of appropriators to insist on a certain silt content in their water. The presence of silt in the water served to seal unlined earthen canals and ditches and prevent seepage losses. When the federal government constructed a dam on the river that was the source of water, silt settled out. The clear water released from the dam seeped from the ditches more readily, resulting in less water being delivered, and the appropriators sought damages. But the court found that they had no right to maintain earthen ditches; the right was solely to divert a quantity of water. Citing the principle of maximum utilization of water it suggested that at some time in the future, the maximum utilization principle may qualify the notion of beneficial use to require installation of pipes or lining of irrigation ditches.

The Colorado decision anticipates incorporation of economic considerations into application of the beneficial use doctrine. A later case indicated that a means of so doing is for the state engineer to require optimum utilization of water through the rules and regulations made upon a consideration of "all significant factors, including environmental and economic concerns." Alamosa–La Jara Water

Users Protection Ass'n v. Gould (1983). The court held that rules could require seniors to construct wells so that more water would be available for juniors.

Requiring owners of inefficient facilities to improve them when they become inadequate because others have appropriated water more efficiently is compelling from a resource allocation standpoint. It should be noted that there are other legal rules in the appropriation system that inhibit efficient uses. For instance, reuse of salvaged water is restricted to uses on the original land, diminishing the value of such improvements to the appropriator. See the next subsection of this chapter. The problem is compounded by the fact that changes in use of water are sometimes inhibited by the no harm rule and other restrictions that prohibit, or increase transaction costs of, transfers that could improve the efficiency of water use. See Section IX of this chapter.

## C. Recapture and Reuse

Most water is "reused." Agricultural water is diverted, spread on fields, and then some is returned through tail ditches or by seepage to a stream. Municipal water is usually returned as treated (or untreated) sewage to a waterway, where others may divert and use it. Maximizing the number and extent of uses promotes efficiency and is an important conservation goal. It is important to consider at what point the right of the original appropriator to continue using water ceases.

Waters originating within the watershed can be recaptured and reused by an appropriator if: 1) the total used does not exceed rights under a permit or decree; and 2) the recapture and reuse occur within the land for which the appropriation was made.

Recapture and reuse of water encourages conservation and maximum utilization of water. Much of the water diverted for irrigation is not consumed by crops. It is needed to saturate the soil sufficiently and for enough time that the plants can benefit from irrigation. It is also used to transport water actually used through ditches subject to seepage and evaporation. This is called "carriage water." In addition to carriage water needs, more water is often applied than is necessary because irrigation practices are notoriously imprecise, farmers may not know exactly how much water the crops require and, if they did, their ability to measure it usually would be limited.

Most unconsumed water seeps into the ground or goes back to the stream as waste or return flow and is appropriated and put to use by others. Such water is not truly "wasted" in the sense that it cannot be used by anyone. Still, significant amounts of water used in irrigation become unusable by becoming "trapped" in marshy areas or unrecoverable groundwater or flowing away from the stream. Much is lost by evaporation from open canals or transpiration through unwanted (non-crop) plants that draw water out of the earth. Because millions of acre-feet of water are "lost" annually, states are seeking ways to encourage greater efficiency through reuse and other methods causing serious problems for those who depend on return flows.

## 1. Total Use Must Not Exceed Water Right

Typically one uses only a portion of the total water diverted and returns the rest to the stream. Water rights are usually expressed as a maximum amount or rate of flow that may be diverted for a certain use on specific land. A right may also be limited by the amount that may be consumed. Within these limits consumption may be increased by reuse so long as nothing occurs that would constitute a change of use—a change in the place, purpose, or time of use or the means or point of diversion. Thus an appropriator ordinarily may "recycle" irrigation return flows or capture seepage and use it within limits imposed by state law. E.g., Cleaver v. Judd (1964). No limits are imposed on reuse of foreign waters imported by an appropriator. See Section VI B 1 of this chapter.

The upstream appropriator's increased efficiency or reuse of water on the original land can reduce the downstream appropriator's supply. This is even allowed when downstream appropriators have become dependent on the upstream appropriator's "waste" as a source of supply. If the increased consumption came about by a change in use it would not be allowed to harm other appropriators. But when it is the result of recapture and reuse or conservation measures on the same land it will be permitted without regard to harm caused to others so long as the amount diverted (and the amount consumed if it has been quantified) does not exceed one's "paper right."

The Colorado Supreme Court has held that one may not enlarge a decreed right by means of a novel water salvage technique. In Southeastern Colorado Water Conservancy Dist. v. Shelton Farms, Inc. (1974), a landowner removed streamside phreatophytes (plants that consume large amounts of water) and filled in marshy areas. The court recognized that the increase in phreatophytes over the years had gradually deprived many junior users of the water to which they were entitled. Since the saved water was originally in the stream and had been appropriated by juniors, the court held that it was error to create a new and senior right in it. See also R.J.A., Inc. v. Water Users Ass'n of Dist. No. 6 (1984) denying an expansion of a senior water right to include water saved in draining a 3000 year old peat bog. Thus the water belonged to the stream and could not be used to enlarge an existing right. Presumably the court would have allowed the senior in each case to have rights to the water if its source had been the senior's diversion and the total amount of the senior's right was not enlarged beyond the decree. The senior also could have made a junior appropriation of the water added to the stream.

## 2. *Reuse Limited to Original Land*

Recapture and reuse of water by an appropriator must occur on the land for which the original appropriation was made. Such waters may be used on the same land to increase yield. But one may not reuse on an adjoining parcel water saved by lining irrigation ditches. Salt River Valley Water Users' Ass'n v. Kovacovich (1966). Of course if the diversion point, means of diversion, or place, time or purpose of use is changed a reuse will be allowed only if no harm occurs to other appropriators. See Section IX of this chapter.

The right to recapture and reuse water can end before the water leaves the appropriator's land if: a) the appropriator no longer intends to use it; b) it becomes so intermingled with other waters destined for the stream (such as seepage from a neighbor's irrigation) that it cannot be identified as part of the appropriator's diversion; or c) the appropriator loses control of the water. At the moment one of these conditions arises, the water becomes part of the stream and is subject to appropriation. Reuse of water recaptured by an appropriator before it leaves the land may also be precluded if state law assumes it has returned to the stream. Colorado does not allow recapture of water once it has entered the ground and begun moving toward the stream, even if the recapture is on the appropriator's land and the appropriator can prove: that the water was part of the original diversion; that control of it has not been lost; and that there was always an intention to recapture the water. Most other states consider the facts in each case.

Any person, including the original appropriator, may intercept seepage water that is considered to have rejoined the stream. It is a junior appropriation subject to the rights of all prior appropriators. An appropriator of seepage water is at the mercy of the person whose activity makes the seepage available. The original appropriator may cause the seepage to stop by making more efficient use of it, by lining, relocating or abandoning a canal or reservoir, or by ceasing the appropriation without liability to the seepage appropriator. Bower v. Big Horn Canal Ass'n (1957).

### 3. Foreign Waters

Foreign waters are waters that would not have been in the stream system except by human efforts, e.g., imported water. See Section VI B of this chapter. They may be used, recaptured, reused and sold by the importer. See City & County of Denver v. Fulton Irrigating Ditch Co. (1972); Thayer v. City of Rawlins (1979).

## VIII. PROCEDURES FOR PERFECTING AND ADMINISTERING RIGHTS

### A. Early Systems

#### 1. Prestatutory Period (1840–1870)

Appropriation of water began several years before statehood in most western states. Miners developed customs and rules for water appropriation whose basic principles were relatively uniform throughout the mining camps. Rights and procedural customs of the prior appropriation doctrine were incorporated into the common law of water rights by the early territorial and state court systems. A miner's right to get water depended upon two acts: posting notice at the point of diversion, and diverting the water to apply it to a benefical use.

The quaint system of appropriation that spread throughout the West reflected the independent-minded miners who conceived it. There was no administration required, no central authority, not even records. But there were conflicts. Courts were called upon to resolve disputes between appropriators competing for the right and priority to water. Litigation, however, was determinative only of the rights of the parties, not of all users of the same water sources. In several states the courts allowed a plaintiff to join all persons claiming rights in a stream to seek a determination of water rights as against them all. This approach was unsatisfactory because of its expense, slowness and difficulty. Further, the resulting decrees were not compiled or easily available to prospective appropriators in search of unappropriated water. Montana was the last to replace the lawsuit system with its 1973 law.

## 2.  Early Statutes

The first state to enact a statutory appropriation procedure was California in 1873. The California statute simply gave legislative sanction to the methods of appropriation previously developed by local custom. It required: a) posting notice of quantity, purpose and place of use of water at the diversion point; b) recording in the county records within ten days; and c) completing the appropriation and applying it to a beneficial use with due diligence. A diligent appropriator was given a priority date relating back to the time of posting notice.

Statutory systems discouraged applications for permits in streams the administrator found to be overappropriated, and served to warn developers of the risks involved. In some states such as Oregon the legislation resolved conflicts between appropriative and superior riparian rights.

Many early statutes anticipated that water users would later have their rights acknowledged by a court. Adjudication of rights could occur many years after rights were established or, under some statutes, not at all.

## 3.  Problems With Early Statutes

The early statutes had several critical weaknesses. Statutory procedures were not exclusive; a water right held under the common law appropriation doctrine was just as valid. This left many water rights unrecorded, and those that were recorded were not filed centrally. On a stream that ran through several counties anyone searching the records had to go to all the county courthouses in the stream basin. This lack of a centralized data bank for record-keeping made day to day administration very difficult. Existing records were unreliable, even as to those who did file. People tended to file for excessive amounts of water, and there was no reasonable way to determine if they had actually applied that quantity to a beneficial use. The posting and filing method caused insecurity for investors. Not only were there evidentiary problems in proving the extent of a water right, but the uncertainties in the court-administered relation back doctrine meant a developer could not be sure of the priority date of a project. Adjudication procedures were slow and left uncertainty about the availability of water for appropriation, sometimes for many years.

## B. Current Permit Systems

### 1. Purpose

All western states have statutory systems to allocate and administer rights to use water. Every state but Colorado has vested authority in an administrative agency. Colorado has a judicial system whose purpose is similar to agencies in other states.

The chief purpose of administrative procedures is to provide an orderly method for appropriating water and regulating established water rights.

Some states allow appropriators the options of applying for a permit or perfecting a common law appropriation by posting notice and diverting water. More typically, state law requires a permit as the exclusive means of making a valid appropriation. Wyoming Hereford Ranch v. Hammond Packing Co. (1925).

## 2. *Constitutionality*

### a. *Source of Authority*

The authority to enact and enforce permit systems is rooted in the broad police power of the state. Water is usually subjected to public control by state statutes or constitutions. Although the state's interest may be expressed in property terms, it is not one of ownership but of sovereignty. See Section III of this chapter. Individual interests in the right to use water may become private property which, like all other private property, is subject to the police power of the state. The definition of property rights, too, is the prerogative of the state. There is no serious doubt that states have the power to enact permit systems; the only question is whether a system adequately provides due process in dealing with vested rights.

### b. *Separation of Powers*

Most state systems for administration of water rights include an adjudication process that casts an administrative body or official in a quasi-judicial role. All systems provide for court review either by appeal or as the last step in the water rights determination process.

The adjudicative function of the agency itself has led to challenges to the mixed executive and judicial role of agencies. As early as 1900 the Wyoming Supreme Court ruled that the Board of Control's adjudication of relative water rights was primarily administrative. The court reasoned that the agency was actually determining evidence of title to a right; claimants were not seeking redress for injury. The court further held that even if the board acted judicially, the power was quasi-judicial, and thus a proper delegation to an administrator or board. Under most statutes a water user also has recourse to the courts if a state official's actions may impair a substantial property right. Farm Investment Co. v. Carpenter (1900). Nebraska enacted a statute similar to Wyoming's, including a provision holding a decree to be final unless appealed to the courts. The Nebraska court upheld the law, stating that the duties of the agency were supervisory and administrative, not judicial. Crawford Co. v. Hathaway (1903), *overruled on other grounds* Wasserburger v. Coffee (1966).

Oregon has a mixed judicial and administrative system in which an administrative determination is made by the state engineer and filed in a court which presides over appeals, makes further modifications and grants final approval. The Oregon Supreme Court held the duties of the engineer to be "quasi-judicial in their character," and the findings only "prima facie final and binding." *In re* Willow Creek (1914), *modified on other grounds* (1915). The U.S. Supreme Court held that proceedings before the Oregon engineer and court were not unrelated but part of a single proceeding, earlier stages of which are before the administrative agency and later ones before a judicial tribunal; that the preliminary proceedings merely paved the way for court adjudication; and "that the state, consistently with due process of law, may thus commit the preliminary proceedings to the board and the final hearing and adjudication to the court is not debatable." Pacific Live Stock Co. v. Lewis (1916).

The Texas Supreme Court held unconstitutional a 1917 water rights statute, which was similar to Wyoming's, pointing out that although the state constitution in Wyoming was ample authority for such a system, Texas had no similar constitutional provision. The executive branch was given powers belonging to the judicial branch without the necessary constitutional mandate. Texas later adopted such a constitutional amendment and a system similar to Oregon's.

## 3. *Permitting Procedures*

The first permit system was adopted by Wyoming in 1890. All appropriation states except Colorado have similar systems requiring permits to appropriate water. The Wyoming act divided the state into four water divisions and established the office of state engineer to collect stream records, make surveys, and provide staff support to the Board of Control. The Board of Control adjudicates all claims and administers the permit system. Under most statutory permit systems a permit will be approved if an applicant follows prescribed procedures and if the state engineer finds that there is unappropriated water and that the appropriation is not detrimental to the public welfare.

### a. Filing

In all permit states a formal written application for a permit to take unappropriated water must be made to the state engineer or an administrative body such as the Department of Natural Resources or Water Resources Control Board. This is almost always the exclusive way to obtain a water right, and must be done before any physical act such as digging a diversion ditch. The time of filing generally becomes the priority date if all later requirements are met.

Montana's water law, the most recently enacted of the western state systems, is typical. Data that must be included under the Montana law include the name of claimant and watercourse, quantity of water, time of use, legal description of point of diversion, purpose of use, date of application to beneficial use and any applicable support such as a map, plat or aerial photograph.

### b. Notice

Typically a notice of filing the application must be published and efforts must be made to contact all affected parties, who have a fixed time in which to file objections. Objections are to be based on an allegation that statutory criteria for issuance of a permit are lacking.

### c. Hearing

The administrative agency holds a public hearing on properly filed objections, serving notice of the hearing on the applicant and objector. The state engineer or equivalent official investigates factual data upon which the agency relies and reports to the agency on whether the statutory criteria were satisfied. The agency then approves, disapproves or approves with modification the permit application. The applicant has a right to due process, i.e., to present any pertinent evidence. The agency's findings may then be appealed to the courts.

### d. Issuance of Permit

The next stage of the process is issuance of a permit. A permit is not a water right but will ripen into one if all conditions of the permit are met. During a stipulated time period the permittee is required to construct diversion works, make a diversion and apply water to a beneficial use. The application to beneficial use is the act that causes a water right to vest; the priority will then relate back to the act of filing. Typical permit conditions include compliance with the time periods stipulated and generally carrying out "due diligence" requirements for completing a diversion project. All states allow extensions of time limits for cause.

Most responsible administrative agencies may impose permit conditions that dictate how the water right is to be exercised. The California statute, for instance, authorizes the State Water Resources Control Board to permit the appropriation for beneficial purposes of unappropriated water under "such terms and conditions as in its judgment will best develop, conserve, and utilize in the public interest, the water sought to be appropriated." Considerable discretion to fashion conditions is allowed. They will be set aside only if a court finds them to be unreasonable or not based on substantial evidence. East Bay Mun. Utility Dist. v. Department of Public Works (1934). In Bank of America National Trust & Savings Ass'n v. State Water Resources Control Bd. (1974), a permit condition requiring the applicant to keep a proposed reservoir open to the public for recreational uses was rejected. The court held that there was no substantial evidence in the record of the need for such a condition.

In addition to regular permits, temporary and seasonal permits are issued by some states. In California such permits create no vested rights and may be issued if there is unappropriated water available, and no harm to downstream users or unreasonable harm to the environment will occur.

The final document issued in the permit process in most states may be called a "license," "certificate," "certificate of appropriation" or "water right certificate." The administrator makes an inspection to see if the water has been applied to a beneficial use and the statute complied with. The certificate is similar to a deed in that it defines the extent of a property right in water. It also may be recorded like a deed.

### 4.  Statutory Criteria

The permit procedures discussed above are to determine whether certain criteria set forth in the statute have been satisfied. In Montana the criteria require evidence of:

    a.  a beneficial use;

    b.  availability of unappropriated water at the time and period of use;

    c.  no harm to prior appropriators;

    d.  adequate diversion facilities;  and

    e.  no interference with reservations of water for future use or other planned uses.

The requirement of available unappropriated water deserves comment. On many streams rights to divert water far exceed the quantity of water flowing in the stream. This is a result of two phenomena: a) many users may depend on the same water, as downsteam users divert water that

has already been diverted and returned by upstream users; and b) the most junior rights may be
exercisable only in years of heavy flow or low
senior usage. Thus, many streams in the West are
"overappropriated." A finding that unappropriated water is available therefore does not mean that
one will have a certain supply of water. Some
states are stricter than others in preventing over-
appropriation. See Lower Colorado River Auth. v.
Texas Dept. of Water Resources (1984).

## 5. *Public Interest Considerations*

The laws of most states authorize the agency to
reject applications not in the public interest. This
power was used by the state engineer of New
Mexico to reject the application of one whose proposed irrigation project seemed too large for the
available water supply and thus might result in
high costs and uncertain supplies for those who
bought land and the accompanying water rights.
The state engineer was concerned that purchasers
might be misled, and that a failed project might
discourage investors in future water development
enterprises. The state supreme court upheld the
engineer's use of these broad policy concerns, specifically rejecting the applicant's contention that
"public interest" concerns should only include matters that are a "menace to public health and safety." Young & Norton v. Hinderlider (1910).

A Utah statute required the state engineer to
determine whether proposed appropriations would
interfere with a "more beneficial use" or "would

prove detrimental to the public welfare." The Utah Supreme Court upheld rejection of an early application in favor of a later one because the interests of the public would be better served by the later appropriation (a federal water project) than by the earlier one (a private power plant). Tanner v. Bacon (1943).

In Washington public welfare considerations have been held to include environmental factors, not simply the effect of the proposed use on quantities available to others. Although these factors were not contemplated by the legislature when it passed the Water Resources Act, subsequent legislation showed an intention to include them. Stempel v. Department of Water Resources (1973).

Western states have begun to charge administrative agencies with applying broad public interest factors in water permitting (and other related water determinations). Alaska has one of the most detailed state statutes requiring such considerations. Factors include: 1) benefit to applicant; 2) effect of resulting economic activity; 3) effect on fish and game and recreation; 4) public health effects; 5) possible loss of future alternative uses; 6) harm to others; 7) intent and ability of applicant; 8) effect on access to navigable or public waters.

Where states have public interest statutes that are relatively inexplicit as to the factors to be considered courts have directed water administrators to look to a wide variety of factors. Idaho's statute says only that the Director of Water Resources is to reject or modify a permit application if the appropriation "will conflict with the local public interest." The state supreme court held that public interest elements to be applied by the Director include those reflected in Idaho laws dealing with instream flows, water quality, water waste and conservation. In addition, "common sense" argues for looking at the factors in the Alaska statute and other state laws. Shokal v. Dunn (1985).

Arguments are increasingly made that an agency not only has authority to reject applications for permits to appropriate water that may be contrary to the public interest, but has a duty to reject them. One court has applied the public trust doctrine to require "at a minimum, a determination of the potential effect of the allocation of water [to major energy projects] on the present water supply and future water needs of this State." United Plainsmen Ass'n v. North Dakota State Water Conservation Comm'n (1976). The ruling requires comprehensive water planning or some other method of weighing the effects of allocating substantial quantities of water to appropriators pursuant to state law.

The most extensive application of the public trust doctrine to limit a state's authority to grant permits to appropriate water was in National Audubon Soc'y v. Superior Court, *cert. denied* (1983). The court found that a state agency's 1940 permit to the City of Los Angeles to use water from tributaries to Mono Lake had been granted without consideration of the effect on public trust factors including fish, wildlife and recreation. Thus the City's established rights to appropriate may be qualified by later agency restrictions to protect the fishery, wildlife and recreational uses dependent on an inflow of fresh water to the lake. The decision is remarkable in that it effectively implies a limitation in every water permit, no matter how long established, to carry out the state's public trust duties. A later case held that the California State Water Resources Control Board, which has authority over both water allocation and water quality in the state, has a public trust duty to exercise its authority to condition water permits to accomplish water quality goals. United States v. State Water Resources Control Bd. (1986). Impacts on water quality appear to be among the most obvious circumstances to incite an application of the public trust doctrine or an exercise of an administrator's authority to control appropriations in the public interest.

## C. Adjudication

There are three general types of judicial procedures affecting water rights.

### 1. *General Stream Adjudications*

All states have adopted procedures for adjudicating the competing rights of all water users in a particular stream system. All persons claiming water rights in the system typically must be joined as parties. In some states, judicial proceedings may be initiated by the users, in others by a state agency and in some states by either users or an agency.

A state agency typically serves as a fact-finder, gathering information, conducting surveys and compiling claims (e.g., in New Mexico, North Dakota, South Dakota, Utah and Washington). The initial hearings and decisions are generally made by an administrative body.

Most states require the administrative determination of rights in a particular stream system to be filed in a court which will embody the determination in a final court decree except to the extent findings may be altered in response to appeals from interested parties. States following this approach include Arizona, California, Idaho, Kansas (no final decree unless there is an appeal), Nevada, Oregon, Texas, Washington and Wyoming. This is usually done a single watershed at a time. Montana provided for a state-wide adjudication of water rights in four large water divisions of the state following a mandatory filing of claimed water rights by April 1, 1982. A water judge in each division enters the appealable decrees embodying all water rights. When a new permit is issued after a general stream adjudication, and there is no ongoing adjudication into which the permit may be integrated, there will be no further adjudication until a new proceeding is initiated.

## 2. Conflicts Among Water Users

One or more water users may sue other water users who allegedly violate their water rights. The decision generally binds only those who are parties. Administrative bodies in some states may have authority to resolve conflicts between individual water users. All decisions of an administrative agency are subject to judicial review either on appeal or as a required step in the process.

## 3. Validation or Review of Agency Permit Decisions

Once an official or agency makes a determination it is final unless someone appeals. Appeals may first go to another level before proceeding to court. In most states the court engages in a trial de novo but most appeals are based on the administrative record.

## D. Regulation of Water Distribution

An administrative agency usually enforces established rights. The manner in which appropriators use water is subject to regulatory and administrative controls.

Wyoming's distribution system is typical of those throughout the West. The state engineer has overall supervision with division superintendents located in each of four water divisions. Each superintendent oversees several water commissioners who physically distribute the water. The commissioner's job, under the guidance of a superintendent and the state engineer, is to make sure the water of each stream under their control is distributed in proper quantities at the right times to those who are authorized to receive it.

The commissioner opens, closes, adjusts and locks headgates in accordance with a list of all appropriators in order of their priority in time, and is a streamside policeman with power to make arrests if necessary. As streamflow wanes in late summer, the commissioner closes headgates starting with the lowest priority (i.e., latest in time), working backward in time towards the first name on the list, always insuring that the earliest appropriators have the best access to water. If streamflow increases, the commissioner can open gates and give juniors the benefit of the increase. Regulation of headgates requires no notice or hearing, because it is purely a ministerial duty of the water commissioner (not a judicial process). Hamp v. State (1911).

The water commissioner also regulates reservoirs, including the exchange of stored water for direct flow. The commissioners feed back reports of measurements on streamflow to the state engineer. In this way data are centralized at the state level so a record of the amount available for appropriation in each drainage and division is obtainable.

In Wyoming an appeal from action of the water commissioner is taken first to the division superintendent, then to the state engineer and finally to the district court of the county where the ditch in controversy is located. The administrative law doctrine of exhaustion of adminstrative remedies does not apply. Neither does the "prior resort" (to administrative official) doctrine apply to suits for damages or injunctive relief between appropriators, and an appropriator may sue another for injury without asking the commissioner, superintendent or state engineer for a judgment. Van Buskirk v. Red Buttes Land & Live Stock Co. (1916). But see Worley v. United States Borax and Chemical Corp. (1967), in which the New Mexico court took an opposing view.

## E. The Colorado System

Colorado was the first state to provide special court proceedings for water rights controversies. The procedure was a refinement of the cumbersome adjudication process in which all claimants could be joined as parties to a lawsuit. By statute the state was divided into districts with each under a blanket judicial decree. The decrees were the result of proceedings that joined all claimants and allowed them to contest one another's claims. New users were added to the decrees as they established appropriations.

Unlike the other western states, Colorado did not later charge an administrative agency with permitting and other determinations. Instead it retained a judicial system and charged it with administrative functions. Colorado is the only prior appropriation state without a permit system, although the system is quite similar to that of the permit states.

One difference is that water users need not ask an agency for a water right. They claim or begin using the water right, then ask a court for a decree. The considerations for the court are similar to those of administrators in permit states.

But the fact that one technically need not seek permission before beginning to use water is considered compatible with the state's constitution, which provides that "the right to divert the unappropriated waters of any natural stream to beneficial uses shall never be denied." (In other states similar provisions have not prevented establishment of permit systems.) In fact, the ability to exercise a constitutional right to divert water means almost nothing unless one has it validated through the statutory system of administration and adjudication. It is always junior to all rights prior to the year of adjudication and therefore is subject to the call of all users with adjudicated rights.

Before 1969, Colorado vested jurisdiction over all water rights adjudication in the district court of each county. The claimant petitioned for an adjudication and notice was given to all parties. The court then ordered the state engineer to supply a list of filings in good standing; the court also could seek additional information about diversion and storage structures from the water commissioner. At the conclusion of the proceeding the court issued a decree. Water rights were determined without active agency participation.

The Water Rights Determination and Administration Act of 1969, C.R.S. §§ 37–92–101 through –602, divided the state into seven water divisions that correspond to the seven major drainages. A division engineer is appointed for each division. "Water courts" in each division have jurisdiction over water rights determinations. They function full or part time depending on the volume of water rights business. Applications for determinations of water rights are made to the clerk of the water court. The clerk prepares monthly resumes of applications that are sent to any potential party and published in local newspapers and other media. After an opportunity for statements of opposition to be filed by those objecting to the application, a referee conducts fact-finding. The state engineer and subordinate officials provide the clerk with a list of decreed and conditional water rights. The referee then approves, disapproves or approves in part the application. In some difficult cases the referee defers to the water judge. If approved, the water right has a priority as of the date of filing the application.

All parties then have an opportunity to protest the ruling to the water judge. Rulings not protested are confirmed unless the water judge finds them to be contrary to law. Protested rulings may be confirmed, modified, reversed or reversed and remanded. Plans for augmentation and changes in use are under the same procedure.

The state and division engineers regulate the distribution of water according to the figures awarded. Appellate review from the judgment and decree of the water judge is available from the Supreme Court.

Division engineers compile and publish tabulations of all water rights in a division every four years, reflecting such matters as abandonment and conditional decrees awarded. The tabulations are subject to protests, on which the water judge conducts hearings.

## IX. TRANSFERS AND CHANGES OF WATER RIGHTS

Appropriation states allow appropriators to transfer water rights to others subject to certain state law limitations. Transfer of rights along with land for continuation of the same uses is a routine matter, but there are restrictions on a transfer for uses in other locations, for different purposes, at different times or involving changes in the points of diversion or return. Some states have special restrictions on water use in another watershed.

A decline in the economic importance of agriculture and urbanization of the West has created a demand for water to be shifted to higher economic uses—uses that return far more economic benefits to society. Agriculture requires vastly larger quantities of water than municipal and industrial uses, so retirement of irrigation water rights can yield plentiful water for such uses. And the typically early priority of irrigation rights makes them especially desirable.

## A. Transfers Generally

A transfer of water rights may be made by sale, lease or exchange. Municipalities often lease rights they hold for anticipated future needs to others for the interim. See Section IV B of this chapter. A transfer of course may not exceed the quantity of rights held by the transferor. It may or may not be accompanied by a change of use (e.g., a different place or purpose of use). For example, if farm land is conveyed along with appurtenant water rights, there may be no change in the purpose, time or place of use or in the point of diversion or return. However, when water rights are conveyed separately (or where the original owner intends a different use), any or all of the above use characteristics may change, thus affecting the rights of other stream appropriators and triggering procedures for determining whether harm to others is sufficient to disallow a change of use.

Water rights in most states pass with the land upon its conveyance unless otherwise provided in the conveyance. And when land is divided, a pro rata portion of water rights accompanies each parcel. Stephens v. Burton (1976). In Colorado the intention of the grantor determines whether water rights pass with the deed to land. Bessemer Irrigating Ditch Co. v. Woolley (1904). Water rights may be granted separately from the land or by a reservation of the water right by the grantor upon conveyance of the land. Water rights may effectively be made nonseverable by statute or severance may be allowed with conditions to protect other users. A portion of an appropriative right also may be sold. Johnston v. Little Horse Creek Irrigating Co. (1904).

## B. State Restrictions on Transfers Apart From the Land

Every prior appropriation state allows transfer of water rights together with the land. But some states restrict transfers for uses away from the land (Montana, Oklahoma, Nebraska, Nevada, South Dakota, Wyoming). Kansas, Arizona and North Dakota experimented with non-severance statutes but later repealed them. Laws restraining transfers apart from the land are based on the riparian-type notion that a water right is appurtenant to a parcel of land. A likely motive for the laws was to prevent appropriators from making claims to water in amounts well beyond the quantity that could be used beneficially on their lands and then selling the early priority water right to others.

Wyoming's 1909 "no-change" statute provides that no severance of water rights from land may be made without loss of priority. This unfortunate rule, however, is riddled with exceptions (e.g., for domestic, transportation, steam power, industrial and highway construction uses, pre-1909 rights, reservoir rights and rotation of waters). Although the 1909 law remains on the books, a 1973 amendment authorizing transfers has negated its effect.

Nebraska's Irrigation District Act of 1895 makes irrigation water rights inseverably appurtenant to land. However, because the statute applies only prospectively, pre-1895 rights (very desirable because of their seniority) may be sold.

In Nevada, Oklahoma and South Dakota, water rights are made inseverable as a rule, but may be severed if their use on the original benefited land becomes economically infeasible. The Nevada statute limits only the transfer of irrigation rights; others are freely transferable. Montana prohibits a change in the purpose of use (of water rights in excess of 15 c.f.s.) from agricultural to industrial uses.

In addition to statutory transfer restrictions, there are private restrictions on stock transfer imposed by mutual ditch companies and irrigation districts. See Chapter Eleven. These restrictions may appear on the face of stock or may be included in the company's by-laws or articles of incorporation.

## C. Restrictions on Transbasin Diversions

Removing water from one watershed to be used in another, variously known as transbasin diversion or interbasin transfer, is generally permitted under the prior appropriation doctrine. Indeed, the seminal case of Coffin v. Left Hand Ditch Co. (1882) involved a diversion of water out of the

basin of its origin. The court recognized that the
appropriation doctrine is fundamentally different
from the doctrine of riparian rights in that it
allows such diversions. A variety of state laws
limit transbasin diversions by placing certain requirements on the diverter to protect the equities
and interests of the area of origin. These limitations are in addition to restrictions imposed by the
rules regarding changes in use that are discussed
below. Restrictions on removing water from within a state may raise special problems under the
commerce clause of the Constitution. See Chapter
Ten, Section IV.

A transbasin diversion is often required because
growth and expansion occur where water supplies
are inadequate. Great investments in diversion
facilities are made in order to bring the water to
the watershed where it is demanded. Southern
California and Colorado's eastern slope have been
able to flourish because of imported water. If
rights are purchased from appropriators in the
area of origin, the "no harm" rule applicable to
changes in use provides some protection for existing appropriators. But the rule does not consider harm to the economy, ecology, lifestyle and
potential for future growth of the area where the
water originates. Because these effects tend to be
severe and lasting when there are massive exports
of water out of a watershed, some states have
created restrictions to protect the interests of areas
of origin. Such protective legislation modifies pri-

or appropriation law and adds costs to transfers, but is justified politically by notions of public policy.

Legislation intended to protect an area of origin often attempts to safeguard existing needs including established water rights and streamflows for fish and wildlife. It also aims to assure some protection for future development, but needs for this purpose are difficult to quantify. California allows transbasin diversions subject to the right of the area of origin to appropriate the water when it is needed with an absolute priority over the exporter. California state law also reserves for the county of origin all the water that may be necessary for its development.

The largest transbasin diversions in Colorado are from the Colorado River basin west of the continental divide to Denver and other heavily populated areas in the east. The legislature enacted a statute to protect the western slope's "present appropriations of water and in addition thereto prospective uses of water for irrigation and other beneficial consumptive use purposes." Those who divert water from the western slope must show that future water supplies for the west slope "will not be impaired nor increased in cost." This is satisfied by providing "compensatory storage" to help meet future needs in the area of origin. See Colorado River Water Conservation Dist. v. Municipal Subdistrict, N. Colorado Water Conservancy Dist. (1979).

A Nebraska statute authorizing interbasin transfers of 75% of the flow of major rivers in the state was interpreted to allow transfers to be denied if they are "contrary to the public interest." Little Blue Natural Resources Dist. v. Lower Platte N. Natural Resources Dist. (1980). Subsequently the statute was amended to set out the factors to be considered by the Director of Water Resources in deciding the public interest.

Texas law provides that interbasin transfers are allowed only if the water diverted is surplus to the reasonably foreseeable needs of the basin of origin for the next fifty years. Oklahoma requires that sufficient reserves be established to meet present and future needs.

## D. Changes In Use

### 1. No Harm Rule

Whenever one seeks to change the point of diversion, or the place, purpose or time of using a water right whether or not a transfer of the right is involved, special protections for other appropriators apply.

An appropriator who seeks to change a use or to transfer a right to another for a changed use must apply to the appropriate administrative body or court for approval.

Changes in use may affect stream conditions upon which other appropriators depend for their beneficial uses. Of course a junior appropriator may do nothing to impair a senior appropriator's prior rights to water, but juniors are protected from changes made by seniors. The doctrine of prior appropriation recognizes a right of junior appropriators "in the continuation of stream conditions as they existed at the time of their respective appropriations." Farmers Highline Canal & Reservoir Co. v. City of Golden (1954).

Irrigation practices typically result in about half, often more, of all water that is diverted returning to the stream. Only a portion is actually consumed by evaporation or by being drawn into plants and retained or transpired into the atmosphere. The rest flows or seeps back to the stream from ditches or fields it is caught in sumps, ponds, groundwater aquifers and the like. The amount that does return to the stream—return flow—becomes available at certain times and places for others to divert. Changes in the point of diversion, or the place, time or purpose of use must not cause material harm to the uses of other appropriators.

Certain actions, however, injure juniors but are not subject to the no harm rule. They include reuse or more intensive consumptive use of the water on the same land for the same general purposes (e.g., agricultural irrigation), changes in use of imported water (see Section VI B of this chapter) and, in some jurisdictions, certain changes in the point of return flow.

## 2. Procedures

An appropriator who wishes to make a change in use or transfer the right to another who will use the right differently must seek permission for the change. In permit jurisdictions the decision whether a change in use will be allowed rests with a state administrative agency such as the office of the state engineer; administrative decisions are subject to review by state courts. In Colorado, a change of use is approved through a statutorily established court proceeding and evidenced by a court decree. In either type of jurisdiction, the main substantive issue in the change of use proceeding is whether the change violates the no harm rule.

In most states the burden of proving that no harm will result is on the person seeking the new use. Other appropriators may contest the change on the ground that it will injure them. The holder of a conditional water right (see section IV B 2 of this chapter) who will be harmed may also contest the change. Rocky Mountain Power Co. v. White River Elec. Ass'n (1962). Once a prima facie case has been made, the burden is on the objector to refute the evidence and prove harm. In Montana the original burden of proving harm is on the objector.

Most permit states also authorize denial of a change on "public interest" grounds. The relevant considerations may include environmental, economic and social effects of the transfer. The Idaho

Supreme Court has said that the loss of a local tax base is not actionable harm. But under Wyoming's change in use statute the Board of Control may consider economic loss to the locality and the state. The Nevada statute allows the state engineer to consider the economic consequences to the state of changes to uses "involving the industrial purpose of generating electricity to be exported."

### 3. Types of Changes

A change in use may take several forms, each with its own potential for harm to other appropriators. Changes may be made in the point of diversion (or point of return); in the place of use (or place of storage); in the purpose of use (e.g., irrigation or municipal); or in the time of use (e.g., seasonal or intermittent or continuous). Harm may occur either from depriving an appropriator of the equivalent quantity or quality of water that was available before the change or by increasing the appropriator's obligations to seniors. It is the possibility of harm, and not a certainty that it will occur, that must be proved.

### a. Change in Point of Diversion

One of the most common types of change in use is a change in point of diversion (which may be accompanied by a change in the place of water use). An irrigator may want to divert through a new ditch or use a surface diversion instead of a well drawing on the same water source. Some potential causes of harm to other appropriators

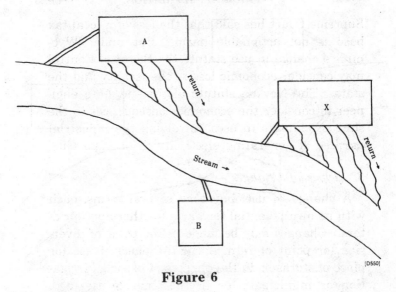

**Figure 6**

that could prevent the change from being allowed are illustated by the following examples.

In Figure 6 senior A moves the point of diversion downstream to point X below junior B (or senior transfers water out of basin); B is deprived of A's return flow.

In the same example B may be harmed if it is a losing stream (e.g., due to seepage). The increased stream losses between points A and X may mean inadequate water is available to junior B. Haney v. Neace-Stark Co. (1923).

In Figure 7 senior A moves the point of diversion upstream to point X. Before the move junior B

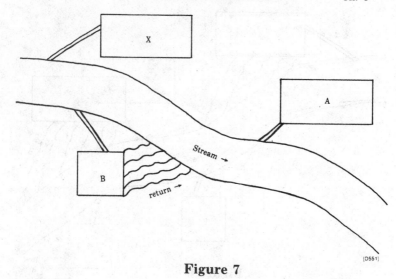

**Figure 7**

could divert and use water, with the return flow supplying A. A's use at point X may deplete the stream leaving inadequate water to supply B. Vogel v. Minnesota Canal & Reservoir Co. (1910).

In the same example there may be another source of harm. If it is a gaining stream (e.g., flow increases downstream because of inflows from seepage or tributaries) between points X and A, senior A may have been supplied in part by the increased flow. After the change junior B may have to reduce use in order to make up for the increased flow no longer available to A. Crockett v. Jones (1926).

In Figure 8 senior A moves the point of diversion upstream to point X. Junior C, who once benefited

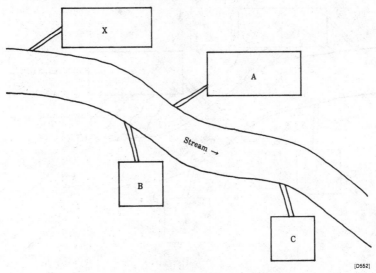

**Figure 8**

from the senior's call (i.e., was able to use water that the senior could prevent intervening junior B from using), now does not benefit if junior B (who is senior to C) uses the water before it reaches C.

In Figure 9 senior A moves the point of diversion downstream to point X. B had been supplied by A's return flow. B must now call C (who is junior to B) in order to get enough water.

A change in the point of return of water may also cause harm to others. Ordinarily such a change accompanies other changes in use, as shown by many of the above examples of changing

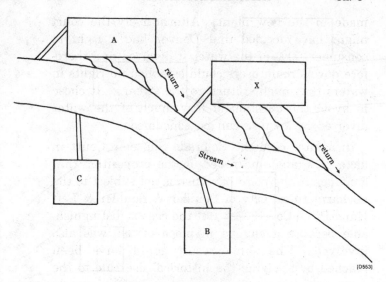

**Figure 9**

a point of diversion. Although cases involving only a change in point of return are rare, one would expect the no harm rule to apply. But in Metropolitan Denver Sewage Disposal Dist. No. 1 v. Farmers Reservoir & Irrigation Co. (1972), the Court held that irrigators who depended on discharges of Denver's sewage effluent suffered no legal harm from Denver's change in the point of return when a new sewage plant was constructed.

The *Metro Denver* case is an aberration that may be limited to the facts. The contest was essentially over who should pay to pump the treated sewage effluent back upstream to where the farmers could use it and perhaps the court did not want to interfere with the investment that the city had made in the new plant. Alternatively the court might have decided that Denver had a right to consume 100% of the water it diverted and therefore downstream users could establish no rights in waters that might return to the stream. It chose to avoid the question of how much of the water diverted by Denver can be consumed.

In a later case the Colorado Supreme Court in dicta reiterated and relied on the proposition that a change in the point of return is not subject to the no harm rule. City of Boulder v. Boulder & Left Hand Ditch Co. (1977). But the case is distinguishable because a change in place of use was also involved. The same result could have been reached by applying the historical use rule to the change in use (see discussion in the following subsection). Instead the court moderated the *Metro Denver* rule by adding a specious and unhelpful distinction between "waste water" and "return flow," suggesting that there is no protectable right to the continued flow of "waste water" (water returning to stream in surface ditches) but is a right to "return flow" (water seeping back to the stream).

### b. *Change in Place of Use*

Juniors are harmed to the extent that the quantity of water available to them is reduced. They may also be harmed if the change diminishes quality of the supply. Heine v. Reynolds (1962) (stream salinity increased by change).

A change in place of use must not increase consumptive use even if the amount diverted remains the same. Enlarged Southside Irrigation Ditch Co. v. John's Flood Ditch Co. (1949). Changes in place of use often change the place or timing of return flows from irrigation. Changing to out of basin uses will yield no return flows, making the new use 100% consumptive.

A change in place of use generally requires a severance of water rights from the land, so if a state has a statute restricting severance it may restrict the change.

A change in the place of storage, such as an alternative reservoir site, is also a type of change in the place of use. The change may be permitted if the new reservoir is at a higher elevation with lower losses than the original site. Lindsey v. McClure (1943). But increased seepage and evaporation loss is harm that can prevent a change. Because a new dam must often be built, dam safety may be considered among the public interest considerations.

Exchange statutes in several western states (including New Mexico, Colorado and Utah) authorize agreements between water users (i.e., to furnish water at one point in the stream and withdraw at another). Exchanges are changes in the manner and place of use that are subject to the no harm rule. Almo Water Co. v. Darrington (1972). A change in place of use may be limited by a state statute restricting severence of water rights from the original land.

## c.  *Change in Purpose of Use*

A change in purpose of use typically involves a change from irrigation use to municipal or industrial use. Municipal uses are among the most consumptive since returns (usually sewage effluent) are a small percentage of the quantity diverted. Hydroelectric power generation and cooling are less consumptive than irrigation. Thus changes from irrigation to municipal use (City of Westminster v. Church (1968)) or from power generation to irrigation use (Hutchinson v. Stricklin (1933), *overruled on other grounds* Rencken v. Young (1985)) may increase consumption. Uses that involve a change from direct use to storage may affect both the timing of usage and amount of consumptive use.

The purpose of use (e.g., agriculture) is not changed if water is used in a new manner for the same purpose. Planting crops that consume more water or using different facilities to irrigate (e.g., sprinklers instead of flood irrigation) are not usually considered changes in the purpose although the manner of use is actually different and others may be harmed (e.g., by a reduction in seepage or elimination of return flows). This seems like a loophole in the no harm rule, but it is built on traditional assumptions of water users, especially irrigators, that they should be able to plant whatever they want and irrigate as necessary so long as the amount of water used does not exceed the amount allowed by a permit or decree. The prevailing rule remains: changes in the purpose of use that necessitate permission of an administrative agency or court and invocation of the no harm rule occur only when water is put to a different type of beneficial use.

### d. Change in Time of Use

A change in the timing of use can harm others. For example, irrigation water rights are seasonal (used only during the irrigation season), although municipal and industrial uses are typically year-around uses. Similarly, a storage right may permit constant diversion into the reservoir although actual uses are intermittent; a direct flow right is occasional, occurring only when there are present uses. A change in the timing of return flows is also a possible source of harm. The slow-moving character of seepage returning to the stream provides a form of "transient storage" which may furnish late-season return flows to juniors (thus extending the irrigation season).

### 4. Limits on Changed Use

A change in use will not be denied or enjoined if conditions can be imposed sufficient to protect other appropriators from harm. To assure maintenance of stream conditions on which others are entitled to rely it may be necessary to restrict the new use. For example, a seasonally used direct-flow irrigation right may be transferred to a continuous storage use, provided diversions are restricted to the irrigation season, Brighton Ditch Co.

v. City of Englewood (1951), and are made under the same conditions as the original direct-flow diversions, Colorado Milling & Elevator Co. v. Larimer & Weld Irrigation Co. (1899). An increasingly common condition requires bypasses or releases of water necessary to maintain stream quality.

### a.  Historical Consumptive Use

A common limitation on a change in use is that water consumption of the new use be no greater than the historical consumptive use (the difference between the amount of water diverted and the amount of water returned). Historical use may be shown by actual records if they exist; expert testimony may be necessary, however, since records are rarely adequate to demonstrate the amount of water that has been beneficially used. Historical use also may be based on evidence of the amount of water that would have been required for the purposes to which it was devoted. Evidence would include soil conditions, proximity to the stream, crop water requirements minus average rainfall, and efficiency of irrigation. See Green v. Chaffee Ditch Co. (1962) (rights sold by farmers to city could not exceed amount of water farmers reasonably could have consumed, as established by expert testimony based on above factors).

Statutes, case law and regulations restricting transfers to historical consumptive use are intended to prevent harm to others. The rules have been applied even if consumption under the new use would be lower. For instance, in one case water had been taken to another watershed where it was used for irrigation, so the old use was 100% consumptive as to the watershed of origin. The new use, however, was entirely in the watershed of origin. One might have expected the change to be approved for the amount "used" historically—all the water diverted. But the court limited the right transferred to the quantity of water that was consumed in the destination watershed (diversion less "returns") although no returns had actually reached the basin of origin. Basin Electric Power Cooperative v. State Board of Control (1978). The decision may be explained by the fact the court was upholding an exercise of administrative discretion by the Board of Control.

Determinations of historical use are complicated by inadequacy of records and the expense of expert advice. The use of experts, then, can make changes in use costly, impeding efficient changes (i.e., changes to higher productive uses). The cost of proof may decide cases if parties are unable to pay for the necessary expertise. See CF&I Steel Corp. v. Rooks (1972) (objectors lost for failure to refute applicant's expert testimony).

## b. *Permitted or Decreed Diversion Right*

The amount diverted can never exceed the diversion right stated in a permit or decree. This is true even if a change in use would result in no greater consumption. If the historical consumptive use of a decreed right of 200 c.f.s. was 100 c.f.s. (50% consumptive), the new user is entitled to consume 100 c.f.s. If the new use is only 40% efficient, however, the new user must divert 250 c.f.s. in order to consume 100 c.f.s. Since the changed use or transferred right is also limited to the original decreed diversion right of 200 c.f.s., the new user will, in fact, only be able to use 80 c.f.s. (200 c.f.s. x 40% consumption).

### c. *Other Restrictions*

It may be necessary to restrict a new use to less than historical consumptive use. For instance, in a change in point of diversion, the no harm rule may dictate further curtailment to assure that the same amount of water actually reaches those who depend on it.

Other possible barriers to changes of use exist, such as federal and state environmental pollution laws (see Chapter Nine, Section V), minimum and maximum streamflow requirements, land use restrictions, area-of-origin protection statutes and state anti-export statutes (see Chapter Ten, Section IV).

## X. LOSS OF WATER RIGHTS

Water rights acquired by prior appropriation may be lost if they are not used. The statutes or applicable doctrines in most states provide that nonuse for a time coupled with intent to relinquish constitutes abandonment. Some states require forfeiture of rights for nonuse in spite of the appropriator's contrary intent. Rights generally may not be lost by prescription because any water not used by a senior appropriator belongs to the stream, to be used for the satisfaction of rights of existing appropriators and for new appropriations.

## A. Abandonment

Most states consider rights to use water established by prior appropriation abandoned and lost if they are not used for an extended time. Mere nonuse is not enough, however. One must intend to abandon the rights. Beaver Park Water, Inc. v. Victor (1982). The burden of proving an intent to abandon is on the person attempting to establish abandonment, but an unreasonable period of nonuse will create a rebuttable presumption of intent to abandon. In some states the period giving rise to the presumption is set by statute. Once the presumption arises the rights holder may rebut it by showing facts or conditions justifying the nonuse. Economic, financial or legal obstacles to water use may justify nonuse. Hallenbeck v. Granby Ditch & Reservoir Co. (1966). But economic infeasibility is not enough to overcome the presumption. CF&I Steel Corp. v. Purgatoire River Water Conservancy Dist.

Some states authorize administrative officials to initiate proceedings to declare abandonments as a way of curtailing paper rights that exist in excess of actual water use. E.g., Colorado, Montana, Texas and Wyoming. An action may be brought by a junior appropriator who stands to benefit. It can be raised in proceedings such as for a change in

point of diversion.  See, e.g., *CF&I Steel*, supra.
Once abandoned, water is again available for appropriation by others.

## B.  Forfeiture

Forfeiture, unlike abandonment, does not require that the appropriator intend to abandon
water rights by nonuse.  Involuntary loss of all or
a portion of one's water rights is triggered simply
by nonuse for a period set by statute.  Thus, forfeiture can be found where there is evidence of abandonment.  Jenkins v. State, Dept. of Water Resources (1982).

Forfeiture statutes usually provide for notice by
a state agency or official that rights will be forfeited if not used within a statutorily specified period.
The New Mexico statute originally provided for
automatic forfeiture after four years of nonuse.
State *ex rel.* Reynolds v. South Springs Co. (1969).
The law was amended to allow a one year grace
period during which use could be recommenced.  A
forfeiture may be avoided if one has an excuse for
the nonuse, generally a showing that it was impossible to put the water to a beneficial use.

Resumption of use or a showing of excuse must
be within the forfeiture period, any statutory grace
period or an extension of either permitted by law.
Some courts have held that the right is lost and
cannot be revived once the period passes.  Baugh
v. Criddle (1967).  In Wyoming, however, the right
continues to exist until there has been a declara-

tion of forfeiture, Sturgeon v. Brooks (1955), allowing additional time for use of the right or for proving an excuse for nonuse.

Forfeiture claims are usually initiated by statutory procedures but also can be decided in private litigation.  Courts may defer to the primary jurisdiction of an administrative agency to decide whether there has been a forfeiture.

## C.  Adverse Possession

One may obtain another's rights in real property by taking actual, open, notorious and hostile exclusive possession of the property.  In the past some courts ruled that a junior appropriator could adversely possess a senior's priority.  E.g., Idaho, Montana and Utah.  However, rights held by prior appropriation generally cannot be lost to others by adverse possession.  First, private individuals can obtain rights only by compliance with statutory procedures; as property of the public, water rights cannot be adversely possessed.  Mountain Meadow Ditch & Irrigation Co. v. Park Ditch & Reservoir Co. (1954); People v. Shirokow (1980) (claim to prescriptive rights not good against the state). Second, one's use of water cannot be adverse to others because everyone has a right to assume that any water use was pursuant to the priority system. Coryell v. Robinson (1948).  This is especially true if the would-be adverse possessor holds some rights on the watercourse.

A junior appropriator who takes water to the detriment of a senior appropriator for an extended period may build a case for the senior's abandonment of the right. If nothing is done to prevent the junior's use, a court might find that the senior intended to give up the right. But the junior would not take the senior's priority; at best the junior could establish a new appropriation in the abandoned water with a priority date no earlier than commencement of the junior's use.

## XI. ACCESS TO WATER SOURCES

Rights-of-way for ditches, canals and pipelines are of critical importance to both individual and corporate water users. Because most irrigated land does not border on a stream, bringing water to a tract may require building facilities on the land of one or more property owners. Even if land is adjacent to a stream, some use of another's land may be necessary in order to use a gravity flow pipe or ditch that must follow contours of the terrain. Recognizing the importance of access, both federal and state governments have acted to facilitate acquisition of rights-of-way across public and private lands.

### A. Across Public Lands

At first virtually all lands in the West were public lands. Congress provided for ditch and canal rights-of-way across public lands in the 1866 Mining Act. In addition to recognizing the right of trespassers to establish water rights by prior appropriation on federal lands, the Act stated "the right of way for the construction of ditches and canals for the purposes aforesaid is hereby acknowledged and confirmed." The 1870 Amendment to the Act made all patents of public lands and all homesteads "subject to any vested and accrued water rights, or rights to ditches and reservoirs used in connection with such water rights." These laws opened the way for construction of all necessary facilities without fear of later dispossession or interruption by the government or its patentees. See Section II A of this chapter.

Today rights-of-way across public land are obtained by special permission. The Federal Land Policy and Management Act of 1976 (FLPMA), 43 U.S.C.A. §§ 1751–71, authorizes the Secretary of the Interior to grant or renew rights-of-way across public lands for water storage and distribution facilities (e.g., ditches, pipelines and tunnels). Securing rights-of-way requires application to the Secretary (or the Secretary of Agriculture in the case of National Forest lands). Permits are granted for a fixed term and are subject to annual rentals and conditions on use.

## B. Across Private Lands

### 1. *Status of Trespassing Appropriators*

Under the appropriation doctrine, use (not land ownership on a waterbody) is the basis of a water right; appropriators may thus take waters from lands not their own. The first appropriations in the West were made by persons entering on the public lands without authority. As indicated above, federal legislation validated the appropriative rights and use of lands for ditch rights-of-way by "trespassers" on the public lands. Lands conveyed to private parties were patented subject to rights of those who already had perfected water rights to use the land for ditch rights-of-way. An 1890 act reserved to the United States rights-of-way for ditches and canals on all public lands patented after that date west of the 100th meridian. 43 U.S.C.A. § 945. A 1964 amendment to the act required the government to pay compensation for any such lands it actually used. Id., § 945a. Thus, many lands were impressed with rights-of-way not only for early private uses established before public lands were patented to private parties, but also for future uses. New appropriators whose water use began after the land was privately patented and who were not acting with the sanction of the federal government generally had to reckon with private landowners when their diversions required crossing private lands.

A number of state laws and cases address whether appropriators may transport water across lands of others. Some state courts (e.g., Idaho and Oregon) have held invalid the appropriation of one who trespasses on the land of another to make a diversion. The right to contest the appropriation may be limited to the non-consenting landowner, however. More typically, trespassing appropriators have their water rights recognized if they come to terms with the property owner. For instance, in Colorado trespass cannot be asserted to prevent perfection of a water right, but the trespasser must compensate the owner for the fair market value of using the lands and any resulting damage to the residue. See Bubb v. Christensen, (1980). This is tantamount to a right of private condemnation, although the owner, if aware of the intrusion when it began, could probably control the choice of a route across the land.

If a trespasser enters the land of another and constructs pipelines, ditches or other facilities without the landowner's permission, and they remain long enough, the use may ripen into a prescriptive right. The period of limitations varies according to state law.

## 2. *Purchase of Rights-Of-Way*

The most common way to obtain a right-of-way to convey water across private land is by purchase. Often the property owner can also be served by the water delivery facilities and an accommodation reached based on the benefits received. The right-of-way for a canal, ditch or pipeline includes a secondary easement for necessary maintenance and repairs.

Grants of easements or rights-of-way, like other interests in land, usually must be in writing and conform to other conveyancing formalities. Yet it has been held that a landowner's oral permission to construct a ditch is valid as a license which the landowner is estopped to contest. See Gustin v. Harting (1912).

## 3. Condemnation of Rights-Of-Way

Sometimes an owner whose land lies in the path of a canal, ditch or pipeline is unwilling or unavailable to grant permission for use of the land. Western states have enacted statutes authorizing certain appropriators to condemn rights-of-way to transport water across private lands.

Private condemnation statutes have been challenged on the ground that they do not further a public use. The United States Supreme Court upheld Utah's grant of eminent domain power against a challenge that the law offended the due process clause of the fourteenth amendment. The Court recognized the great importance of water development under conditions prevailing in the West. Clark v. Nash (1905). Western state courts have upheld similar statutes. In Kaiser Steel Corp. v. W.S. Ranch Co. (1970) the Supreme Court of New Mexico said that any beneficial use pursuant to state law (coal mining in that case) would suffice to support a valid "public use." The only remedy of the landowner against the appropriator who crossed private land without permission was damages for inverse condemnation.

## C. Appurtenancy of Ditch Rights to Water Rights

The right-of-way for a ditch and a water right are usually considered appurtenant to one another so that the conveyance of one carries the other with it. This does not prevent one from being sold apart from the other, however, if the parties express that intention.

## XII.  STORAGE

Without storage, beneficial use of water would be limited to short runoff periods throughout most of the West. Storage is an important way to maximize the use of scarce water resources.

On-channel storage means that the facility is physically part of the appropriated stream. Most major dams and projects are examples of on-channel storage; their function is to retain some of the natural flow, while allowing enough water to stay in the stream to satisfy rights of downstream appropriators. Off-channel storage requires diversion and transportation works to get water to the storage location away from the stream channel. There is no legal distinction between off-stream and on-stream storage rights. Retention of water in the streambed by artificial means constitutes a "diversion" for purposes of perfecting a water right.

## A. Acquisition of Storage Rights

Permission to store water and permission to maintain a dam involve distinct issues.

### 1. *Storage Water Rights*

Some states make statutory distinctions between diversions for immediate use, "direct flow water rights" and diversions for subsequent uses, "storage water rights." A right to use water directly from the stream does not entitle the user to store any water and a right to store water does not mean that water can be used directly from the stream. Handy Ditch Co. v. Greeley & Loveland Irrigating Co. (1929). Nevertheless, courts have often upheld storage of water appropriated under a direct flow right as a sensible conservation measure if no harm is caused to others. E.g., Ackerman v. City of Walsenburg (1970). The ability to capture and store unappropriated water beyond one's appropriation has also been upheld because it would otherwise go to waste. E.g., Federal Land Bank v. Morris (1941).

A permit or decree for a storage water right is obtained from the same agency or court that administers other water rights. The storage right is not complete until water is actually put to a beneficial use. Separate permits are required by some states for storage and for application to a beneficial use, e.g., Arizona, Nevada, Wyoming and Nebraska. This approach recognizes that often the entity diverting and holding the water (e.g., reservoir company) is different from the entity or persons using the water (e.g., irrigators). Some states consider the two joint appropriators. Board of County Comm'rs v. Rocky Mountain Water Co. (1938).

## 2. Permission to Construct Storage Facilities

Besides perfecting a right to store water, one seeking to impound it in a reservoir must have permission to build the facility. Most states require plans for construction of dams and reservoirs to be approved by the same agency that administers water rights. The agency or official (e.g., state engineer or director of water resources) may consider factors related to the public interest such as safety, impacts on fish and wildlife and aesthetics. Most states exempt small storage facilities like stock watering ponds from permit requirements.

## B. Use of Storage Rights

The holder of a storage water right can use stored water for any beneficial purpose. Cf. Basey v. Gallagher (1874). Appropriative rights on a stream, whether for storage or direct flow, are governed by the same rules of priority that apply to other appropriations. Donich v. Johnson (1926). Storage and direct water rights are integrated; neither is given preference. An exception is Nebraska, where water may not be impounded, even by holders of senior rights, when needed for direct irrigation.

Some states allow exchanges between appropriators. For instance, water stored downstream may be exchanged for direct flow diversions upstream. Exchanges among rights holders maximize the use to which water can be put, allowing the benefit of storage to be shared with those who have no storage rights. In Colorado an appropriator can devise a plan for augmentation that provides for such an exchange, which will be approved so long as others are not harmed. Exchanges are permitted in most states upon compliance with conditions imposed by an administrative agency. Stored water may also be used under a contract, lease or other arrangement. E.g., Kearney Lake, Land & Reservoir Co. v. Lake DeSmet Reservoir Co. (1970).

## C.  Limits on Storage

A widely applied limitation on holders of storage water rights is the "one-fill rule." The rule allows an appropriator to fill a reservoir only once annually and not to use it over the course of a year to store more than its full capacity. Windsor Reservoir & Canal Co. v. Lake Supply Ditch Co. (1908). The purpose of the one-fill limitation was ease of regulating but its application can be terribly inefficient. A series of several fillings and drawdowns may be necessary to even out flows throughout the year. A small regulating dam can release many times its capacity during a year. This is prohibited whenever the one-fill rule is strictly applied. If applied to restrict control of water by hydroelectric dams, the result could greatly reduce their utility. In fact, there is a dearth of cases except in the irrigation context.

Water diverted to a reservoir but not used may be retained for future use by the appropriator. Known as "carryover storage," this practice helps balance out wet and dry years. Some states do not allow the appropriator to use the amount of carryover storage plus the reservoir's full capacity of carryover storage the following year; the limit of one filling still applies with the amount carried over debited against the single filling.

# CHAPTER FOUR

# HYBRID SYSTEMS AND OTHER VARIATIONS

Ten states employ a mixture of riparian and appropriation doctrine in their water laws. They include the three West Coast states (California, Oregon and Washington) and the six states that straddle the 100th meridian—the dividing line between the arid West and the relatively wet East (Kansas, Nebraska, North Dakota, Oklahoma, South Dakota and Texas). These states flank a cluster of eight of the nine states that embrace the pure appropriation doctrine. (Alaska is the other appropriation state.) Mississippi also has a hybrid system. Hybrid states are sometimes said to follow the "California doctrine" because California developed such a system first and most fully.

There is no pervasive doctrine that fits all the hybrid system states. California adopted a dual system from the beginning but the others originally were riparian and later converted to a system of prior appropriation. Each hybrid state has its own mixture of the systems. Riparian rights are important in each mostly for historical reasons because substantial riparian water rights had been established by the time appropriation laws were passed. Appropriation law is more important today in the hybrid states, since it is the basis of new rights. Only in California can riparians originate new uses superior to appropriators by virtue of a riparian location.

The chapter considers several special water allocation schemes existing in the United States. Unique features of the water law of Louisiana and Hawaii are discussed, followed by a consideration of pueblo water rights which have relevance in several southwestern states.

## I.  DEVELOPMENT OF HYBRID SYSTEMS

The historical roots of hybrid systems vary among jurisdictions. The common denominator is that each state recognized riparian rights at first, but eventually adopted the prior appropriation system because it was believed to be more suitable for allocating rights to use water. For states on the West Coast and central states that lie between higher elevation arid land and lower land with greater rainfall, neither the riparian system nor the appropriation system was entirely fitting; hence they developed hybrid systems. In all hybrid states it has been necessary to develop accommodations between the two rather inconsistent systems of water allocation.

## A.  California's Early Recognition of Both Appropriative Rights and Riparian Rights

In Irwin v. Phillips (1855), the dispute was between the owner of a canal supplying water to

early miners located away from the stream and
subsequent miners located along the stream. All
were located on federal lands. The subsequent
miners argued that their riparian location entitled
them to use water without regard to earlier appropriations of the canal owner. The Supreme Court
of California rejected this contention. Since none
of the parties actually owned the land they occupied, the court reasoned that the subsequent miners were not riparian landowners and therefore
could not complain about the canal owner's diversion. The court concluded that on the public domain the rule of prior appropriation established by
the early miners had become so firmly fixed as to
be "looked upon as having the force and effect of
res judicata." In reaching this conclusion the
court noted that the state legislature had recognized canals for mining purposes as property subject to taxation, thereby implicitly approving the
prior appropriation doctrine.

Shortly after the decision in *Irwin*, the California Supreme Court acknowledged the continuing
viability of the riparian doctrine in that state. In
Crandall v. Woods (1857), as in *Irwin*, the parties
were all trespassers on the public domain. In
*Crandall*, however, defendants had occupied lands
adjacent to a stream prior to the time the plaintiff
water company built its diversion works, but they
started taking water later. The defendants did not
own the land but had settled there under federal
public land laws, yet the court held they were

absolute owners of their lands as against all but the United States. Thus they were entitled to exercise riparian rights subject only to the rights of appropriators who diverted water prior to the time defendants claimed their lands. From the two cases the rule emerged that between appropriators on the public domain the prior appropriator acquired the superior right. But one who settled on riparian land in the public domain, even without taking water, could not be defeated by an appropriator whose water use began after the riparian settler claimed land.

The California Supreme Court later suggested in dictum that the rights of riparians whose land was patented (conveyed) by the United States after the Mining Act of July 26, 1866 could not be defeated by appropriations made after the Act but before the patent. Lux v. Haggin (1886) (riparian plaintiffs whose land was patented before the Act held to have vested rights that would defeat any appropriator).

## B. Federal Recognition of Appropriative Rights

The California Supreme Court assumed that water on federal land belonged to the federal government and passed with the land to settlers. Courts in Colorado and other appropriation states held that water law was entirely a state matter and that a federal patent carried with it no riparian rights. Were the Colorado doctrine states depriving landowners of riparian rights the federal government intended to convey to them? A few federal land statutes helped to clarify the situation.

The 1866 Mining Act, codified at 30 U.S.C.A. § 51 and 43 U.S.C.A. § 661, reads in relevant part:

Whenever, by priority of possession, rights to the use of water for mining, agricultural, manufacturing, or other purposes have vested and accrued, and the same are recognized and acknowledged by the local customs, laws and decisions of courts, the possessors and owners of such vested rights shall be maintained and protected in the same.

By the Act, Congress recognized the validity of rights established under the appropriation doctrine that many western states had been applying on the public domain. The statute should have made clear that the rights of an appropriator on the public domain could not be defeated by a patentee of riparian land. To eliminate any doubt, the Placer Act of 1870 (amending the 1866 Act) said that future patentees of riparian land would take subject to the vested rights of appropriators.

Another federal statute important to western water law is the Desert Land Act of 1877, codified at 43 U.S.C.A. §§ 321–29. The law was originally intended as an incentive program in which the federal government gave desert lands to persons who irrigated them. After providing for establishment of the program, the Act stated:

. . . that the right to the use of water by the person so conducting the same on or to any tract of desert land of 640 acres shall depend upon bona fide prior appropriation, and such right shall not exceed the amount of water actually appropriated and necessarily used for the purpose of irrigation and reclamation; *and all surplus water over and above such actual appropriation and use, together with the water of all lakes, rivers, and other sources of water supply on the public lands and not navigable, shall remain and be held free for the appropriation and use of the public for irrigation, mining, and manufacturing purposes, subject to existing rights.* [Emphasis added]

The italicized portion of the Act was probably intended only to limit the amount of water an appropriator could claim. But the Supreme Court of Oregon interpreted it as removing riparian rights from all federal land patents. Hough v. Porter (1908), *supp. op.* (1909). In other words, a patentee who received a patent after March 3, 1877, acquired no riparian rights under the Oregon rule. South Dakota adopted the Oregon rule in Cook v. Evans (1921), *modified* (1922). But the courts of Washington and California interpreted the Desert Land Act as applying only to specified desert lands and continued to hold that one who received a patent to riparian lands (other than desert lands) acquired riparian rights subject to the rights of prior appropriators. Still v. Palouse Irrigation & Power Co. (1911); San Joaquin and King's River Canal & Irrigation Co. v. Worswick (1922), *cert. denied* (1922).

The issue of whether the Desert Land Act extinguished all riparian rights on federal lands patented after March 3, 1877 was before the Supreme Court of the United States in California Oregon Power Co. v. Beaver Portland Cement Co. (1935). An Oregon landowner, whose property bordered on a stream, claimed riparian rights. The Court upheld Oregon's construction of the Desert Lands Act in Hough v. Porter as applied to the particular Oregon case but left other states free to define water rights as they pleased. The Court said that federal land laws recognize that each state has "the right . . . to determine for itself to what extent the rule of appropriation or the common law rule in respect to riparian rights should obtain."

## C. Limitations on Riparian Rights

Unlike California, other hybrid states did not start out with dual systems of water law. Either by statute or adoption of the common law each originally embraced only the riparian doctrine, then before the turn of the century enacted legislation implementing a system of prior appropriation. Such statutes usually contained some provision recognizing the continued validity of vested rights of riparian landowners existing on the effective date of the act.

## II.  MODIFICATIONS OF RIPARIAN RIGHTS IN HYBRID SYSTEMS

All hybrid states limited the extent to which present riparian rights could be exercised and future riparian rights asserted.  The ability of riparians to insist on the continued flow of a watercourse and to begin and cease using water as they pleased was incompatible with successful operation of an appropriation system.

### A.  Reasonable Use Limitations

In an early case the California Supreme Court upheld the right of riparians to enjoin diversions by subsequent appropriators even in the absence of actual harm.  Lux v. Haggin (1886).  The practical difficulty with the rule was shown by Herminghaus v. Southern California Edison Co. (1926), *cert. dismissed* (1927), where riparian landowners on the San Joaquin River who relied on the heavy spring flows of the river to flood their lands successfully enjoined the defendant from building an upstream hydroelectric power plant which would have deprived the plaintiffs of natural irrigation. *Herminghaus* led the California legislature to amend the state constitution in 1928.  The amendment limited water rights "to such water as shall be reasonably required for the beneficial use to be served  . . ."  Limiting riparian rights to reasonable uses was sustained as a valid exercise of police power in Tulare Irrigation District v. Lindsay-Strathmore Irrigation District (1935).

All hybrid states now follow some form of the reasonable use rule; thus a riparian cannot defeat an appropriation unless undue interference with the riparian's reasonable use of the water is proved. Some states legislatively adopted the reasonable use rule or judicially adopted it without the concern expressed in *Herminghaus* that made necessary a state constitutional amendment. E.g., Brown v. Chase (1923) (judicial adoption).

## B. Extinguishment of Unused Riparian Rights

The essential conflict between riparian and appropriation systems was that riparian rights—being appurtenant to riparian land—do not depend on use. Appropriators had no assurance that their rights would not be defeated by formerly inactive riparians who suddenly decided to exercise their rights. This uncertainty provided little incentive for appropriators to undertake expensive water projects. As a result all of the hybrid states have effectively eliminated unused riparian rights by statute.

Typically, unused riparian rights were eliminated by a statute adopting the prior appropriation system, but "vested rights" were recognized. Riparians were sometimes required to obtain permits or file statements that reflected rights to the amount of water they actually put to use. The last of the hybrid states to enact a prior appropriation statute was Mississippi, which abandoned the ripa-

rian doctrine in favor of a system of prior appropriation in 1956.

## C.  Constitutional Challenges

Legislation limiting or extinguishing riparian
rights has generally been upheld when challenged
as a taking of property without just compensation.
The 1928 California constitutional amendment restricting riparian rights to waters reasonably used
was sustained.  More substantial questions were
presented by statutes that terminated unused riparian rights.

Kansas adopted a statute that said: "Subject to
vested rights, all waters within the state may be
appropriated for beneficial use as hereby provided
. . ." and required riparians to obtain permits to
preserve their vested rights, which were limited to
water applied to a beneficial use at or within three
years of the law's 1945 enactment.  Constitutionality of the statutory scheme was tested when the
United States refused to proceed with a major
irrigation project that depended on appropriative
rights under the statute unless the law was found
constitutional.  The Kansas Supreme Court upheld
the legislation.  State *ex rel.* Emery v. Knapp
(1949).

The Kansas scheme is typical of others that
limited "vested rights" to those applied to a beneficial use some time prior to passage of the statute
or, in the case of works under construction at the
time of enactment, within a reasonable time after-

wards. Such laws have generally been upheld and compensation denied for extinguishment of unused rights. E.g., Hough v. Porter (1908) *supp. op.* (1909).

A few state courts had difficulties with laws limiting riparian rights in favor of a new appropriation system. In 1913 South Dakota's 1907 appropriation law was declared to be an unconstitutional taking of riparian property without just compensation. In 1964 a subsequently enacted system of appropriation in South Dakota was upheld in light of several intervening U.S. Supreme Court decisions distinguishing police power regulation from takings. Knight v. Grimes (1964).

Although California still recognizes unused riparian rights, a 1979 decision interpreted the 1928 constitutional amendment to mean that legislatively authorized adjudication of water rights of all water users in an entire river system can limit riparian users to the amount of water currently being applied to a beneficial use, plus a quantified future right (discussed in Section III B of this chapter).

Although language in the Nebraska Constitution and water statute resembles language construed in other states to cut off future riparian claims, the Nebraska courts have declared that riparian rights have not been abolished and that riparian uses can still be claimed on riparian lands. Wasserburger v. Coffee, *modified on other grounds* (1966). Ripar-

ians are limited to a quantity reasonable for their
purposes relative to the purposes of appropriators.

## III.   ADMINISTRATION OF HYBRID
SYSTEMS

Because of the substantial differences between
riparian and appropriation systems, courts have
struggled to give effect to both systems of water
law. Riparian doctrine differs from prior appropriation in several ways. One of the most important
differences is that in times of shortage riparians
must cut back their uses ratably; early appropriators may take their full entitlement, placing the
burden of shortages on junior appropriators.
Courts must resolve disputes among competing riparians and appropriators based on inconsistencies
between the two systems.

## A.   Resolving Disputes Among Water Users

In states where permits for riparian rights state
a specific quantity, these rights can be treated as
part of the hierarchy of appropriative water rights.
If no fixed quantity is set, it may be necessary to
quantify unused riparian rights (discussed in the
next subsection). The priority date of riparian
rights ordinarily is ahead of appropriators, since
appropriative rights ordinarily were created pursuant to a statutory scheme adopted to replace a
riparian system.

California limits the circumstances in which an
appropriator on the public lands can defeat a ripa-

rian. Only if water rights were appropriated *after* the 1866 Act and the appropriation was *before* the patent will the appropriator prevail. See Lux v. Haggin (1886). A diversion made on private land, however, even for use on public land, will not defeat the rights of a riparian. San Joaquin and Kings River Canal & Irrigation Co. v. Worswick, *cert. denied* (1922). Thus in California a riparian will prevail over an appropriator whenever: 1) the riparian land was claimed or patented before the appropriation; or 2) the riparian land was patented before 1866 (regardless of when the appropriation was made).

In Nebraska, the only other state to protect unused riparian rights against appropriators, the courts have allowed competing rights of riparians and appropriators to be determined based on their relative reasonableness. The issue arises only as to riparian lands patented before the 1895 Nebraska Irrigation Act; prior appropriation prevails as to later patented lands. Wasserburger v. Coffee, *modified on other grounds* (1966). Riparian uses can commence at any future time on pre-1895 patented riparian land and will be prior to appropriative rights unless the appropriator's use is more reasonable.

## B. Adjudication of Unused Riparian Rights

Most appropriation states have procedures for adjudicating water rights among users. In hybrid states, riparians must be made parties to general adjudications to have their rights reflected in a final determination of all rights on a stream system. Riparian rights may be specifically quantified based on past usage and unused rights may be extinguished.

A number of hybrid states (Kansas, Oklahoma, South Dakota and Texas) that have extinguished unused riparian rights have made exceptions allowing riparians to claim water rights for future "domestic" purposes that are superior to all appropriative rights. The quantities involved are small, so the uncertainties about unquantified, unused rights are minimal.

California is unique in allowing the future exercise of unused riparian rights, but recent decisions have allowed administrative limitations. In the case of *In re* Waters of Long Valley Creek Stream System, (1979) a riparian owned several thousand acres but was irrigating only eighty-nine when the State Water Resources Control Board began an adjudication. The riparian urged that unused riparian rights could not be quantified, but if they were they should include enough water to irrigate the entire tract with the same early priority date attached to the rights already in use. The Board awarded riparian rights to irrigate only eighty-nine acres and "extinguished" any future exercise of riparian rights for the other lands. On appeal the California Supreme Court held that the Board exceeded its powers in abolishing unused riparian rights, but said their future exercise could be limited in "scope, nature and priority" to assure that uses were reasonable and beneficial (in accordance with the 1928 constitutional amendment). Thus unused riparian rights may be put to any reasonable, beneficial use in the future, but can have a lower priority than all intervening rights recognized by the Board to exist.

## C. Prescription

Appropriation is the sole method of acquiring water rights in prior appropriation states; acquisition of a water right by adverse possession is generally not allowed. See Chapter Three, Section X C. In riparian states upper riparians can gain prescriptive rights as against lower riparians. Further, an upstream non-riparian may gain a prescriptive right as against a downstream riparian. See Chapter Two, Section VII C.

Rules governing prescriptive acquisition of water rights in hybrid systems are illustrated by the case of Pabst v. Finmand (1922) (Figure 10). Four tracts of land were each owned by different parties. Pabst and Prior sued to quiet title to the waters of Eagle Creek. The California Supreme Court held that H. H. Finmand, a non-riparian, had acquired rights by prescription against both lower riparian plaintiffs by virtue of diversions for the statutorily required period of five years. This was so although the plaintiffs had not suffered actual harm. The court said, "the slightest use by the owners of these lands being notice to all riparian owners that a hostile right was being asserted, a prescriptive

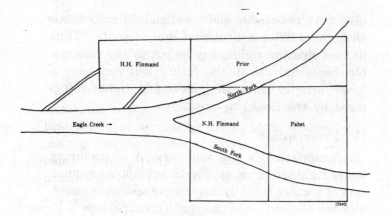

**Figure 10**

right was acquired by such adverse use on those lands." The court held that N. H. Finmand could not gain a prescriptive right unless the use caused actual harm to lower riparians. Since Prior's lands were only riparian to the north fork of the stream, N. H. Finmand's use from the south fork could not have harmed Prior. N. H. Finmand also failed to acquire a prescriptive right as against Pabst because "In the absence of showing that the upper owner [N. H. Finmand] is using the water under a claim of prescriptive right, the lower owner [Pabst] has the right to presume that such owner is only taking that to which he is entitled as a riparian owner by virtue of his riparian right."

If a non-riparian acquires a prescriptive right in a hybrid system state, the right acquired is essentially a riparian right not subject to the appropriation scheme.

## IV.  OTHER WATER LAW VARIATIONS

Some water law systems are not easily characterized as prior appropriation, riparian or as a hybrid of the two.  They include Hawaii's ancient system, remnants of civil law in Louisiana and pueblo rights applicable in some parts of the southwestern United States.

### A.  Hawaiian Water Law

Water law in Hawaii springs from the ancient Hawaiian system of land tenure.  Traditionally Hawaiian lands were held by chiefs in units known as *ahupua'as*.  The typical *ahupua'a* was a wedge-shaped parcel that began at the top of the mountains and widened toward the sea generally following watershed lines.  Lands and waters were controlled by *konohiki* (land chiefs).  Commoners were allowed to work lands and raise crops but had to give a share of what they produced to the chiefs and, after unification of the islands under a single king, to the king.  Rights to sufficient water to cultivate taro (the mainstay of the Native Hawaiian diet) were appurtenant to the land for use of those who lived there.  The *konohiki* in charge of each subdivision of land allocated any surplus waters remaining after basic needs were satisfied.  Water distribution was based on recognition of the mutual dependence of the *konohiki* and the commoners who produced crops for the *konohiki*.

At the urging of westerners, individual titles to most of the land were established by a process known as the Great *Mahele* (division). The most significant accomplishment of the *Mahele* was to make land titles (and certain "appurtenant" water rights) alienable.

The Kingdom of Hawaii became a republic for a while, then a United States territory and finally a state. Judicial decisions under Hawaii's various governments announced principles of water law that now apply to creation of individual, privately held water rights. The decisions dealt with "appurtenant" and "surplus" waters.

Appurtenant rights are based on the amount of water used for taro cultivation. Early cases responded to the water demands of sugar plantations and allowed transfers of appurtenant rights, but only upon a showing by the party seeking the transfer that the change would not harm others in the exercise of their water rights or in their means of diversion. Kahookiekie v. Keanini (1891). Thus courts scrutinized changes in place of use, Peck v. Bailey (1867), and type of use or point of diversion, Carter v. Territory (1917).

Appurtenant rights also could be obtained by prescription by adverse use for the statutory period. Lonoaea v. Wailuku Sugar Co. (1895). Of course prescriptive rights cannot be obtained in waters on state-owned lands because adverse possession does not run against the government.

"Surplus" waters generally include all waters not needed to satisfy appurtenant water rights. Early courts disagreed about whether the rights to surplus waters belonged to the proprietor ("*konohiki*" or successor in interest) of the *ahupua'a* where the water originated or to the *konohikis* of all the *ahupua'as* through which the water passed.

Uncertainty also existed concerning whether "storm and freshet" waters are "surplus." An early case specifically included storm water as "surplus," holding its use to be within the control of the *konohiki* of the *ahupua'a* of origin. Hawaiian Commercial & Sugar Co. v. Wailuku Sugar Co. (1904). But when a case arose concerning who was entitled to the storm waters that increased streamflow well beyond its normal levels, the territorial court did not follow its earlier dictum. Instead it held that storm waters were to be divided between the bordering *ahupua'as* as they would be under the riparian doctrine. Carter v. Territory (1917). The same court later reiterated its decision that surplus waters belonged to the *konohiki* of the land (*ahupua'a*) of origin, declining to say anything about the distinction in *Carter* between flood waters and other surplus waters (the parties had limited the issues by stipulation to "normal daily surplus waters"). Territory v. Gay (1931), *cert. denied* (1931).

In 1973 the Hawaii Supreme Court made several major changes in existing law. It applied riparian principles to hold that surplus water rights could not be used or transferred on any land except the riparian parcel and that appurtenant rights by their nature could not be used on other lands. The court also held that appurtenant rights could not be obtained by prescription. The court accepted the "natural flow" doctrine of riparian law in that it best fit the language of an 1895 statute vesting rights to free-flowing streams in "the people." Mc-Bryde Sugar Co. v. Robinson, *aff'd on rehearing* (1973), *cert. denied* (1974). A short time later the court changed its view, holding that the modern reasonable use test and requirement of actual harm to the plaintiff applied to riparian rights in Hawaii. Reppun v. Board of Water Supply (1982), *cert. denied* (1985).

The *McBryde* court also held that an 1850 statute could not allow uses of surplus water away from the original land because the water did not belong to the landowner. Rather, it had been "reserved for the people of Hawaii for their common good in all of the land grants." Prescriptive rights were defeated because prescription is void against the state, which holds the water in trust for all the people.

The effect of *McBryde* was to prohibit parties who had acquired extensive rights from exercising water rights on their lands outside the watershed. This led to vigorous challenges. On rehearing, the parties urged that the court's decision amounted to a taking of their property rights in violation of the due process clause of the Constitution because it departed from earlier declarations of water rights, but the court reaffirmed its decision. The parties then took their cause to the federal district court, which enjoined the state from carrying out the state court decision. Robinson v. Ariyoshi (1977).

On appeal of the *Robinson* case the Ninth Circuit Court of Appeals certified several questions of state law to the Hawaii Supreme Court. The most important was whether "the issue of who owned surplus water" was a "settled question in Hawaii law" before *McBryde*. The court replied that its earlier cases were in conflict about who was entitled to use surplus waters and *McBryde's* announcement of riparian doctrine for Hawaii had settled the confusion. Instead of adhering to the kind of riparianism that exists in other states, the court specially characterized Hawaiian riparian law as rooted in ancient Hawaiian custom giving the state, as trustee for the public, much greater authority to allocate Hawaiian riparian rights "than exists in other states." Robinson v. Ariyoshi (1982).

The court explained that as successor to the kings and chiefs who formerly held all the lands, the state is obligated to assure a fair distribution of waters among all the people who put it to productive use. At the *Mahele* lands had passed to private parties subject to a reservation of rights in the king (now the state) to allocate water among all those needing it. The waters are held in a public trust for common usage of the citizenry, including diversion and use, analogous to the public trust doctrine that obligates states to protect waterways for public uses such as navigation, recreation, wildlife, and fish. The state supreme court also said that Hawaiian rights are more akin to federally reserved water rights for Indian reservations (see Chapter Eight) than to true riparian rights. Reppun v. Board of Water Supply, supra.

During pendency of the *McBryde-Robinson* cases the state constitution was revised to recognize the state's trust obligation to assure water resource use for the public benefit and to require establishment of a water resources agency to regulate resource use and conservation. In 1987 a sweeping new state water law was adopted. Existing and new water rights must have permits and the common law is largely supplanted once an area is designated as a water management area triggering the requirements.

## B. Water Law in Louisiana

Although Louisiana is often listed as a riparian state, its system of water law is based on a civil code with French and Spanish origins; it is the only state in the Union that has a civil code system. The relevant rules for settling water disputes are found within the code, which specifies a scheme of regulation. The courts are not bound by

the principle of *stare decisis* but may refer to
common law precedents if they are on point.

The code sets forth rudiments similar to a riparian system, such as:

Article 657: The owner of an estate bordering
on running water may use it as it runs for the
purpose of watering his estate or for other purposes.

Article 658: The owner of an estate through
which water runs, whether it originates there or
passes from lands above, may make use of it
while it runs over his lands.  He cannot stop it
or give it another direction and is bound to
return it to its ordinary channel where it leaves
his estate.

Article 657 is a nearly verbatim adoption of the
French Civil Code implemented by Napoleon.  It is
not clear whether the provision expresses the natural flow rule or the reasonable use rule.  The early
case of Long v. Louisiana Creosoting Co. (1915)
applied a reasonable use rule in a water pollution
context.  The court said:

. . . whether a use that pollutes a water course
is a reasonable or an unreasonable use is for the
judge or jury to determine from all of the circumstances of a case, including the nature of the
water course, its adaptability for particular purposes, the extent of injury caused to the riparian
owner, etc.

By statute Louisiana has various types of water districts that supply customers with water for purposes such as domestic use, municipal use, industrial use and irrigation. Municipalities also have statutory authority to maintain their own waterworks systems.

Until recently groundwater in Louisiana was almost totally unregulated. The Civil Code states:

Article 490: Unless otherwise provided by law, the ownership of a tract of land carries with it the ownership of everything that is directly above or under it.

The owner may make works on, above or below the land as he pleases, and draw all the advantages that accrue from them, unless he is restrained by law or by rights of others.

Adams v. Grigsby, *writ denied* (1963) held that water under a person's land is not owned until it is reduced to possession by pumping. The *Adams* decision was criticized for not providing incentives to conserve water. A 1972 act responded by authorizing the Department of Public Works to regulate wells producing in excess of 50,000 gallons per day. Smaller wells still appear to be governed by the rule of Adams v. Grigsby.

## C. Pueblo Water Rights

In a few places in the Southwest pueblo water rights held by some municipalities and the Indian pueblos are superior to the rights of appropriators. The present-day successors to agricultural villages recognized by the Spanish or Mexican governments have rights to use all the naturally occurring water within their boundaries they need for the villages and their residents. Existence of pueblo water rights has been acknowledged in cases arising in New Mexico (Cartwright v. Public Service Co. (1958)) and California (Vernon Irrigation Co. v. City of Los Angeles (1895)). They may also have some viability in other states where such rights had originally existed (e.g., Arizona, Texas and Colorado). Pueblo rights are held in addition to rights established under the prevailing water rights system in the state, usually prior appropriation rights.

Pueblo rights are traceable to rights recognized by the Spanish crown or the Mexican government. Spain ruled portions of the Southwest prior to 1821; the Republic of Mexico then governed the area until 1848. In that year the territory was ceded to the United States by the Treaty of Guadalupe Hidalgo. The treaty confirmed property rights then existing under Mexican law, including pueblo rights. Under Spanish law, water rights were held by municipalities, as common property for their inhabitants. Grants of pueblo rights were intended to encourage settlement in the New World by facilitating growth of villages and agricultural production. Where settlements already were established they assured some protection for the rights of settlers. In the case of the Indian pueblos, which for hundreds of years had inhabited parts of an area now in New Mexico, the grants seem to have had the dual purposes of evidencing respect for their aboriginal rights as governments and of defining the areas outside which settlement by others would be possible.

Pueblo water rights are superior to other rights in surface flows and groundwater. They extend from the source to the sea, and to any amount of water reasonably required by the city's (or Indian pueblo's) inhabitants, including water for expansion or new uses, even if the entire supply is demanded. In this respect the pueblo right is similar in extent to Indian reserved water rights, discussed in Chapter Eight. See New Mexico v. Aamodt (1976), *cert. denied* (1977) (certain Indian pueblos do not hold reserved rights but may have comparable rights under Spanish and Mexican law).

Use of the waters is not required to keep the right alive; a successor city may displace long-established uses even if it has not historically used the water. Thus Los Angeles, as the successor to a pueblo, was able to assert rights to meet its growing needs from groundwater supplies. The California Supreme Court held that the city's rights were superior to established rights of other appropriators (including other cities). City of Los Angeles v. City of San Fernando (1975).

# CHAPTER FIVE

# RIGHTS TO USE THE SURFACE OF WATERWAYS

Rights in water are not exclusive in the same sense as other property rights, real and personal. First, others may share rights to use the same resource. Second, members of the public have rights to use the surface of many waterways. Surface use of waters has deep historical importance. Public rights to use the surface of waterways are rooted in ancient Roman law and were reflected in the common law.

Historically, many waterways were chiefly valuable as avenues for commerce and for fishing and hunting by members of the public. These public rights have always qualified the rights of those who own the beds and banks of waterways and the rights to consume waters from such sources. Navigation for commerce remains significant but the public value of surface use of many waterways today lies more in the satisfaction of recreational needs than commercial needs.

Navigability of a waterway is a benchmark for defining a federally protected realm of public use. Navigability concepts, under various definitions, also retain importance in some states for describing the reach of public rights. But most states have developed other concepts for asserting public rights and exerting their police powers over private landowners and water rights holders.

The principles in this chapter apply whether a state has a riparian, prior appropriation or hybrid system of water rights. In each kind of jurisdiction private rights to use water are limited to the extent necessary to allow for exercise of surface use rights of the public and of other private water rights holders.

# I. PUBLIC RIGHTS IN NAVIGABLE WATERS

The English common law rule allowed any person to navigate waters and to make uses incidental to navigation such as hunting and fishing. "Navigable" has been defined for different purposes at both the state and federal levels. Generally, state law governs which waters are available for public uses such as navigation.

## A. Definitions of Navigability

### 1. *Federal Definitions*

The federal definition of "navigable" waters determines title to the beds underlying streams and lakes. If water was "navigable" under the federal test at the time of statehood, title to the bed of the stream or lake passed to the state upon admission into the Union. Second, federal classification as navigable or non-navigable determines the permissible extent of congressional regulation of waters under the commerce clause.

Early American decisions adopted a test of navigability that turned on whether the tide ebbed and flowed in the water body in question. The rule was based on an apparent misunderstanding of the common law that considered ebb and flow of the tide as evidence, not the test, of navigability. This rather unrealistic test eventually was rejected.

In Gibbons v. Ogden (1824), a case dealing with Congress's power to regulate navigable waters, Justice Marshall wrote that the commerce clause "comprehends navigation within the limits of every state in the Union, so far as that navigation may be, in any manner, connected with commerce with foreign nations or among the several states, or with the Indian tribes." Another commerce clause case dealing with Congress's regulatory powers held that navigable waters are any waters that are navigable in fact. The Daniel Ball (1870). Federal power to legislate concerning commerce based on navigability is developed more fully in Chapter Nine, Section II.

The federal tests of navigability for determining title and for defining Congress's power under the commerce clause differ slightly. Both determine whether the waterbody was navigable in fact as of the date a state came into the Union, not the time the determination was made. Navigability for title is determined by the natural and ordinary condition of the waterbody at statehood; navigability for commerce clause purposes is determined by whether the waterbody could be made navigable by reasonable artificial improvements. Navigability for commerce clause purposes requires use only in intrastate commerce, not necessarily in interstate commerce. Like the definition itself, the rules for deciding whether a waterway is navigable for determining the extent of title to submerged land are a matter of federal law. Hughes v. Washington (1967).

## 2. *State Definitions*

States do not necessarily base their definitions of "navigability" on whether waterways can sustain commercial navigation. Some have used a "saw log" definition based on whether a stream would allow passage of logs on their way to the mill.

Several states have adopted expanded definitions of navigability that are directly related to recreation—the "pleasure boat," People v. Mack (1971), or the "recreational use" test, Arkansas v. McIlroy, *cert. denied* (1980). Other states following this approach include Idaho, Massachusetts, Minnesota, New York, Ohio and Oregon. A waterway that is useful for rowboats, canoes, inflatable rafts or the like is considered navigable and subject to public use. Property rights of riparians are qualified to the extent necessary to allow these public use rights. Michigan has expressly rejected this approach, though the case dealt with private lakes that the court found to

be too small for recreation. Bott v. Michigan Dep't. of Natural Resources (1982).

## 3. Ownership of Beds

If a waterbody was navigable under the federal test at the time of statehood, title to the bed of the stream or lake passed to the state upon admission into the Union. State ownership is a valuable asset though the state's authority over disposition of the bed is limited by the federal power to use and regulate the waterway for navigation and by the public trust doctrine.

In Pollard v. Hagan (1845), the Supreme Court held that states acquired title to noncoastal tidelands upon admission into the Union. It said that prior to admission, tidelands were held in trust by the federal government for the people of future states. Later the Court held that coastal tidelands remained in federal ownership. United States v. California (1947). Congress responded by passing the Submerged Lands Act which turned over control of tidelands to the states.

The curious doctrine that granted new states title to ribbons of land through large expanses of federal public lands has origins in the common law. The original thirteen states took their sovereignty from foreign nations, principally England. Historically the Crown held complete title to the beds and waters in all navigable waterways. Ownership of rivers passed to the original states as England's successors, but upon formation of the

United States control of the waters flowing in navigable rivers was given up by the states. In the United States Constitution the states agreed to the commerce clause, granting the national government the power to regulate commerce. Because commerce was then primarily waterborne, the clause was understood to establish national control of navigable waterways. The states retained title to the beds; the title was subject, however, to the government's navigation servitude. Rights in the flow were necessarily surrendered.

Submerged land beginning at the mean high tide line belongs to the state. This line is determined by an average of the high water marks over all seasons. Along a navigable waterbody, riparian property ownership extends to that line; the state owns the bed of the river beginning at the line. The line also delineates the area in which the federal navigation servitude may operate to destroy private property interests without compensation. See Chapter Nine, Section II B.

Title to the beds of waters not navigable under the federal test usually passed to riparian landowners. Under the law of a few states, such as Wisconsin and Iowa, the state retained title to the beds beneath waters navigable under a state law test even if they were not navigable under the federal test.

## B.  Rights of the Public to Use the Surface of Navigable Waters

If a waterway is navigable for commerce clause purposes, the federal government can regulate navigation and otherwise decide the terms of public use of the waterway.  The public right to navigate on a navigable river or lake clearly includes the right to use it for transportation.  The right to use the flow of the stream in aid of commerce is not limited to travel by commercial vessels.  For example, it includes floating logs to the mill.

People exercising public rights must respect the rights of riparian owners.  On the other hand, a riparian landowner may only make uses, such as consumption of water, that do not unreasonably interfere with the rights of the public.  Bridges and dams must allow for the right of passage.  The right of a riparian owner to wharf out, discussed in Chapter Two, Section III B, must be exercised consistent with public use rights.  Ownership of the bed does not allow a riparian to prevent public use of the surface of a navigable waterbody for the purposes and in the manner permitted by state law.

To accommodate increased public demand for water-related recreational opportunities, some state legislatures and courts have broadened the scope of permissible public uses of navigable waters.  In Diana Shooting Club v. Husting (1914), a riparian owned the bed underlying a stream navigable under state law.  The defendant floated down the river in a small boat to hunt ducks. The riparian sued for trespass. The court ruled for the defendant, holding that the rights of hunting and fishing are incidental to the right of navigation. The court further held that riparian owners on streams navigable under state law have only a qualified title to the beds of those streams. The title is subordinated to a state's authority to secure for its people full enjoyment of navigation and other incidental rights.

## II.  THE PUBLIC TRUST DOCTRINE

Although each state took title to the beds underlying its navigable waters, it has been held that when such lands are in state ownership they are held subject to a public trust and cannot be conveyed unless it would promote a public purpose. This rule is known as the "public trust doctrine."

The leading case is Illinois Central Railroad v. Illinois (1892). In that case the Illinois legislature granted the railroad title to part of the bed of Lake Michigan in return for the railroad's promise to pay the state a percentage of its gross earnings from wharfs, piers and docks to be built over the land. The legislature later repealed the act granting title to the railroad, but the railroad claimed that the repeal was invalid. The state filed suit for a judicial determination of title to the submerged lands. On appeal the United States Supreme Court upheld the repeal and found the original grant to be invalid. The court reasoned that the state held title to the lands beneath the navigable waters of Lake Michigan in trust for the citizens of the state for navigation and other public purposes and could not convey the lands inconsistently with the trust.

Where the doctrine applies, private uses will be continually scrutinized to determine if they are inconsistent with the trust. Kootenai Environmental Alliance v. Panhandle Yacht Club, Inc. (1983) (state lease of lake surface for construction of private sailboat slips).

The public trust doctrine has been expanded to allow protections for public rights in a variety of contexts beyond the conveyance of submerged lands. Courts have applied the trust concept to afford the public easements for navigation, commerce, fishing and hunting, bathing, swimming and recreational uses. E.g., Marks v. Whitney (1971). The doctrine has also been applied to limit diversions from nonnavigable tributaries of a navigable watercourse under the prior appropriation system. National Audubon Society v. Superior Court, *cert. denied* (1983).

## III. STATE–RECOGNIZED PUBLIC RIGHTS OF SURFACE USE OF "NON–NAVIGABLE" WATERS

A number of states have recognized use rights in waters that have recreational capacity, but where the beds are privately owned, without denominating them "navigable." Section I explains that some states have expanded their definitions of navigability to allow public recreational uses of waterways for recreational boating, fishing and hunting even where beds are in private ownership. The rationale and result in states that base public use on recreational capacity are similar but they do not indulge the fiction and the sometimes difficult evidentiary problems of proving navigability.

Since colonial times in what is now Maine, Massachusetts and New Hampshire, large, freshwater lakes known as "great ponds" (having a surface area over ten acres), although non-navigable, have been considered open to public use with a limited right of public access across private lands to reach the ponds. A Minnesota statute declares certain defined waters that are managed or accessible for public purposes to be public.

The modern approach is exemplified by Montana Coalition for Stream Access v. Curran (1984). The court held that streambed ownership was irrelevant because "the capability of use of the waters for recreational purposes determines their availability for recreational use by the public." Although the river involved in the case was navigable, a case involving a non-navigable stream was decided by the same court a month later and it said explicitly that navigability for recreation (or any other purpose) was not an issue. After the cases, sweeping legislation specified extensive public rights in recreational streams of various types. Portions of the statutes that allowed camping and even construction of duck blinds below the high water lines of privately owned streams were held unconstitutional as was a provision requiring property owners to construct portage routes at their own expense.

The Montana court relied in part on a state constitutional provision that is similar to provisions in most western states which declares all state waters to be "for use of its people . . . subject to appropriation for beneficial uses." Wyoming cited such a provision to hold that riparian title on non-navigable streams is limited by a right-of-way for the water to pass and for the public to use it for navigation, hunting and fishing. Day v. Armstrong (1961). New Mexico follows the same approach.

A nearly identical provision in the Colorado constitution has been interpreted as having the opposite effect. People v. Emmert (1979). In *Emmert,* the court declined to read any right of public use into the portion of the constitution that declares unappropriated waters to be "the property of the public, and the same is dedicated to the use of the people of the state." The court said that the constitutional provision was "historically concerned with appropriation" and should not be used to limit the otherwise absolute property rights of riparians to use the surface. Thus, the public "has no right to the use of waters overlying private lands for recreational purposes."

Colorado is among a small minority of states that deny public use. Only Alabama, Pennsylvania and Indiana also hold that riparians have absolute rights to exclude others from the surface. A few other states grant no public fishing or hunting rights in non-navigable waters (e.g., Louisiana, Missouri, Virginia). Some old cases limit public rights to an easement for passage over privately owned beds (e.g., Connecticut, Illinois, Maine, Massachusetts, New York, North Carolina, Tennessee). But most modern decisions allow at least some public recreational use.

Awaiting a judicial decision as to which waters are subject to public use can cause uncertainty for property owners as to their rights and property values. Some states have opened private waters to the public by legislative act, allaying such uncertainty. A Minnesota statute lists as public waters a variety of waterbodies including all large waterbodies, those that are classified by state agencies for uses such as fishing and those which are bordered or accessible by public lands. In Alabama and Pennsylvania such statutes have been held to effect a taking of vested property rights of the private owners of streambeds.

## IV.  ACCESS TO WATERWAYS FOR LAWFUL SURFACE USE

The public right to use the surface of waterways, whether they are navigable or are otherwise considered open to the public, often cannot be exercised without crossing private lands or touching the banks, sides or bottoms of the beds. The problem of public access to beaches is closely related.

## A. Condemnation

States are free to take land by eminent domain to provide public access to waterways. Branch v. Oconto County (1961). Though there may be disputes over the amount of compensation due, there is little question that governments have the power to condemn easements and other rights of public access to waterways that are open to public use. The more difficult cases involve legislative and judicial decisions that such rights exist without the need to compensate landowners.

## B. Implied Rights of Access

Some courts have held that riparian property bordering waterways that are open to the public is burdened with an easement of public access. Oregon has held that riparians can be prevented from fencing the dry sand areas adjacent to the ocean. State legislation declared the area between high and low tide lines to be a state recreation area. The court found that the public has an easement to use the dry sand area (above the high tide line) based on customs of the people going back to earliest times. The court cited Blackstone. State *ex rel.* Thornton v. Hay (1969).

Custom has also been cited as the source of beach access rights in Florida and Hawaii. New England statutes dealing with public use of great ponds allow public access across private land but have been interpreted to apply only to unimproved or unenclosed lands. These laws were based on colonial practices and are arguably rooted in custom.

The California Supreme Court has held that dedication of an easement of public access for recreational uses can be implied where members of the public used private land adversely for over five years. Gion v. Santa Cruz (1970). The doctrine has also been applied in New York. Dedication is the donation of land or an easement for public access. It requires both an intention on the part of the landowners to dedicate and an acceptance by the public.

Wisconsin recognizes that a right to moor boats may be acquired by prescription. Prescription occurs when the public has used an access way openly, continuously, and adversely for the prescriptive period of time.

Other courts have applied the public trust doctrine as a rationale for a public right to cross private property and to use the dry sand area adjacent to the ocean. Matthews v. Bay Head Improvement Association (1984).

Some coastal states impose extensive regulations upon property owners. Among the most extensive are those of the California Coastal Act. Conditions may be imposed on those seeking to build or modify structures within the coastal zone, including exactions of easements for view and for public access. The Act withstood constitutional attack where the exactions were related to the legislative purposes. Sea Ranch Ass'n v. California Coastal Comm'n (1981). However, the United States Supreme Court held that a condition requiring the provision of lateral access along the shoreline of an objecting property owner who was remodeling a house was not tailored specifically enough to satisfy the statutory purpose. Nollan v. California Coastal Comm'n (1987). The case may have serious implications for the Act and for other state attempts to secure public access to waters otherwise available for public use.

The United States Supreme Court also has held that a privately owned lagoon connected to the ocean by dredging does not thereby become open to public navigation unless the government compensates the owner for a taking of property. Kaiser Aetna v. United States (1979).

Fewer cases have dealt with access to streams and lakes than to beaches, but generally the same principles apply. There is, however, an additional issue concerning the right of members of the public to touch privately owned beds in the course of their surface use. Michigan and Missouri allow wading in the stream on privately owned submerged lands and the adjoining banks. Wyoming limits the use of streambeds to incidental contact necessary to exercise the right of flotation. In Montana the public can use the bed and banks of streams for recreational purposes and has the right to use upland areas to portage around obstructions.

## V. RECIPROCAL RIGHTS OF RIPARIAN OWNERS

A riparian owns the bed of a non-navigable waterway to its center. This means to the centerline of a stream and to the center of a lake by extension of lines drawn from the points where the property lines of the riparian land meet the shore. Traditional property law principles recognize a land owner's rights in real property to extend "from heaven to hell"—that is, into the air space above as well as into the earth below. This absolute ownership concept recognizes rights in owners of riparian land on a waterway to exclude as a trespasser anyone seeking to use the water (or bed and banks) for recreational or other waterborne activities. Many early cases so held, but, as the above authorities show, the rule persists only in a few states (Alabama, Pennsylvania, Indiana and Colorado).

The rights of riparian owners are qualified to the extent that they must tolerate the public's exercise of surface use rights. In addition, the property rights of riparians in waters overlying privately owned beds are qualified by the common right of other riparians to use all of the water surface.

The general rule is that riparians may make reasonable use of water overlying the land of other riparians on the same waterbody. Although a technical trespass may be involved, the law has accommodated the practical need for mutual access to water resources in which several persons have a common interest. Most courts have held that all landowners surrounding a lake may use the entire surface if the use does not interfere unreasonably with the same rights of other owners. E.g., Johnson v. Seifert (1960); Snively v. Jaber (1956).

The common right of the owners of land surrounding and beneath a waterbody may not apply to "artificial waters"—those created by structures (dams and dikes) rather than natural features. Anderson v. Bell (1983).

Because all riparians have rights to use a lake surface, an owner of littoral land may not fill or build out into a lake on submerged land. The owner's right to use private land is subject to the common rights of others to use the surface. Bach v. Sarich (1968). However, the court in that case said that the result might have been different if it had involved a "water-related" construction project (e.g., a dock or boathouse) and not an apartment house. A property owner is prohibited from filling land if it obstructs the public right of navigation. One Washington case enforced this rule even where the level of a natural lake was raised by an artificial dam causing the land to be inundated part of every year. Wilbour v. Gallagher (1969).

In applying the reasonable use rule to non-navigable lake surfaces, the courts have held that a riparian (e.g., a resort owner) can permit guests to use the lake, but must limit their numbers and activities to prevent unreasonable interference with rights of other riparians. The rule applies if the state itself purchases or condemns lakefront land and opens it to the public. Only reasonable use by members of the public, as the state's licensees, will be tolerated. Botton v. State (1966). The reasonable use standard has also been applied to the construction of a series of canals and the granting of easements to permit public access to a small lake for recreational boating. Thompson v. Enz (1967); Thompson v. Enz (1971).

# CHAPTER SIX

# GROUNDWATER

## I. BASIC HYDROLOGY

### A. How Groundwater Occurs

### 1. Underground Streams and Percolating Water

An *underground stream* has been defined as waters that flow underground within "reasonably ascertainable boundaries" or as "a constant stream in a known and well-defined natural channel." Hayes v. Adams (1923). Underground waters not part of an underground stream are said to be *percolating waters*. Both are "groundwater" but underground streams generally are subject to the law of surface streams; percolating waters are subject to groundwater law. See Herriman Irrigation Co. v. Keel (1902). Factual determination of whether waters are percolating is often difficult, making the burden of proof onerous. The burden may be met by circumstantial evidence, such as vegetation growing above, indicating the course of the alleged stream. The stream may be audible at the surface, or well withdrawals may produce downstream effects. Drilling and hydrologic studies are also methods of proof.

## 2. *Permeability of Rock Formations*

Occurrence and movement of groundwater are governed by laws of physics and local geological conditions. Although groundwater can occur in the form of defined underground streams, most groundwater is percolating water stored in the pores, or interstices, of rock formations. The size of these interstices varies with the size of the rock particles; a bed of gravel has interstices visible to the naked eye, but clays have very minute particles and interstices. Interstices may be formed by geological processes at the time the rock was formed, or created later by cracking or erosion.

*Porosity* is the measure of the amount of open space within rock. It is defined as the percentage of the rock's total volume occupied by pore space. Other factors being equal, the greater the porosity, the more freely water can move through the rock and the more water that can be stored within.

The force of gravity can cause water to move "downhill" through rock formations. Opposing and slowing this movement are the forces of *molecular attraction*. Molecular attraction is proportional to the surface area of the rock particles, which increases as their size decreases. To illustrate, compare the movement of water through gravel and through sand. The gravel is made up of large particles so the surface area of all the particles is cumulatively smaller than the surface area of all the particles of sand. Thus, water moving through the minute interstices is slowed by powerful forces of molecular attraction. The porosity of a volume of sand may equal that of gravel, but the *permeability* of the sand (its ability to transmit water) is lower.

Although permeability varies across a spectrum, rock formations are grouped into broad categories, described as "permeable" or "impermeable." Whether water percolates through rock, and the speed at which it does so, are functions of the pressure created by gravity and the permeability of the formation. Groundwater is stored in permeable formations bounded and contained by impermeable formations.

## 3. *Zones of Groundwater Occurrence*

The geological strata may be divided into two zones of groundwater occurrence: the *zone of aeration* and the *zone of saturation.* In the zone of aeration, nearest the surface, moisture is present in the soil and accessible to the root systems of plants, but is held by molecular attraction, and thus cannot readily be captured by pumping.

Below the zone of aeration is the zone of saturation where groundwater saturates the interstices completely. In this zone water flows in response to gravity and can be withdrawn by pumping. The upper boundary of the zone of saturation is the *piezometric surface,* or *water table.* Water is at atmospheric pressure at the piezometric surface. Underlying the zone of saturation is a layer of impermeable *bedrock*. Bedrock is under tremen-

dous pressure from the formations above and its
interstices have been crushed, giving the rock a
very low porosity. Almost all usable groundwater
occurs within two miles of the surface, and is
commonly within a half mile in depth.

## 4. Aquifers

Aquifers may be thought of as underground reservoirs. They are rock formations that yield water
in significant quantities. Thus, a formation with
low permeability may not be an aquifer, even if
porous and saturated with water, because the
water is liberated at a rate too slow to be of use.
Aquifers may be confined or unconfined. Most
common are *unconfined aquifers*, in which the
water exists under normal atmospheric pressure.
Unconfined aquifers must be pumped to withdraw
the water. *Confined* or *artesian aquifers*, by contrast, are under a pressure greater than that of the
atmosphere. This pressure is generated when the
aquifer is squeezed between overlying and underlying impermeable strata. If the positive pressure is
great enough the water in a well may rise to the
surface without pumping, but any pressure sufficient to raise the water above the top of the zone of
saturation (water table) is sufficient to make the
aquifer artesian. This often occurs when a portion
of the aquifer lies above the point where the well
(or spring) is located; the pressure is caused by
gravity.

Aquifers may be perched. A *perched aquifer* is
an unconfined aquifer underlain by an impermea-

ble stratum that is perched above another aquifer in the *zone of aeration.* Perched aquifers are often hydrologically unaffected by withdrawals from the zone of saturation. Where perched aquifers outcrop on hillsides, springs may result. The term *spring*, however, applies to any concentrated discharge of groundwater that appears on the surface as flowing water.

Aquifers are initially filled with water either by geological processes occurring when the rock was created (*connate water*) or by subsequent sources such as rainfall (*meteoric water*). Typically an aquifer is recharged by precipitation falling where the aquifer outcrops on the surface; it may also be recharged by surface or underground streams. The rate of recharge, like the rate of water movement, varies greatly and is a function of geologic conditions. Some aquifers get no recharge; others recharge so slowly that it takes millions of years to fill them.

Geologists call the amount of water an aquifer will yield without depletion "*safe yield*." The term has also been used by economists, courts and legislatures to describe rates of depletion in excess of recharge, but which are viewed as reasonable in light of current demands for the water. When withdrawals from any aquifer exceed its recharge, an overdraft or *mining* condition is said to exist. Some harmful effects of sustained overdraft are discussed in the next section.

Aquifers may be isolated from other aquifers and from surface streams. If aquifers are hydraulically interconnected, the term *groundwater basin* is used to describe the physiographic unit usually consisting of a large aquifer and one or more smaller, interconnected aquifers. Recognition of the interconnection between aquifers has led planners to think in terms of groundwater basins and to engage in basin-wide groundwater planning.

If an aquifer is hydraulically connected to a stream so that groundwater withdrawals affect the stream supply, the groundwater is sometimes said to be *tributary* to the stream. Whether groundwater is tributary may have important legal consequences: sound management dictates that the tributary groundwater and the stream be managed as a single system. Thus, a court in a prior appropriation state may enjoin pumping to prevent injury to senior appropriators on the stream. If groundwater use does not affect a stream, there can be no such harm, and groundwater need not be administered in conjunction with the surface water allocation system. Integration of groundwater and surface water uses are discussed in Section IV of this chapter.

## B.  How Wells Work

### 1.  *Drilling and Pumping*

Water wells are commonly drilled by truck-mounted rotary drilling rigs. Drilling through layer after layer of rock is an expensive process. In addition, the deeper a well is, the greater pump lift and attendant energy costs. Wells sometimes must be deepened because water tables are lowered by pumping in the area. The cost of deepening wells and of pumping from greater depths can force marginal water users out of business.

As the technology of groundwater diversion has developed, the character of use has changed. The spread of pump-irrigated agriculture in the West was hastened by invention of the windmill. Shallow aquifers could be tapped, giving irrigators a reliable supply in the face of uncertain surface flows and precipitation. Development of the high-pressure pump ushered in a new era of intensive groundwater use; deeper aquifers became accessible. Junior appropriators with deep wells were able to draw down water tables beyond reach of the seniors' often primitive apparatus or to cause increased costs of pumping the groundwater from greater depths.

## 2. Effects of Well Use

### a. Cone of Influence

Once a well begins operating, a number of effects result from the water withdrawal. Water from the surrounding aquifer begins percolating through the formation to replace the water being withdrawn. This creates a *cone of influence*, a cone-shaped region from which the water has temporarily been removed. The cone is inverted; its tip is at the point of withdrawal and its base is the surface of the water table. As the cone of influence broadens, it may affect the wells of neighboring users, forcing them to deepen or move their wells to avoid losing their supply.

## b. *Effects of Depletion*

In addition to the localized cone-of-influence effect, rate and extent of pumping also may affect the capacity and ability of the aquifer to produce water.

*Salt water intrusion* can contaminate groundwater as salty water from the ocean or underground deposits intrudes to replace the water withdrawn from an aquifer. Some coastal areas have dealt with salt water intrusion by injecting a barrier of fresh water into the zone of intrusion.

Depletion of a finite supply of groundwater may also cause *subsidence*—sinking of the land surface overlying an aquifer. Subsidence occurs when certain formations (e.g., compressible, low-permeability clays) are unable to support the weight of overlying strata unless they are saturated with water. As the support provided by *hydrostatic pressure* is removed, the formation collapses irreversibly. The resultant sinking of the overlying land surface may damage buildings, highways, railroads, ditches and wells. Natural structures may also be harmed; aquifer storage capacity may be reduced and cracking of the earth surface can lead to erosion. Coastal areas may be flooded as they sink. There is some evidence that geological faulting may result.

The most severe subsidence within the United States has occurred in Florida, Texas, Arizona and California in areas experiencing heavy groundwater overdraft.

Subsidence, like other consequences of groundwater overdraft, is usually an economic externality of the pumper; that is, the cost of subsidence damage to others is not a part of the individual pumper's costs. Some jurisdictions provide legal remedies for such damage to help internalize the costs of subsidence. E.g., Friendswood Dev. Co. v. Smith-Southwest Indus., Inc. (1978) (pumper liable for damage caused by subsidence).

A variety of theories of subsidence liability have been approved: negligence, groundwater law principles, nuisance and the obligation for subjacent support. None, however, seems to offer a satisfactory solution to widespread, regional subsidence such as experienced in Galveston, Texas. A few states control subsidence as part of the groundwater management scheme. Texas confers powers over subsidence on groundwater conservation districts. Arizona's 1980 Groundwater Code authorizes establishment of Active Management Areas in regions affected by overdraft.

## 3. Optimum Yield

Probably the most significant effect of groundwater mining is the economic burden imposed on pumpers by a declining water table. Groundwater, a common-pool resource, is available to a number of individual users each of whom may make unlimited use of it. A person who owns an entire aquifer might want to reduce current consumption to save part of the groundwater for future uses, obtaining the maximum economic benefit over time. If a number of users have access, however, little incentive exists to conserve for the future. The individual user who foregoes present uses takes the risk that others will consume any water saved; thus each individual is induced to pump as much water from the common pool as can be used for any purpose, even a wasteful or marginal use, before other pumpers use up the supply. This disincentive to conserve results in a "race to the bottom of the aquifer," preventing optimal economic utilization of the resource. Garrett Hardin has called the phenomenon the "tragedy of the commons."

Localized effects of overdraft can be significant to individual water users. As water tables fall, progressively deeper wells are required, increasing drilling and pumping costs. Entities such as municipalities and large farms may enjoy economies of scale enabling them to pump from great depths; small, individual irrigators, however, are caught between high pumping costs and comparatively low economic return per unit of water applied. For example, if the cost of pumping is $100/acre-foot and the yield per acre-foot of water applied to crops is only $90, the irrigator cannot justify continued pumping.

The groundwater rules applied will determine the obligation of the new pumper to the existing well owner. The newcomer may have to cease all pumping under a system of strict priority administration. Or the junior may also be required to pay the well-deepening and increased pumping costs of the senior, or furnish the senior with water from the junior's well.

## II. ALLOCATING RIGHTS IN GROUNDWATER

### A. Nature of Rights

A number of legal rules and procedures treat the difficult problems of establishing rights to use a common-pool resource such as groundwater. Rights and obligations pertaining to use of groundwater may be considered to spring from property ownership concepts or from the notion that water is a shared public resource, or both. Rules adopted by a state usually reflect more than a single theory of rights in groundwater. Thus a state may recognize "ownership" of groundwater by an overlying landowner but limit the owner to reasonable uses and provide special protections for earlier users against subsequent pumpers and for all pumpers against those who contaminate aquifer waters.

States in which the resource is relatively plentiful give less attention to allocation of legal rights in groundwater. But recent problems with groundwater pollution have caused even those areas to focus on rights in groundwater. Generally, one having a right to extract groundwater has a right to protect it from pollution by others. Statutory protections and administrative agencies dealing with pollution problems are usually separate from the mechanisms for allocating rights to use groundwater, however. An integrated approach may be desirable from a policy standpoint.

## 1. Rights Based on Land Ownership

### a. Absolute Ownership Doctrine

Under this doctrine a landowner is said to own, and has an unlimited right to withdraw, any water found beneath the owned land. Also known as the "English Rule," the doctrine was set forth in Acton v. Blundell (1843). The court in *Acton* based its holding upon the ancient right of a landowner to the airspace above and the soil beneath the land and groundwater was viewed as part of the soil. Another reason for the holding, however, seems to have been the mysterious character of groundwater; the primitive state of hydrology at the time made it difficult to establish a causal connection between withdrawals by a defendant and harm to a plaintiff. See Roath v. Driscoll (1850).

As scientists have come to understand groundwater better, legal doctrines have evolved. The absolute ownership doctrine was widely adopted in the United States during the 1850's. It is still said to be the law in Connecticut, Georgia, Illinois, Indiana, Maryland, Massachusetts, Mississippi, Rhode Island and the District of Columbia. But nearly all of these jurisdictions temper its effects with regulatory legislation or common law interrelations.

The doctrine was rejected in a series of American cases, beginning in 1862 with Bassett v. Salisbury Mfg. Co. (1862). Courts found it harsh and impractical to recognize "absolute ownership" rights in groundwater, which leads to premature depletion of the resource and leaves groundwater users at the mercy of nearby high-capacity pumpers.

Even malicious withdrawal of water for the purpose of injuring a neighbor was not actionable under strict application of the absolute ownership rule. Today, however, even states following the absolute ownership doctrine allow remedies for wilful injury. In addition, a number of states that follow the English Rule impose liability for land subsidence caused by negligent pumping (e.g., Massachusetts). Many absolute ownership states subject groundwater use to regulation under some of the rules discussed below.

### b. Correlative Rights

Under the correlative rights doctrine rights to groundwater are also determined by land ownership. However, owners of land are each limited to a reasonable share of the total supply of groundwater. The share is usually based on the amount of acreage owned. The correlative rights doctrine was applied in Katz v. Walkinshaw (1902) *reversed*.

In that case the court ruled that in times of shortage each overlying owner must limit withdrawals to a "fair and just proportion" of the supply, a proportion based on the ratios of the landowners' acreage overlying the aquifer.

California allows surplus groundwater (in excess of landowners' needs) to be used on other than overlying lands. Rights to export water are based on prior appropriation. The court in *Katz*, supra, held that as between two exporters, the doctrine of prior appropriation applies. In conflicts between overlying owners and exporters, an overlying owner is entitled to a reasonable share regardless of priority relative to the exporter, but any surplus is allocated according to priority. Other jurisdictions adopting correlative rights have not adopted the full *Katz* allocation scheme; they have only adopted the generalized notion of pro rata reductions based on land ownership.

California has introduced another appropriation concept into the law of correlative rights. In a case involving a basin subject to serious overdrafts because combined pumping for overlying and export uses far exceeded safe yield, the court held that all pumpers had used water contrary to the rights of one another. Consequently, the continuous adverse uses had resulted in "mutual prescription." City of Pasadena v. City of Alhambra (1949), *cert. denied* (1950). Such rights are proportionate to actual historical use. The mutual prescription approach announced in *Pasadena* was developed to avoid the hardship of completely cutting off some large users such as municipalities and public utilities. But it resulted in a scramble to pump large amounts of groundwater in order to establish (and minimize loss of) prescriptive rights.

The mutual prescription doctrine was significantly qualified by the decision in City of Los Angeles v. City of San Fernando (1975). There, the court held that municipalities (which had stipulated to the mutual prescription approach in *Pasadena*) are exempt from prescription and required that owners be put on notice of the adversity caused by commencement of the overdraft. The court also altered the correlative rights allocation formula. Under the new formula, prescriptive rights (against private owners) are determined and a correlative rights allocation then made, subtracting the amount of prescriptive rights from each private owner's allocation. Any surplus remaining is allocated by priority of appropriation.

## 2. *Rights by Prior Appropriation*

Prior appropriation doctrine recognizes the best legal rights in the person who first begins using water. Some of the reasons for affording rights to early users of surface water apply to groundwater use. Investments in wells, irrigation equipment, land and businesses based on an expectation of a water supply should be protected. Thus, the law has recognized special rights in established users of groundwater. The rules of liability discussed in Section II B of this chapter respond primarily to injury of existing users caused by a new user's pumping. Groundwater use permit systems usually protect equities of pumpers whose use predates the establishment of the permit system by giving them "grandfather rights" to the extent of their use. Permits for new uses are allowed only when they do not harm rights under earlier permits.

Allocation of rights in groundwater strictly based on prior use is not practical. A senior groundwater appropriator theoretically could demand that no pumping be allowed because virtually any new pumping causes some effect. Application of prior appropriation doctrine to groundwater would ignore other equities of individuals and interests of society. It may be unfair to deny rights in groundwater to a junior pumper who owns overlying land and has no other readily available source. Most important, the state may have an obligation to protect and regulate use of a limited or nonrenewable public resource that would be frustrated by laws allowing the first users to monopolize rights in groundwater. In short, a strict application of prior appropriation could deprive other users—and society—of the ability to make full beneficial use of the resources.

States must determine the extent to which new uses will be allowed to interfere with established uses. Appropriators also must be limited in the uses they may make of groundwater in order to prevent an aquifer from being used too heavily. This may mean that no more than the average annual recharge can be pumped. Where there is little or no natural recharge the state must decide whether the resource can be "mined" and, if so, at what rate and for what purposes. See Section II E of this chapter. Appropriation concepts are often modified by statutes that set reasonable pumping levels for all or parts of a state. E.g., Alaska, Colorado, Idaho, Kansas, Montana, Nevada, North Dakota, Oregon, South Dakota, Washington and Wyoming. The objective is to balance the interests in protecting senior users, optimizing new economic uses and assuring a sustained supply.

### 3. *Groundwater as a Public Resource*

Private property notions do not inhibit state control of groundwater in most jurisdictions. Most states recognize no private ownership rights in groundwater and consider it subject to management as public property. Rights to use it are typically created under permits granted by the state. They may be allocated as the legislature sees fit, usually by an administrative agency or official. Changes in the law ordinarily do not result in a taking if they deprive landowners or former users of the right to use groundwater. Town of Chino Valley v. City of Prescott (1981).

The Colorado Supreme Court held that non-tributary groundwater is neither subject to the right of all citizens to appropriate water secured by the state constitution nor owned by the overlying owner. Thus the legislature is free to decide how to manage the resource. State Dep't of Natural Resources v. Southwestern Colorado Water Conservation Dist. (1983), *cert. denied* (1984).

In states where groundwater is not considered "public property," the exercise of private rights of landowners or appropriators is governed by doctrines of reasonable use, correlative rights and other bases for imposing liability for harm to other users. States may exercise their police power to protect competing users and to allocate the groundwater resource in the public interest. The police power is extensive enough to justify permit systems and strict regulatory schemes so long as any vested property rights are respected.

## B. Rules of Liability

Most groundwater disputes arise when an existing pumper alleges that new or increased pumping by another is causing harm. The principal rules applied are described below. The rules of liability are influenced by the theory defining the source of rights in the particular jurisdiction. Most states use permit systems (described in Section II D of this chapter) and thus avoid the complexities involved in disputes among groundwater users.

### 1. No Liability Rule

States that recognize absolute property rights to groundwater in overlying landowners often allow groundwater to be pumped without liability to existing users. Theoretically, every landowner has a right to take whatever water may be pumped from the land by paying only those costs directly incurred (e.g., drilling, equipment and electricity); no obligation is incurred for harm or expenses caused to others.

## 2. Prior Appropriation—"Junior-Liable" Rule

Many states, particularly those that adhere to the prior appropriation doctrine in allocating surface waters, impose liability on new pumpers for harm caused to existing pumpers with vested senior rights. The rule was applied in Current Creek Irrigation Co. v. Andrews (1959).

Few states impose a pure prior appropriation system on groundwater not hydrologically connected with surface water. But notions of priority may be built into statutory systems for groundwater allocation. Liability among well owners is based on the extent to which statutory rights to appropriate groundwater have been violated. Generally only "unreasonable harm" is actionable.

## 3. Reasonable Use Doctrine

### a. Common Law

The reasonable use doctrine was eventually adopted by so many American jurisdictions that it has become known as the "American Rule." The reasonable use rule is nearly identical in purpose and effect to the rule applied to surface waters in modern riparian jurisdictions. A landmark case is Forbell v. City of New York (1900).

The doctrine prefers uses on overlying land. Traditionally, any beneficial use on the overlying land (short of actual waste) was considered reasonable and any use off the land was considered unreasonable unless it was for purposes incidental to the beneficial enjoyment of the land. Higday v. Nickolaus (1971). Although the common law reasonable use doctrine imposes a place-of-use restriction it, like the absolute doctrine, imposes little restriction on the nature and amount of use on overlying land. Nor does it seek to balance the comparative utilities of the competing uses and the comparative hardships imposed on competing well-owners.

### b. Correlative Rights

Where the correlative rights doctrine applies, the rule of reasonable use is further qualified. A well owner's reasonable use of water on overlying land may deplete an aquifer to the point that uses by others are difficult or impossible. The doctrine of correlative rights was designed to accommodate all overlying owners when water supply is insufficient to meet reasonable needs of all. Therefore, all users must ratably reduce their use of water. The allocation goal is to give each landowner a fair and just proportion of the supply.

### 4. Restatement (Second) of Torts § 858

The Restatement (Second) of Torts Section 858 is an attempt to balance equities and hardships among competing users. It imposes liability only for withdrawals that affect other users unreasonably. The Restatement approach differs substantially from the "reasonable use" rule discussed above because it involves inquiries into the nature of the competing uses and the relative burdens imposed upon each party by a particular remedy. It differs from the correlative rights approach in that allocation of rights can depart significantly from proportions of land ownership. Finally, the Restatement rule does not attach special significance to use of the water on overlying land.

No jurisdiction adheres exactly to the Restatement approach. Most courts in reasonable use jurisdictions apply some of the Restatement considerations. Furthermore, some courts that continue to espouse the absolute ownership doctrine have tempered it by application of reasonable use principles and elements of the Restatement approach in cases where one's pumping damages another's property or person. In Smith–Southwest Indus. v. Friendswood Dev. Co. (1977), the Texas Supreme Court relied in part on Section 858 in imposing negligence liability for subsidence caused by pumping, in spite of the fact that Texas then followed the absolute ownership doctrine.

Section 858 is phrased as a rule of non-liability. It states that a well owner is not liable for withdrawal of groundwater unless the withdrawal:

    a. causes unreasonable harm by lowering the water table or reducing artesian pressure, or

    b. exceeds the owner's reasonable share of the total annual supply, or

    c. has a direct and substantial effect on surface supplies.

The first limitation requires a balancing test to determine "unreasonable" harm. It seems to require that plaintiff's well be reasonably efficient in light of the type of use. A court applying the balancing test may inquire into such issues as relative wealth of the parties (e.g., municipalities vs. small farmers), relative ability to obtain financing and relative value of the uses.

In Prather v. Eisenmann (1978), the court looked to the nature of use in determining the reasonableness of harm. In that case a high-capacity irrigation user was held liable for lowering the artesian pressure of a domestic well. The court interpreted the state preference statute to say that harm to domestic users caused by irrigation may be *per se* "unreasonable." In dicta the court noted that there would be no liability between domestic well owners for similar harm if there were an adequate supply deeper in the aquifer.

The second limitation in § 858 incorporates a "correlative rights" notion. In adopting this as an additional basis of liability, the drafters of the Restatement rejected the contention of the Wisconsin Supreme Court in State v. Michels Pipeline Constr., Inc. (1974) that high administrative costs militate against adoption of a correlative rights scheme.

The last limitation in § 858 contemplates administration of groundwater use in conjunction with surface appropriation systems, discussed in Section IV of this chapter.

## 5. "Economic Reach" Rule

The economic reach approach is similar to the Restatement in attempting to strike a balance between junior and senior rights. The leading case exemplifying this approach is City of Colorado Springs v. Bender (1961). In *Bender*, a senior groundwater appropriator sought to enjoin a junior pumper who interfered with the senior's shallow well. The court looked to the law of surface streams, which does not protect a senior's means of surface diversion against diversions by juniors unless it is reasonably adequate (a suggestion made by the Supreme Court in Schodde v. Twin Falls Land & Water Co. (1912)). See Chapter Three, Section VII B 2. The court in *Bender* held that a senior well owner's well must be "reasonably adequate" in light of historical use. This may imply that a reasonably adequate domestic well need not be as deep as a reasonably adequate irrigation well.

The *Bender* rule, like the Restatement, invites inquiry into issues such as wealth of parties and value of competing uses. The court observed that although seniors ". . . cannot reasonably command the whole source of supply merely to facilitate the taking by them of the fraction . . .", they ". . . cannot be required to improve their extraction facilities beyond their economic reach, upon a consideration of all the factors involved." The *Bender* rule has been applied in Idaho and Utah. Baker v. Ore-Ida Foods, Inc. (1973); Wayman v. Murray City Corp. (1969). The *Bender* rule reflects a policy compromise concerning the extent to which seniors should be protected against loss of pumping ability.

## C. Economic Analysis of Rules for Allocating Rights

Since groundwater is a "common-pool" resource, difficult problems arise in allocating the supply and providing proper incentives for conservation. The conduct of well users is influenced greatly by the rules governing rights to pump and liability for harm caused to others. Economics is useful in identifying the incentives for water use provided by various legal regimes for groundwater management. Groundwater use involves two kinds of costs: internal costs, borne directly by the individual, and external costs ("externalities"), passed on to third parties and the public. Internal costs of groundwater include costs of drilling and pumping (e.g., construction, equipment, electricity, pipe); external costs include harms to all users resulting from the withdrawal (e.g., costs of drilling deeper, buying more powerful pumps or paying for more power to draw water from a lowered water table; a share of the value of water that will not be replaced). Every user inflicts "reciprocal externalities" on all other pumpers in the form of higher pumping costs and depletion of the physical supply.

If an individual pumper's comparison of costs and benefits includes only internal costs, decisions about whether and how much to pump will not take into account harm suffered by other pumpers and society as a whole. The law, by setting rules of liability, can internalize (pass on to individual pumpers) some or all of the external costs. This affects the degree of demand placed on an aquifer since, theoretically, every prospective pumper will compare the marginal cost (cost of producing a unit of water) to the marginal return (value of crops or products from use of the unit of water), in deciding to pump. But many legal rules allow a pumper to externalize some of the marginal cost of producing water, yielding a net gain for the pumper, but deflecting that cost onto others, often to society's detriment.

This is not to say that an individual pumper should internalize all external costs resulting from pumping a unit of water. If that were the rule, the cost to a new pumper of producing water would be driven up artificially by inclusion of costs resulting from earlier pumpers' activities in pumping from the same aquifer.

The law may seek to allocate to each pumper an appropriate share of the total marginal cost, including indirect pumping costs, so that each will make the most economically justified decision. Presumably at that point the optimum or "best" decision is made for society, since water will not be "wasted," i.e., more produced than will yield a net gain or less produced than could be used to yield a net gain. Legislatures or courts may fix liability on new pumpers for all costs, impose no liability on new pumpers (senior and junior pumpers paying only their own direct expenses), or impose liability in a way that considers factors like priority and efficiency.

If no liability is imposed on new pumpers for harmful effects on others there is little incentive to conserve because each user pays only the internal costs of pumping; rapid and uneconomic exhaustion of the aquifer also results.

The junior-liable rule that fully protects vested senior rights will discourage juniors. All the seniors' costs are passed on to the junior, including external costs partially attributable to the seniors' own use (the water table would decline due to the seniors' use even without new junior pumping). Further, the seniors' inefficiency can be protected by this system; seniors have no incentive to improve their means of diversion.

The rule of the Restatement (Second) of Torts § 858 holds a junior liable only for unreasonable harm to seniors. Determination of reasonableness may involve many factors, including value of the competing uses, efficiency of competing wells and wealth (economies of scale and ability to finance improvements) of the parties. The Restatement rule has potential for correcting the inequity of the junior-liable rule by making seniors responsible for a share of the marginal costs attributable to their pumping (thus achieving desired incentives for optimal resource allocation). The balancing test is subjective, however, and far-ranging enough to consider non-economic factors; results may be dictated by equities rather than by economic goals.

## D. Permits

Permit systems are simply administrative means to protect rights to use of groundwater. Rights embodied in permits can be based on any of several doctrines or rules of liability (absolute ownership, prior appropriation, correlative rights, reasonable use or the Restatement rule) discussed in Section II B of this chapter. Groundwater statutes establishing permit systems were enacted in an attempt to replace piecemeal litigation between water users with a unified administrative scheme. The central objective of permit systems is to regulate development and use of groundwater so that it is used most beneficially. Such systems also provide for public knowledge and community control of pumping activity.

Permit requirements vary depending upon the source of water. States commonly apply separate permitting procedures to different types of groundwater; many distinguish groundwater connected with ("tributary" to) surface streams and lakes. Most western states require a permit for all groundwater withdrawals, excepting small domestic and stock watering wells. Other states require permits only for withdrawals of groundwater from certain sources. For example, California requires permits only for withdrawals from underground streams or the underflow of surface streams (although special restrictions apply in many areas such as municipal water districts and where there are adjudicated rights in a groundwater basin). Texas requires no permits for groundwater withdrawals, but provides for voluntary formation of local management districts.

Statutory restrictions and permit requirements often are not imposed until overdraft problems develop. Many states have designated "critical areas" where permit requirements and other regulations apply. Although economic tools such as pump taxes could be used to remedy such problems, permit systems administered by a state engineer's office or its equivalent are far more common. Most permit requirements include criteria designed to prevent overdraft and protect existing wells.

There are two types of permits, and both are usually required.

## 1. Well Permits

Permits are often a prerequisite to well drilling. Well drillers also have to be licensed and to report information on geological structures, locations and depths of aquifers for all wells drilled.

Information on applications for well permits is mandated by statute or administrative rulemaking.

Required data typically include: type of use and amount of water to be withdrawn; legal descriptions of well location and land on which the water is to be used; type of well; and description of geologic strata through which it is drilled. Most states have laws governing well construction, such as the requirement that all wells be cased (sealed) as they pass through and may tap other waterbearing formations or allow migration of pollutants into or from another aquifer. Proximity of wells to one another also is regulated. Other than the casing requirement, there is surprisingly little regulation of whether the well will produce contaminated water or cause contamination of other waters.

## 2. *Permits Evidencing a Water Right*

Besides a well permit, a separate permit may be required to use water. In evaluating applications for water rights, administrators are primarily concerned with whether the granting of additional water rights will impair existing pumpers' rights. Determination of "impairment" is based in part upon hydrologic data on aquifer recharge and the extent of existing uses. Administrators also make value judgments as to the permissible rate of aquifer depletion, usually guided by statutory criteria. Such criteria reflect policy choices made by the legislature in reconciling priority of use rights, with rights of overlying owners, economic efficiency and other social goals.

Statutes often specify the type of public notice and hearing required and provide procedures for potentially injured parties to file objections. Many provide for appealability and judicial review of administrative decisions to grant or deny water rights. Permits may contain conditions on well use designed to protect existing rights. Once a prospective user's well and water use permits are issued, the user must proceed with reasonable diligence to drill the well and apply the water to a beneficial use. The right vests when the water is put to use, and a certificate is usually issued evidencing it. Permits are subject to loss by abandonment, forfeiture or violation of conditions.

## E.  Statutory Limits on Pumping

Every jurisdiction provides some protection for existing uses. Many states also statutorily limit the rate or volume of groundwater pumped. Several states have enacted laws to deal with areas having special groundwater pumping problems.

### 1.  *Protection of Existing Rights*

Most statutory systems regulating groundwater include some measures to protect existing wells. Potential interference is possible from any new well, so absolute protection is not contemplated. Usually "unreasonable" interference will be prevented. At a minimum such protections prevent the inequities that would result if the state authorized new wells to interfere with older wells that were lawfully established and relied upon. Statutory systems are designed to bring order and reliability to groundwater management and protection of existing wells is an important means to that end.

In some states a statutory system has replaced the system of appropriation or land ownership system; protections are often built into the statute for wells predating its enactment (even those that would not have been authorized under the statute) as well as for those permitted under the statute.

The 1965 Colorado Groundwater Management Act seeks to reconcile protection of vested appropriative rights with full economic utilization of groundwater. The statute employs a "modified" appropriation doctrine to govern administration of designated basins. In contrast to the pure appropriation doctrine, under which a new use would be denied if any harm resulted to seniors, the statute requires refusal of a permit only if unreasonable harm to senior rights or unreasonable waste would result. Unreasonable harm is defined to include "the unreasonable lowering of the water level, or the unreasonable deterioration of water quality, beyond reasonable economic limits of withdrawal or use." Criteria for determining unreasonable harm or waste include geologic conditions, average annual yield and recharge rate of the supply, priority and quantity of existing claims to the water, proposed method of use and all other appropriate facts. Existing well owners are required to have reasonably deep and efficient wells. The Colorado Groundwater Commission developed complex regulations to implement its vague statutory mandate.

New Mexico case law has addressed the question of what constitutes impairment of existing rights in a critical area. In Mathers v. Texaco (1966), the New Mexico Supreme Court rejected the argument that any pumping whatsoever by juniors in a closed basin constitutes impairment, stating that a lowering of the water table is not impairment *per se*. But in City of Roswell v. Reynolds (1974) the court upheld conditions on use imposed by the State Engineer to protect seniors, stating, ". . . it does not follow that the lowering of the water table may never in itself constitute an impairment of existing rights."

## 2. *Legislative Schedules for Groundwater Mining*

Several states have provided for controlled mining of aquifers so that depletion occurs over a predictable number of years. The term "safe yield" in its strictest sense means a level of withdrawals that does not exceed recharge. In the case of aquifers that are not rechargeable or which take many years to recharge appreciably, the concept has been modified so that "safe yield" refers to a level of withdrawals that will allow depletion of an aquifer over a period thought to be socially optimal. The choice of time period reflects policy judgments. For example, a long depletion period preserves groundwater for future uses, but requires more severe curtailment of present withdrawals; thus it imposes a hardship on well owners who must invest large sums in well drilling and irrigation equipment. By contrast, a shorter period allows larger withdrawals for the benefit of current users, but may allow depletion so rapid, for instance, that an established irrigation economy fails suddenly as pumping costs exceed economic returns from the water. Usually a compromise is reached under which investors have time to recover their equipment costs and aquifer life is also prolonged. Oklahoma's 1972 Groundwater Management Act allows a comparatively rapid 100% depletion within 20 years. In Nebraska, local districts may establish their own timetables for depletion. Pumping in nontributary aquifers outside depletion basins in Colorado must provide for a 100 year aquifer life.

## 3. Critical Area Legislation

Even where there are not statewide problems of groundwater overdraft, there may be localized overdrafts that demand strict management. Many western states statutorily provide for identification and management of "critical areas," in which new well drilling and pumping may be severely curtailed or prohibited. States providing for designation of critical areas include Arizona, California, Colorado, Hawaii, Idaho, Kansas, Nebraska, Montana, Nevada, New Mexico, Oklahoma, Oregon, Texas, Washington and Wyoming. Critical areas are commonly regulated by the State Engineer's

Office or an equivalent administrative body and
tend to be geographically defined by the boundaries of an aquifer or groundwater basin.

Requirements for critical area status vary. In
Montana, Oregon and Wyoming a critical area
may be designated if withdrawals from the basin
exceed recharge (the definition of "overdraft"). In
Colorado, an overdraft condition need not be shown
to establish an area as a "designated groundwater
basin," if the basin is non-tributary or located in
an area where groundwater has been the principal
water source for fifteen years prior to the application for designation. Other states, such as Kansas
and Nebraska, provide for formation of groundwater management districts by local option.

Critical area legislation also varies in the remedy applied to correct the overdraft. For example,
under the Idaho Groundwater Management Act,
groundwater is deemed unavailable and appropriation permits denied where further withdrawal
would: 1) affect present or future use of any
groundwater right; or 2) cause overall withdrawals
to exceed recharge. This statute was held to prohibit junior pumping if it would involve mining of
groundwater. Baker v. Ore-Ida Foods (1973).

Washington, Colorado and Nevada statutes also
provide for pumping reductions, but the reduction
is made on the basis of priority; senior appropriators may continue to pump, while juniors are shut
down. Oklahoma's 1972 Groundwater Management Act adopts a doctrine of "correlative rights"

similar to California's doctrine. Scarce supplies are allocated based on land ownership.

Kansas allows formation of local Groundwater Management Districts by petition of local residents. Management plans are subject to approval by the Chief State Engineer of the State Department of Water Resources. Each local district applies its own standards for well spacing and safe yield.

Phoenix and Tucson in Arizona constitute the largest metropolitan areas on earth to depend so heavily on groundwater. Years of unregulated pumping led to severe overdrafts. Accordingly, Arizona's 1980 Groundwater Management Act contains the strictest controls of any state statute. It provides for establishing "active management areas," that now encompass eighty percent of the state's population. These areas may be designated if overdraft exists, withdrawals threaten to create subsidence or groundwater quality is threatened by saltwater intrusion. The management goal for critical areas is to achieve safe yield (withdrawals not in excess of recharge) within forty-five years. To reach this goal, the state director of water resources is required to formulate a management plan including: mandatory conservation by "reasonable reductions" in per capita use by municipalities and individuals; pump taxes with revenues earmarked for expenses of administration and augmentation plans; retirement of irrigated lands; and a requirement that new subdivisions demonstrate adequate water supply and quality for 100 years (or have a contract for Central Arizona Project water).

## III. CONTROLLING GROUNDWATER CONTAMINATION

There are several state and federal laws controlling the discharge or use of materials that may cause pollutants to enter groundwater and other waters. Federal laws are the most influential. States have had a few laws to prevent groundwater contamination until recently, though common law remedies have been available to well owners to redress aquifer pollution.

## A. Regulation of Groundwater Pumping

Groundwater extraction can cause pollutants to migrate from a contaminated aquifer into a relatively pure one. The problems of improperly constructed wells and wells that draw out water in such large quantities or at such high rates that they attract contaminated water into the aquifer have been mentioned previously. The sources of contaminated groundwater include seawater intrusion, other salty or otherwise naturally contaminated water, land disposal of pollutants, waste injection wells, surface storage and activities, and runoff from agriculture, city streets and industry.

The use of groundwater once it is extracted can also cause pollution. Some groundwater is already contaminated and its application to land or other use will affect other aquifers or surface sources.

As indicated above, some states will deny or condition well permits to prevent groundwater contamination. Some impose conditions on the right to use water that control the rate and extent of extraction. Overdraft problems may lead to the creation of special districts or imposition of state controls under critical area legislation. In states like Arizona, Colorado and Kansas criteria for imposing permit conditions include prevention of groundwater contamination. Prevention of contamination is also a factor in setting allowable rates and volumes of water that can be pumped from an aquifer. Critical areas are rarely designated specifically to deal with contamination problems.

State permitting agencies often examine the effects of an application for a new well or for a change in well location to see if it will draw saline or other lower quality water into parts of an aquifer used by existing pumpers. If serious degradation is likely, the agency may deny or condition the permit. But minimal increases in the rate of intrusion or concentrations of pollution may be considered reasonable and the permit granted in the interest of allowing full development of water resources. Stokes v. Morgan (1984).

Virtually no jurisdictions deny the right to use groundwater because the use, as opposed to the extraction, of water will cause contamination. The

Oklahoma Supreme Court has ruled, however, that an agency decision to allow withdrawal of fresh groundwater to be used in a waterflood operation (spreading water in old oil fields to help produce secondary recovery of oil) required a finding that it would not cause "waste" by either pollution or depletion. Oklahoma Water Resources Bd. v. Texas County Water Resources Ass'n, Inc. (1984).

## B. Regulation of Polluting Activities

### 1. State Regulation

Most states have long regulated well construction. The oil producing states also control oil and gas drilling and production to prevent saline water from getting into freshwater wells. Most states are now adding new regulatory programs, many in response to federal incentives or requirements.

Comprehensive groundwater quality laws must regulate land use and other activities as well as construction and use because they are the major sources of contamination. The laws may classify certain aquifers according to the uses that can be made of them and allow more or less pollution to occur as necessary to protect the actual or anticipated uses. States that have enacted somewhat comprehensive groundwater protection laws include Arizona, Florida and Wisconsin.

It is rare for the same agency that regulates groundwater allocation to regulate polluting activities. Thus, there can be interagency conflicts. E.g., Matador Pipelines, Inc. v. Oklahoma Water

Resources Bd. (1987) (Corporation Commission has exclusive authority over pollution so Water Board did not have jurisdiction to order clean-up after break in oil pipeline).

## 2. Federal Regulation

Federal regulation of groundwater quality has not pursued a fixed strategy but there are many environmental laws that have the effect of protecting groundwater.

The Clean Water Act, described in Chapter Nine, Section V A, controls discharges of pollutants from point sources. Although the Act has not been applied specifically to protect groundwater it does regulate many industrial and other activities that are sources of groundwater contamination. The Surface Mining Control and Reclamation Act (SMCRA), 30 U.S.C.A. §§ 1201–1328, regulates coal mining activities started since 1977 to prevent water pollution.

Non-point sources cause pollutants to seep into aquifers and run down wells. Irrigation return flows and runoff from farming, construction activities, city streets and mine sites are all considered "non-point sources" of pollution outside the scope of the Clean Water Act. The Clean Water Act has been amended to require states to develop plans to control these sources though there are no sanctions for failing to implement effective programs. The Safe Drinking Water Act, 42 U.S.C.A. § 300h, has a wellhead protection program that provides for designation and protection of wells and wellfields used to extract drinking water. This program motivates some control of non-point sources.

Placing or spilling waste on or in the ground causes enormous amounts of pollutants to seep into groundwater. Protection of groundwater necessitates control of dumps and, in many cases, clean-up of old sites. The law that most directly protects groundwater quality is the Solid Waste Act, also known as the Resources Conservation and Recovery Act (RCRA), 42 U.S.C.A. §§ 6901–6991i. It controls every aspect of hazardous waste generation, transportation, storage, processing and disposal. It also sets guidelines for state regulation of other (nonhazardous) wastes. A program under the act regulates underground storage tanks (such as gasoline tanks).

A common way to dispose of liquid waste, including some hazardous wastes, is by injecting them into deep wells. The Safe Drinking Water Act includes an underground injection control (UIC) program that requires permits and adherence to certain standards. States are allowed to take over the administration of these programs.

Past disposal of wastes causes contamination of many groundwater resources and threatens others. The Comprehensive Environmental Response, Compensation and Liability Act (CERCLA), 42 U.S.C.A. § 9605, also known as the "Superfund", establishes a federal program to clean up hazardous substances in inactive or abandoned sites. CERCLA also allows governmental entities to bring actions against almost anyone connected with past disposal activities for damages to resources and the resource most frequently harmed is groundwater. Even private parties have a cause of action to recover the costs of cleaning up hazardous waste spills.

Indirect protection of groundwater results from legislation controlling the production and use of toxic substances. The Federal Insecticide, Fungicide and Rodenticide Act (FIFRA), 7 U.S.C.A. §§ 136–136y, requires federal registration of pesticides. It also allows the Environmental Protection Agency to limit the distribution, sale or use of pesticides to protect the environment. The Toxic Substances Control Act (TSCA), 15 U.S.C.A. §§ 2601–2671, regulates the manufacture of chemicals that EPA finds may present a risk to health or the environment.

## C. State Judicial Remedies

Most state courts entertain liability suits by well owners against persons, including oil well owners, whose activities cause pollution of water wells. Some state laws, like Oklahoma's Oil Well Pollution Act, create special rights of action. Common law remedies for groundwater contamination include nuisance, trespass and negligence suits. Mowrer v. Ashland Oil & Refining Co. (1975); City of Attica v. Mull Drilling Co. (1984).

Some cases involve questions of whether the enactment of federal statutes and programs preempts state programs and actions. The outcome depends on a reading of the individual federal statute to determine if Congress intended to preempt state laws. In some cases state remedial programs and causes of action will be allowed as a way of making pollution control more effective. In others Congress intended, for instance, not to burden interstate commerce with varying requirements. E.g., Attorney General v. Thomas Solvent Co. (1985) (CERCLA did not preempt state public nuisance suit).

## IV. CONJUNCTIVE USE

The term "conjunctive use" refers to the joint use or management of groundwater and surface water sources. It is especially important if the two sources are hydrologically interconnected. The term sometimes also refers to use of two unconnected sources to maximize available supplies. Joint management of connected surface and groundwater sources is the only reasonable way to deal with what is in fact a single resource. Nevertheless, laws in many states manage water use from wells and streams separately, ignoring the fact that they may derive from the same source. As discussed below, an increasing number of states are managing interconnected groundwater and surface sources as a single system.

In some instances conjunctive use involves influencing or compelling water users with rights and access to both wells and surface sources to adjust their use of each to an optimum mix. In other situations the vested rights of different surface and groundwater users must be observed but regulated in a manner consistent with maximizing overall beneficial uses. One promising approach is to create a centralized water management agency with powers over conjunctive use. There is often political resistence, however, to giving agencies substantial powers to tax, incur bonded indebtedness, own property, take legal action and exercise broad administrative powers.

## A. Regulation of Groundwater Connected With Surface Sources

### 1. *Interaction of Groundwater and Surface Water*

Groundwater is often hydrologically connected to surface streams. For example, seepage from a stream may charge an underlying aquifer. The surface flow of a stream may "ride piggyback" upon the groundwater contained in the aquifer beneath the stream. Or a stream may be fed by seepage from aquifers. See Section I A of this chapter. In these situations stream water use may diminish recharge to the aquifer and withdrawals of groundwater may diminish surface flow. Colorado calls such interconnected groundwater sources "tributary."

Although the scientific community has long recognized the interconnection of groundwater and surface water, the law has been slow to catch up. Some early cases enforced rights based on this truth. Smith v. Brooklyn (1899) (riparian entitled to prevent interference with streamflow from use of groundwater). Laws of many states are still founded on the misconception that the two types of water exist in isolation from one another; thus they mandate separate regulatory systems for groundwater and surface water.

Several states, including Colorado, New Mexico, California and Utah, administer groundwater sources affected by or affecting surface flow as part of the surface appropriation system. The 1973 Report of the National Water Commission recommended wider adoption of this approach. Some states do not use separate systems, but empower regulatory agencies to impose special conditions on groundwater withdrawals that interfere with surface rights. E.g., Oregon.

Timing and magnitude of the effect of well pumping on streamflow are expressed by the United States Geological Survey as a "stream depletion factor." Since groundwater may percolate very slowly through aquifers, there is often a delay between groundwater withdrawals from a connected aquifer and their effect on the surface stream. In addition, the effect may be less in amount than the groundwater withdrawal. The stream effect is defined as a percentage of the streamflow (not of the amount withdrawn). For example, a thirty-day, five percent stream depletion factor means the pumping will diminish the streamflow within thirty days by an amount equal to five percent of the streamflow. Calculation of stream depletion factors involves use of computer models and stream depletion contour maps.

The length of the delayed effect of well pumping on streamflow determines how far in advance of the needs of senior surface rights holders junior well-owners must be shut down, and when juniors will be allowed to pump even if a senior surface user is deprived of water, under the "futile call" doctrine (see Chapter Three, Section V C). The length of delay also helps define which waters have a sufficient hydrologic connection to be conjunctively managed, since stream effects very remote in time may be considered de minimis.

## 2. Definition of Hydrologically Connected ("Tributary") Groundwater

The word "tributary" is convenient shorthand terminology for groundwater that has a hydrologic connection with a surface stream sufficiently direct to warrant legal attention. Though tributariness (by whatever name a state chooses) has important legal consequences proof of this factual issue is often a difficult and expensive hydrologic issue. By Colorado statute, non-tributary water is water "the withdrawal of which will not, within one hundred years, deplete the flow of any natural stream. . . . at an annual rate greater than one-tenth of one percent of the annual rate of withdrawal." As a practical matter the presumption operates in favor of stream appropriators, since the expense of proof is borne by proposed junior groundwater users. To simplify fact-finding, Colorado courts have adopted a "presumption of tributariness." Safrenek v. Limon (1951).

### 3. Conjunctive Use Management

Interrelation of ground and surface supplies gives flexibility to users with access to both. A senior stream appropriator may be able to "follow the source" and get a more reliable supply by sinking a well to tap water flowing under the stream. This procedure was approved in Templeton v. Pecos Valley Artesian Conservancy Dist. (1958). An owner of senior water rights unable to divert sufficient surface water because flows had been diminished by groundwater pumping sought to drill a well to tap the alluvial aquifer supporting the stream. The court held that the well used the same water from a deeper source, so it had the original surface priority rather than a recent priority as of the time the well was drilled. See also Langenegger v. Carlsbad Irrigation Dist. (1971) (extending the "follow-the-source" rule to allow surface appropriator to tap deep aquifers that feed more shallow aquifers).

Colorado, which integrates management of tributary groundwater with surface sources under prior appropriation law, allows wells as alternate points of diversion for surface sources. A Colorado statute even requires seniors who have both wells and surface diversions to use their wells as alternate points of diversion before they "call the river" (require upstream juniors to shut down). It is not clear how much expense courts will require seniors to bear in operating or deepening a well as an alternate point of diversion. It is likely that the Colorado courts will follow the same approach they use in well interference cases: requiring that the senior's well have a reasonable economic reach before a junior will be shut down. See Section II B 5 of this chapter.

Another management advantage of surface-groundwater interconnection is the "transient storage" provided by delayed stream effect. A junior well owner on a tributary aquifer may have weeks or months of delay between the time of withdrawals and resulting stream effects. In states with flexible administrative policies the junior may continue to pump so long as the senior is provided with sufficient supplemental water by the time the stream effect is felt.

Stream effects may not only be delayed, but the magnitude of the measurable stream effects may be only a fraction of the amount withdrawn from the tributary aquifer. For example, the withdrawal of ten acre feet from an aquifer underlying a stream may reduce streamflow by only two acre feet; other sources of recharge make up the difference at least for a long time or in the immediate vicinity. In this situation, a pumper may furnish seniors on the surface stream with a substitute water supply of sufficient quantity and quality, thereby making a much larger supply of groundwater available. In the example given, the pumper might withdraw ten acre feet while bypassing two acre feet directly into the stream to avoid stream depletion effects on surface water users, a technique known as "bypass pumping." Its effectiveness is limited by the physical recharge to the aquifer, and by possible effects on adjacent wells. Stored or imported surface water may also be used to satisfy surface priorities, thus allowing greater amounts of groundwater to be pumped without adverse effects on senior rights in the connected stream.

The Colorado 1969 Water Rights Determination & Administration Act provides for conjunctive use management by means of "augmentation plans." Junior appropriators of groundwater (or surface water) may satisfy senior rights by use of a comprehensive plan utilizing various augmentation methods, including development of new diversion and storage facilities, alternative points of diversion, pooling of water resources, water exchange projects, substituted supplies and development of new sources of water. The plans are subject to terms and conditions designed to protect senior appropriators and must be approved by the Colorado State Engineer. Typically, augmentation plans are entered into and costs shared among groups of junior appropriators, all of whom would otherwise be threatened with shutdown. Some augmentation plans are administered by a central water manager, who relies on hydrologic studies and computer models to formulate a basin-wide water budget. Although there is some risk to seniors that their rights will not be satisfied because hydrologic data may be in error or the plan will fail for other reasons, the validity of augmentation plans was upheld in Cache La Poudre Water Users Ass'n v. Glacier View Meadows (1976).

### 4. Regulation of Tributary Groundwater: The Colorado Example

The 1965 Colorado Groundwater Management Act directs the State Engineer to administer tributary waters as part of the system of surface priorities. The Act protects vested rights, subjecting junior well owners to potential mass shutdowns in the event of a senior call. The Colorado Supreme Court has mandated that the State Engineer's power to protect senior rights be used judiciously, however, in order to maximize economic use of water. In Fellhauer v. People (1968) the court set aside an order of the engineer shutting down junior wells because it was not shown that seniors would benefit. This is the tributary groundwater equivalent of the "futile call" doctrine (Chapter Three, Section V C). For example, if a junior's pumping does not affect streamflow within twenty days, and if a senior's use would end within the twenty days (e.g., at the end of the irrigation season), the junior is allowed to continue pumping. Recognizing the inefficiency of strict priority administration, the court in *Fellhauer* noted the beginning of "a new drama of maximum use and how that use may constitutionally be integrated with the protection of vested rights."

*Fellhauer*'s mandate of maximum use and acceptance of the futile call doctrine for groundwater was reaffirmed by the Colorado Legislature in the 1969 Water Rights Determination and Administration Act. The Act recognized vested water rights of well-owners, but effectively required appropriators to have a reasonably efficient means of diversion. No one is permitted "to command the whole flow of the stream merely to facilitate his taking of a fraction." One administrative response to the policy directives of the 1969 Act is the Colorado State Engineer's "zone system" for administering wells in tributary aquifers. Areas may be divided into zones based on the delay between groundwater withdrawals and streamflow effects. Wells can then be shut down in advance of anticipated senior calls on the river, with wells in the most distant zone shut down soonest, then wells in the next zone, and so on, so that shutdowns relate to the timing of effects on streamflow and senior needs. The system was approved as a fair and reasonable administration scheme in Kuiper v. Well Owners Conservation Ass'n (1971). The court later went farther and said that the State Engineer can require seniors to develop well water before calling juniors. Alamosa-La Jara Water Users Protection Ass'n v. Gould (1983).

## B. Imported Supplies and Intensive Management: The California Example

Southern California's rapid population growth long ago created demands exceeding the capacity of local supplies. Large aquifers were overdrafted and threatened with saltwater intrusion and subsidence. Local water users responded by implementing a unique water management system based on increasing the physical supply and managing for conjunctive use.

The Metropolitan Water District (MWD) was formed by an act of the state legislature in 1929 to meet the supplemental needs of its public agency members—several southern California municipalities and municipal water districts. MWD imports water from northern California and the Colorado River and wholesales it to MWD members, who distribute it to local users and water companies. Some imported water is used to recharge aquifers by means of spreading basins or injection wells, so that it may later be withdrawn from storage by pumping.

Transbasin diversion projects provide most of southern California's water supply. Since 1941, Colorado River water has been imported through a system of aqueducts built by MWD. Surface collection and storage facilities in northern California, part of the massive California State Water Project, now supply additional water by aqueducts to southern California users according to a contract with MWD. In addition, the Owens Valley aqueduct of the City of Los Angeles was opened in 1913.

Institutional allocation and economic incentives are necessary to avoid inequities among competing users and damage to aquifers through subsidence and saltwater intrusion. A number of approaches have been taken. One is to adjudicate groundwater rights of everyone in a particular basin as a predicate to limiting their use of the aquifer. Once basins have been adjudicated, special water districts are formed to manage basin-wide development and use of water. Pumping allocations are made among users and pumping assessments levied to provide for purchase of imported water to replenish the basin as needed. Imported water is made available to those without direct access to it by an exchange agreement with those who do.

Another method of adjusting uses of groundwater and imported water in southern California is by market mechanisms. The Orange County Water District (OCWD) buys imported water from MWD, then allocates imported water and groundwater by pricing incentives, attempting to achieve an economic solution to conjunctive use problems. A basin-wide goal is set for the proportional use of groundwater and more expensive imported MWD water. Users who pump more groundwater than the indicated proportion of their total entitlements are subject to a special pump tax; the amount of tax is the difference between the cost of pumping an acre foot of groundwater and the cost of buying an acre foot of MWD water. Taxes are credited to those who use a greater share of imported MWD water, so everyone effectively pays the same for an acre foot of water, whether groundwater or MWD water. This leads to economic optimization and maximizes water use benefits.

## V.  GROUNDWATER STORAGE

Storage capacity greatly enhances flexibility in water planning decisions. Erratic surface flows can be accumulated through the year and released as needed. The conventional method of storage is impoundment of surface waters behind a dam, creating a surface reservoir. Aquifer storage avoids many disadvantages of surface reservoirs such as alteration of the temperature and silt content of streams, land use impacts of damsites, flooding of wildlife habitat, threat of dam failure and flooding, evaporation losses, pollution of stored water and high construction costs. Storage of water in groundwater aquifers is becoming increasingly important. Southern California uses underground storage in conjunction with an ambitious program of importing surface waters from the Colorado River and the northern part of the state.

Imported water may be introduced into an aquifer by several methods. Natural recharge may be augmented by imported surface water. Water may be placed directly into the aquifer through injection wells or may be spread on the overlying lands to allow waters to percolate down.

Despite its advantages over surface storage, underground storage may be infeasible unless the importer has legal rights in the stored supply. A public agency will be reluctant to undertake an expensive importation scheme unless it has the right to reclaim, and exclude others from taking, waters it has captured or imported and stored. California, which has taken the lead in developing underground storage and administering the stored water in conjunction with surface uses, has encouraged such efforts by providing the importer/ storer with firm rights in the stored supply, thus protecting the importer's investment. In City of Los Angeles v. City of San Fernando (1975), the court held that the City of Los Angeles has the exclusive right to recapture imported water it adds to the groundwater basin. The right is limited to imported water and to storage by public agencies. Similarly, Washington has held that commingling stored and naturally occurring groundwater does not cause the stored water to lose its separate identity. Jensen v. Department of Ecology (1984).

In Alameda County Water Dist. v. Niles Sand & Gravel Co., *cert. denied* (1974), the water district was engaged in a groundwater storage program. Niles pumped water out of its sand and gravel pit which was hydrologically connected to the storage aquifer. The dewatering operation drew down the level of the stored water in the aquifer while the water district was attempting to recharge it to prevent salt water intrusion. The court enjoined pumping, ruling that there was no compensable taking of vested property rights. It found not only that the storage plan was within the police power of the water district but that the district had a "public duty" to maintain the water level. Thus the gravel company's use was burdened with a "public servitude" in favor of storage.

The cases support the existence of three types of storage rights:

1. The right of a public agency to import and store water without obligation to overlying land-owners;

2. The right to protect the stored water against use by others; and

3. The right to recapture the stored water.

New Mexico has followed a contrary line of reasoning in cases holding that once imported water percolates into an aquifer, it becomes public water subject to appropriation. Kelley v. Carlsbad Irrigation Dist. (1966). The New Mexico approach, if strictly followed in subsequent cases, may frustrate efforts to develop groundwater storage.

Statutes in several states facilitate storage. California statutes provide that underground storage is a beneficial use for which surface supplies may be appropriated, and that private parties may not acquire rights in stored water as against storage entities. Similar statutes are in effect in Utah (provides for appropriation of water for storage) and Washington (stored water held out from appropriation).

An unresolved issue concerns priorities among those using groundwater storage. The issue may arise if several public agencies are competing for the limited storage capacity of a groundwater basin. Priorities could be embodied in storage agreements negotiated between competing public agencies.

# CHAPTER SEVEN

## DIFFUSED SURFACE WATERS

Watercourses are subject to the applicable state water allocation system—riparian, appropriative or hybrid. Diffused surface waters are generally those waters that have not yet joined a watercourse, such as runoff from rainfall to which different rules apply.

A landowner may be concerned with surface flow that can threaten the safety of persons or property on that or nearby land, or that can make the land less valuable or useful unless channelled, controlled or drained. A landowner responding to such concerns may direct surface flow toward another's land, creating conflicts between landowners. Generally one may take reasonable measures to protect property or persons from harm.

Another type of issue, arising mostly in arid areas, is whether a landowner has the right to take and use surface flows unrestrained by state laws concerning appropriation of water. The laws of most jurisdictions, although differing in rationale, allow rather unrestricted use of diffused surface waters captured on a landowner's property.

291

## I. WATERCOURSES AND DIFFUSED SURFACE WATERS DISTINGUISHED

### A. Watercourses

Theoretically, almost all waters may be included in the definition of a "watercourse." A great river includes tributaries, which in turn include not only small streams, but gullies and washes that feed them rainwater and snow melt. And the snowpack, falling rain, clouds and evaporating water not yet formed into clouds are all "tributary" in a sense. But there are limits to the confidence with which science can trace water destined for streams and lakes, and to the state's practical and political ability to impose controls on water use. Thus, there are some generally accepted criteria for defining "watercourses" that come under state regulatory authority. Once water has gone underground it usually becomes subject to allocation as groundwater.

States generally seek to exert authority over "natural watercourses." A natural watercourse is most often defined as a body of water flowing in a defined channel with bed and banks. Most states say that water must be present a substantial portion of the time, but will occasionally consider dry steams or lake beds to be "natural watercourses." Water flowing in a surface depression only as the result of rainfall or snowmelt usually is not considered to be in a watercourse (see Chapter Three, Section VI A).

## B.  Diffused Surface Waters

Surface water not in or connected with a "watercourse" is considered "diffused surface water." The Restatement (Second) of Torts § 846 defines diffused surface waters as "water from rain, melting snow, springs or seepage, or detached from subsiding floods, which lies or flows on the surface of the earth but does not form a part of a watercourse or lake." This usually includes water flowing in draws, swales, gullies, ravines and hollows. It may include water collected in puddles, depressions, marshes and small ponds. Springs may not be considered diffused surface water if they run directly into a stream or have a large enough flow to constitute a stream. Generally, if water flows with some frequency and historical regularity and carves a recognizable channel or reaches a lake or pond having some permanency, it is considered to be in a watercourse. Floodwaters, usually considered to be in a watercourse, become diffused surface waters when they lose their connection with a stream, such as by overflowing the banks, and settle elsewhere.

## II.  PROTECTION FROM DAMAGE BY SURFACE FLOWS

Some of the earliest reported cases dealing with water have to do with drainage. The law allows landowners to protect or develop their land even if it causes drainage problems for others. An upper landowner may augment natural drainage to make

marshy land useful, divert flood waters to protect
land or buildings, or fill, build on or pave land as
part of developing it.  In each case drainage patterns are altered, affecting lower landowners.
Lower landowners can raise their land level or
construct dikes, buildings or other obstructions to
the flow of surface waters that bank water up onto
the lands of upper neighbors.  Disputes often arise
if avoided water cannot be placed directly into a
watercourse without causing harm to others.
American jurisdictions have historically split between two rather extreme and opposite rules to
resolve such disputes: the common enemy doctrine
and the civil law doctrine.  Most now follow a rule
of reasonable use.

Water other than diffused surface water may
need to be disposed of or drained from one's land.
For instance, a person using water diverted from a
stream or lake (*e.g.*, for irrigation or to power a
mill) may need to dispose of the unconsumed
water, often known as tail water.  That water is
not diffused surface water and may not be released
on or drained across the land of another without
permission, usually accomplished by acquiring an
easement or right of way.  Cf. Loosli v. Heseman
(1945).  The right can also be acquired by prescription.

Water impounded on one's land, such as in a
reservoir, is treated under different rules than
diffused surface water, whatever its source.  Care
must be taken to protect property of others in

maintaining a reservoir and in releasing water from it. Many jurisdictions impose absolute liability for harm caused by artificial storage of water, such as when a dam breaks. Rylands v. Fletcher (1868). The right of a landowner to back up water behind a dam causing the land of another to become flooded is also limited.

## A. Common Enemy Doctrine

The common enemy doctrine holds that landowners may take any action they see fit in order to avoid diffused surface waters, without liability to others. This includes building a barrier to water flowing down from adjoining land, such as a dike along one's upper boundary, or altering natural drainage patterns by a system of berms, ditches or pumps to keep it out of a basement or away from a field. It may also allow development of drainage systems to augment natural drainage. Excavations can be made for drains and channels to collect and divert flows or accumulations of water. The only apparent limitation is that one may not store surface water (as in a dam or reservoir) and then release it upon another.

The common enemy rule is sometimes called the "Massachusetts rule," because of its acceptance there as early as 1851, though it now has been rejected even there. The doctrine has been attributed to the common law of England where, as in much of the eastern United States, development or agricultural use of land may depend on avoiding surface runoff and draining saturated land. In

England, where drainage was early centralized by statute under a system of common drains, no clear common law developed and decisions contain some support for both the common enemy and civil law rules.

The absolute right of landowners to use their lands as they please, as embodied in the common enemy rule, ignores an equally important principle in our jurisprudence: landowners must use their property in a manner that does not harm others. Very early it became apparent that although the doctrine encouraged development of property needed for a growing nation, unhindered development often was at the expense of other owners. It also promoted nasty drainage contests among landowners and breaches of the peace. Nearly all states that purport to follow the common enemy rule today have modified it to include familiar tort concepts of reasonableness. Courts have altered the rule by holding that deflection or other activity causing surface water to flow onto lands of another must be in good faith, not be negligent and not cause "substantial harm." Jurisdictions that employ a modified common enemy doctrine are Arizona (as to floodwaters), Arkansas, Connecticut, Nebraska, South Carolina and the District of Columbia. In addition, courts in New York, Missouri, Oklahoma, Virginia and Washington invoke the doctrine but have modified the rule so extensively that they effectively apply the reasonable use rule (discussed below in Section II C of this chapter). The Massachusetts court has indicated an intention to follow the rule of reasonable use in future cases. See Tucker v. Badoian (1978). In spite of the anomaly presented by the doctrine in its unmodified form, it is still controlling in Maine, Indiana and Montana. See Argyelan v. Haviland (1982) (suggesting that channelling water onto a neighbor's land would not be covered by the rule).

## B. Civil Law Doctrine

The civil law doctrine, traceable to the Code Napoleon, entitles every landowner to have natural drainage maintained. Each owner has a reciprocal duty to refrain from damming, channelling or diverting diffused surface waters that would change or increase drainage affecting others. The rule thus places a servitude upon adjoining lands for natural drainage. The civil law rule is unsuited to settled areas because it prevents most development; construction of a building or paving a parking area displaces natural runoff and would not be permitted under literal application of the doctrine; and in rural areas, cultivation for agricultural use often depends on altering the natural drainage pattern.

Although the language of the few reported cases is often ambiguous, the following states appear to follow the civil law doctrine without significant modifications: Delaware, Florida, Georgia, Idaho, Kansas, Louisiana, Michigan, Mississippi, Nevada, New Mexico, Tennessee, Texas, Vermont and West Virginia.

As with the common enemy doctrine, courts have modified the civil law doctrine to fit the society it is supposed to serve. In addition to employing reasonableness concepts, some states employ elements of the common enemy doctrine. For instance, Arizona has generally followed the civil law doctrine for diffused surface waters but has held that "floodwaters" are subject to the common enemy rule.

A few states have incorporated notions of reasonableness into the civil law doctrine to allow for some alteration of natural drainage patterns. Colorado and Iowa allow deviations that do not change the quantity or manner of flows. And an Illinois court modified the rule to employ reasonableness as a criterion for judging liability of a housing developer, citing the policy behind a special agricultural exception from the civil law rule.

Some states have made exceptions to the civil law doctrine to accommodate development in urban areas where lots are typically small and close together. They include Alabama, Nevada, Ohio, South Dakota and Pennsylvania. In Oregon a similar exception has been allowed for agricultural drainage if required for "good husbandry" and water is not diverted from natural channels. The Illinois statute mentioned above also permits artificial drainage necessitated by good husbandry. In Texas the civil law doctrine applies to private parties while the reasonable use rule applies to municipal corporations.

## C. Reasonable Use Doctrine

Courts have crafted numerous exceptions to both the common enemy and civil law rules insofar as they allow landowners to disregard the property of others or tend to stifle future development. Permitting landowners to affect natural drainage in ways that are reasonable under the circumstances creates both benefits and burdens. The existence of reciprocal rights, however, increases uses that may be made of all property, to society's benefit, and enhances land values.

The reasonable use doctrine is embodied in the Restatement (Second) of Torts §§ 822–31, 833. It has become the majority rule as courts have rejected or modified the common enemy and civil law doctrines. Some states purporting to follow one of those rules have so modified it that principles of the reasonable use doctrine in fact control.

The reasonable use doctrine was first invoked to determine rights in cases involving interference with diffused surface waters in New Hampshire. Bassett v. Salisbury Mfg. Co. (1862). It now appears to be followed in more states than either of the other rules: Alaska, California, Connecticut, Delaware, Hawaii, Kentucky, Maryland, Massachusetts, Minnesota, Mississippi, Nevada (urban growth), New Hampshire, New Jersey, New York, North Carolina, North Dakota, Missouri, Ohio, Oklahoma, Rhode Island, South Dakota (urban areas only), Texas (municipal corporations), Utah, Virginia, Washington and Wisconsin.

In applying the rule of reasonable use, courts generally balance gravity of harm against utility of the conduct. To determine the gravity of harm a court may consider extent and character of the injury, social value of the activity harmed, suitability of the harmed use to the location and difficulty for the injured party to avoid the harm. In evaluating utility courts may consider the social value of that activity for the location, impact on the activity if compensation for harm were required and difficulty of avoiding the injury.

Often "reasonableness" criteria will not point clearly to a particular result. Several jurisdictions that employ the reasonable use rule then refer to the common enemy or civil law doctrine. For example, in California the reasonable use doctrine is considered to be a modification of the civil law rule previously used. The California Supreme Court, discussing considerations of reasonableness in deciding disputes over diffused surface waters said there must be a case by case judgment. Keys v. Romley (1966). If the conduct and uses of both parties are reasonable and necessary, the burden of any harm will fall on the landowner who changes the natural drainage system, consistent with the civil law rule.

## D. Public Control of Surface Drainage

### 1. *Public Drainage Projects*

For centuries England has administratively regulated surface drainage. In the United States

there are numerous special districts that administer drainage projects. They are typically formed
under state law after a local election or petition
showing consent of a majority of affected landowners. The projects are usually publicly financed
and assessments are made against all property
benefited, whether or not all individual landowners
have consented. Such projects can increase the
agricultural capacity of drained lands and provide
"new" land for buildings and other improvements.
Indeed, many thousands of acres of marshes and
swamplands in drainage districts have been re-
claimed for productive use. Nearby lands can be
protected from floods by these projects, too.

Special statutes governing drainage districts generally exempt them from restraints imposed by the
various doctrines discussed above. But if private
property rights are taken or if others are damaged,
compensation must be paid.

## 2.  *Public Restrictions on Draining Wetlands*

Marshy areas long considered useless are important habitat for migratory waterfowl and other
types of birds, fish and wildlife. Drainage may
have an adverse effect on recreational opportunities, increase fluctuations in streamflows and flooding problems and can lower groundwater levels.
Consequently, many states and the federal government have passed laws regulating private activities
that would impair desirable qualities of swamps,
marshes and other wetlands.

State and local control of private land use for
environmental protection is surely a proper exercise of police power. Although regulation may
interfere with an owner's ability to put land to the
most lucrative use, it is not a taking vulnerable to
constitutional challenges or claims for compensation. See Just v. Marinette County (1972). But
see State v. Johnson (1970).

Section 404 of the Clean Water Act, 33 U.S.C.A.
§ 1344 (see Chapter Nine, Section V A) requires
that a "dredge and fill" permit be obtained from
the Army Corps of Engineers before constructing a
project affecting any wetlands or other "waters of
the United States." The definition of "waters of
the United States" is so broad as to include remote
reaches of the tiniest streams that eventually flow
into a navigable stream. Before issuing a dredge
and fill permit the Secretary of the Army must
find that there will be no unacceptable effects on
fish or wildlife or their habitats and that values
protected in other federal statutes will not be impaired. As administered, the Act is a major limitation on drainage or other such activity in wetlands.
States may apply to administer the federal permit
system, but must follow federal guidelines and
standards. Coverage of § 404 is so broad that
there is no room for conflicting state or local regulation. But the Clean Water Act expressly allows
states to impose more stringent standards for
granting wetlands permits than those in the Act.

## III.   USE OF DIFFUSED SURFACE WATERS

Diffused surface waters subject to capture are generally not regulated by the state; thus no one can demand continuation of their flow. Although a landowner is entitled to impound and use such waters at will, a higher landowner may intercept the waters, for which there is no remedy.

### A.   Right to Capture Diffused Surface Waters

Most states recognize an absolute right in landowners to any diffused surface waters on their lands, including waters from ravines and gullies, rainfall, snowmelt and any standing water. This entitles them to dam, store, use or sell the water and consequently to prevent it from flowing to adjoining lands. The unlimited right to capture diffused surface waters is in accord with the rationale of the common enemy doctrine: a landowner who owns all water above and below the land and may deal with it without incurring liability to other landowners. Broadbent v. Ramsbotham (1856). The civil law doctrine of natural flow would seem to allow adjoining owners to demand that surface waters be allowed to flow unimpeded. Nevertheless, the rule of capture has been embraced in virtually all civil law jurisdictions as well.

Because almost no states attempt to regulate or restrict a landowner's use of diffused surface water, no legally enforceable rights or responsibilities arise concerning diffused surface waters, except to the extent that avoidance rules (discussed in the preceding section) may apply. Water rights generally cannot attach until the water has joined a watercourse.

## B. State Control of Use of Diffused Surface Waters

States seeking broad control of waters are likely to define diffused surface waters narrowly, since watercourses are subject to state regulation. A few states recognize no distinction between water in watercourses and diffused surface waters for the purpose of regulation. This is done by express, all-inclusive legislation or by interpretation of constitutional or statutory language defining the state's authority.

A Texas statute explicitly exerts state control over all "storm water, floodwater, and rainwater of every river, natural stream, canyon, ravine, depression and watershed in the state" by making it the "property of the state." The Texas Supreme Court limited the effect of the statute by holding that it cannot apply to lands granted (presumably to private owners) prior to the effective date of the law because the right to such water had vested in the landowners. Turner v. Big Lake Oil Co. (1936). The decision relies on the statute's reference to state "property" as an assertion of ownership. Typically such language in statutes and constitutions refers to a state's sovereign power over water. If interpreted in this way, the Texas law should

have been held valid as an extension of police
power over all diffused surface water. Other Texas decisions have expanded state control of diffused
surface waters by relaxing the definition of watercourse to include any water found present at times
and quantities that make it "practicable and valuable to irrigate therefrom." Hoefs v. Short (1925).

A Utah constitutional provision asserting jurisdiction over all waters in the state has been interpreted by the state supreme court to preclude use
of diffused surface waters outside the state regulatory scheme. Richlands Irrigation Co. v. Westview
Irrigation Co. (1938). The court held that all water
destined for a stream is effectively part of the
stream.

Colorado's Constitution provides that "natural
streams" are within the state's power. This has
long been judicially and legislatively interpreted to
deny property owners the use of surface water,
however. All water tributary to a natural stream
affects the streamflow and the courts presume that
all flowing water is tributary. A statute asserts
that all "water . . . which is in or tributary to
a natural surface stream" is public property subject to appropriation in accordance with the state
constitution. Even precipitation has been claimed
as subject to administration. Case law indicates
that in Colorado capture and use by a landowner of
diffused surface water destined for a stream is not
allowed. Nevius v. Smith (1929).

The Colorado and Utah approach is based upon the realization that streamflow depends on runoff. Although this may seem to deny property rights to landowners, in fact water rights in surface waters can be perfected and assured by complying with state appropriation law, by which one acquires an enforceable water right, not subject to the whims of other landowners. Whether strict state control of surface waters would prevent minimal uses such as small stockwatering ponds (or even rainbarrels) has not been decided; if the use is trivial the case probably will not arise. Technically, lawful use of a stockwatering pond created on a natural stream by human effort depends upon the landowner's conformity with the state's prior appropriation system.

Some riparian states control diffused surface waters by subjecting them to the reasonable use rule (e.g., New Hampshire, Minnesota). A statute in Iowa affirms the right of a landowner to use diffused surface waters, conditioned on a continuation of minimum flows necessary to protect rights of lower water users (presumably on a watercourse that depends on the surface flow).

Most states afford all landowners a right to capture waters outside a natural stream. The rule is embodied in statutes of some states (e.g., Indiana, South Dakota); Oklahoma and North Dakota expressly exclude diffused surface waters from state control. In Arizona and New Mexico the omission of diffused surface waters from the definition of

waters subject to appropriation effectively excludes
them from state control. Most states confine control to "natural streams" or use similar terminology construed to mean "watercourses" as opposed to
diffused surface waters. A few states (e.g., Nevada,
Oregon) claim control over all waters but only
Utah and Colorado actually extend control to diffused surface waters. Many jurisdictions simply
have not yet dealt with the issue of a landowner's
right to use diffused surface water.

# CHAPTER EIGHT

# FEDERAL AND INDIAN RESERVED RIGHTS

## I. RESERVED RIGHTS DOCTRINE

The reserved rights doctrine was created to assure that Indian lands and public lands set aside by the government for a particular purpose would have adequate water. The doctrine recognizes rights to a quantity of water sufficient to fulfill the purposes of the reservation. Although most water rights in the western United States have priority based on when they first were put to a beneficial use, rights on federal and Indian lands have a priority dating back to at least as early as when the reservations were established, even if water use begins long after others have appropriated waters from the stream. Congress has consented to joining the United States as a party in state court stream adjudications, but reserved rights are not generally subject to state law.

## A. Origin of the Doctrine—*Winters v. United States*

The reserved rights doctrine is rooted in the Supreme Court decision in Winters v. United States (1908). The case grew out of a conflict between Indians of the Fort Belknap Reservation

in Montana and nearby non-Indian settlers over
waters of the Milk River. In 1888 the Indian
tribes agreed to cede a large area of land to the
United States that was part of the lands reserved
by them in an earlier treaty and agreed to remain
on a relatively small reservation. The federal government induced settlers to take up homesteads on
the ceded lands. The homesteaders began using
water from the Milk River for irrigation, perfecting their water rights under Montana law. A
short time later the Indians began diverting large
quantities of water for irrigation. The settlers
diverted water upstream from the Indians, preventing them from getting sufficient water. The
United States then brought suit against the settlers on behalf of the tribes.

The Supreme Court held that although the settlers had established rights under state law and
had begun using water before the Indians, the
Indians held a prior water right. The right was
based on an implication drawn from the circumstances. Because it was government policy to
make the Indians "pastoral and civilized people,"
and because the reserved lands were arid, the
Court found it inconceivable that either the Indians or the government would agree to the vast
land cession unless enough water were reserved to
make the remaining lands useful. Although the
agreement was silent on the subject, water rights
were found to exist by "necessary implication."
Further, the Court had to reconcile the conflicting

inference that the government had intended settlers to cultivate the ceded lands, which purpose would be defeated by denying the settlers' water rights. The Court resolved the conflict by applying the established rule of construction that ambiguities in an Indian agreement or treaty should be resolved in the Indians' favor to compensate for the typically unequal bargaining positions of the Indians and the United States.

It was many years before the full impact of the landmark case was realized because few Indian tribes asserted their rights. Although Indians theoretically held rights under the *Winters* doctrine to waters developed by others, they lacked facilities to divert and distribute the waters and legal representation to assert their rights.

Indian tribes are in a fiduciary relationship with the federal government that causes them to look to it for protection of their property and assertion of their legal rights. Since the federal government invested heavily in water development projects that enabled non-Indians to use vast quantities of water subject to inchoate Indian rights, a conflict of interest exists. The Secretary of Interior plays a dual role as administrator of the Bureau of Reclamation and trustee for Indians but must exert uncompromised efforts to secure sufficient water to the Indians, not simply seek an accommodation between the interests. Pyramid Lake Paiute Tribe v. Morton (1972). Nevertheless, once the government has represented Indians in a water rights adjudication third parties can rely on the determination; the Supreme Court has refused to modify such determinations even if the tribes were inadequately represented. See Nevada v. United States (1983).

Once asserted, Indian reserved rights can have an important impact on the quantity of water available to non-Indians in the future. Arizona v. California (1963) held the reserved right extends to protecting future reservation uses not limited by the population or needs of the Indians.

Once the Indian reserved right arises it will not be extinguished even after the reservation is terminated and the land sold off. There is a continuing purpose to be served unless there is express federal legislation. United States v. Adair (1983), *cert. denied* (1983) (tribe retained unextinguished fishing rights).

## B. Application to Federal (Non-Indian) Lands

The reserved rights doctrine has been extended to public lands reserved for a particular governmental purpose. The rationale of *Winters* is apt: if Congress authorizes creation of a park, wildlife refuge, national forest, military base, wilderness area or another use of public land that demands water for its success, that act of establishing or reserving the land implies an intention to reserve sufficient water to carry out the congressional purposes.

Although Congress has power to reserve waters from appropriation for reserved federal lands, a legitimate question existed as to whether a reservation of federal land, silent as to water rights, should imply a reservation of water rights. The Supreme Court held in Federal Power Comm'n v. Oregon (1955) (the *Pelton Dam* case) that a reservation of federal land for particular purposes (not merely the existence of public land available for homesteading or other dispositions) removed water sources on that land from appropriation pursuant to state law. The decision foreshadowed the Court's unequivocal decision announced eight years later in Arizona v. California (1963), that the reserved rights doctrine applied to federal lands.

Courts imply a reservation of waters in each reservation of federal public lands to the extent necessary to fulfill the purposes of the reservation. Thus, the Supreme Court upheld the government's claim to the amount of water in a limestone cavern at Devil's Hole National Monument required to preserve the habitat of the pupfish, a prehistoric species mentioned in the proclamation setting aside the monument. Cappaert v. United States (1976).

The quantity of water reserved is limited to the amount necessary for the reservation's specific purposes. Only purposes encompassed by the grant of congressional authority at the time the reservation was set aside will be considered. In United States v. New Mexico (1978), which involved reserved rights for a national forest established in 1899, the Supreme Court rejected government claims of reserved rights for instream flows needed for wildlife, recreation, aesthetics and stockwatering because purposes stated in the 1897 Organic Act of the Forest Service included only furnishing a timber supply and protecting watersheds. On the other hand, reserved water rights are created for instream flows when Congress creates a wilderness area because the purposes of the Wilderness Act include preserving lands in their natural condition. Sierra Club v. Block (1985).

## C. Federal Power

No Supreme Court decision has questioned the existence of federal power to reserve water from appropriation under state law. Rather, the persistent question has been whether, in the absence of an express reservation, Congress intended to exercise its powers.

### 1. Constitutional Bases

Congress has power to reserve water for use on public lands under the property clause of the Constitution, art. IV, § 3, which authorizes it "to dispose of and make all needful Rules and Regulations respecting the Territory or other Property belonging to the United States." The power of the United States to regulate navigation under the commerce clause, art. I, § 8, cl. 3, has also been cited as authority for protecting water for federal purposes.

In United States v. Rio Grande Dam & Irrigation Co. (1899), the Court upheld the ability of Congress to regulate the flow of a non-navigable stream that affected the navigable capacity of navigable waters. The navigation power was also cited in Arizona v. California (1931), but the property clause, mentioned in dictum in *Rio Grande Dam*, is the most commonly cited source of power for federal reservations of water. Water rights can also be reserved in the exercise of other federal powers, such as the defense power (in the case of a military installation or a dam needed to generate electricity for defense purposes).

Reservation of water for Indian reservations is generally based on the Indian commerce clause, art. I, § 8, cl. 3, granting Congress authority "to regulate Commerce . . . with the Indian Tribes," but also may be based on the treaty power, art. II, § 2, cl. 2, which is sometimes cited as authority for establishing Indian reservations.

## 2. *Exercise by Congress or the Executive*

The reserved rights doctrine was created by the Supreme Court to construe the extent of federal power that has been exercised by Congress. Close questions arise concerning whether Congress intended to exercise its power and, if so, whether it intended to supersede the operation of state water law.

Congress can take the water rights it needs in the exercise of its eminent domain power. This requires paying just compensation to persons holding rights established by state law, since those rights constitute property. But if Congress reserved the rights for future federal uses at a time before private rights were established, no compensation need be paid. Before private rights are established by appropriation the government can reserve them expressly or implicitly and thereby remove them from availability for appropriation.

Congress exercises its power to reserve waters whenever it sets aside land for purposes that require water. The land can be set aside by an act of Congress, or a treaty or an executive order made pursuant to a delegation by Congress of authority to the President. Arizona v. California (1963). Although Congress may not have considered whether it was delegating authority to reserve water when it gave the executive the authority to establish Indian reservations, national forests or other reservations, courts have had no trouble implying the reservation of water rights from establishment of executive order reservations.

## D. Relationship to State Water Law

The federal government has long deferred to state law in the allocation of water, even on public lands (see Chapter Three, Section II). The 1877 Desert Land Act was interpreted in California Oregon Power Co. v. Beaver Portland Cement Co. (1935), as confirming a federal policy of recognizing only those water rights on public lands that had been perfected according to state law. Yet the

Supreme Court's reserved rights doctrine acknowl-
edges the prerogative of the federal government to
establish and exercise water rights in ways that
may not be in accord with state law. The states
never had power to alienate rights to water that
was needed for federal uses on public lands. Federal recognition of state-perfected water rights did
not abdicate the federal property interest in unappropriated waters (waters not yet allocated to private parties) on the public lands. A state's authority to allocate rights in water, then, should be seen
as applying to all waters in the state except those
that the federal government reserves before they
are appropriated.

State law cannot prevent exercise of federal
property rights or defeat federal purposes and programs. As unremarkable as this proposition may
seem, the notion that state control of water is
limited by the exercise of federal power causes
great concern to state water law administrators
and holders of state water rights because federal
reserved water rights often remain unused for
many years and exist in uncertain quantities.
This creates a possibility of disruption of a state's
water rights system and displacement of state
water rights holders economically dependent on
those rights.

## 1. Prior Appropriation

The prior appropriation doctrine operating in
most western states recognizes water rights based
on historical beneficial use. That is, the earliest

user has a right to use the amount that has been continuously diverted, superior to rights of subsequent users. Each user is ranked according to when water use began, with the earliest continuous users securing the highest priority rights. See Chapter Three. All water rights holders who began their uses after a reservation was created have rights lower in priority than the reservation. The federal government can enter the picture at any time to assert its unusual water rights; if a stream is fully appropriated before the federal use commences, junior rights may become worthless when federal rights are asserted. Thus, anyone who established rights after the date public land was reserved for a particular use holds rights clouded by a degree of uncertainty. The value of those rights depends upon the quantity of prior rights, the potential size of federal uses and the available supply.

Possible federal uses are limited by the "purposes of the reservation." A federal use may be the basis of a reserved right even if it does not constitute a beneficial use under the state definition; the federal government need not comply with the state system of water administration to exercise a reserved right. In addition, the federal government cannot be restrained or regulated by state law in exercising its reserved water rights to carry out federal purposes.

## 2. Riparian Rights

Winters v. United States and other cases dealing with reserved rights were concerned primarily with preserving federal rights where the prior appropriation doctrine was applicable. Thus, the government "priority" for uses on a reservation as of the date the reservation was established. But under riparian water law no special significance attaches to the order in which people began using water. See Chapter Two. Generally every landowner bordering on a stream has a right to use a reasonable quantity of water. In times of shortage, available supplies are shared by all riparians.

The courts have not decided how the concept of reserved water rights applies in a riparian jurisdiction. If the federal government must share the burden of shortage equally with other users no assurance exists that federal purposes can be carried out. One solution would be to exempt the government from sharing shortages, imposing the burden only on private riparians. This may be unfair to the early riparians.

Professor Eva Hanks has recommended a solution to the problem of protecting federal uses in a riparian system during shortages without building in unfairness: allow the federal reservation its full use; allow riparians whose ownership predates the reservation to the share they would have gotten if all water users including the government had shared the shortage equally; limit riparians who acquired rights after the reservation was established to shares diminished further by sharing among themselves the burden caused by the government's taking its full water needs.

## II.  PRIORITY OF RESERVED RIGHTS

### A.  Date of Reservation

The federal government obtains a water right with a priority as of the date a reservation is established, that is, the date of the statute, executive order, agreement or treaty setting aside the reservation.  Private rights existing on a stream when a reservation is established are superior to the reserved rights of the federal government; federal reserved rights are superior to subsequently established private rights.  This greatly limits the federal government's rights for newer reservations on heavily or fully appropriated streams.

### B.  Early Priorities Based on Aboriginal Indian Rights

Many Indian treaties are grants of land from tribes to the United States.  If a tribe is seen as reserving all rights except those specifically granted away, priority may attach to the reserved right as of some time in prehistory.  Some lower courts have so indicated, although the Supreme Court has not yet decided the question.  Whether the priority date of an Indian reservation is the date of a treaty creating the reservation out of a much larger aboriginally held tract or time immemorial is usually of little consequence, however;  most Indian reservations were created before other rights were established. The rationale for the earlier, immemorial priority would not apply to Indian reservations established unilaterally by the government from land not aboriginally held by the tribe.

## III.   QUANTITY

### A.   Purposes of the Reservation

The quantity of water subject to federal or Indian reserved rights is limited to the quantity necessary to fulfill the purposes of the reservation. The amount may change over time as needs change, so long as they are within the original purposes for establishing a reservation.

### 1.   *Limitation on Quantity Reserved*

The Supreme Court in Cappaert v. United States (1976), said that the government impliedly reserved "only that amount of water necessary to fulfill the purpose of the reservation, no more." In United States v. New Mexico (1978), the Court said that the purposes to be considered in imposing this limitation are the specific purposes for which the land was reserved.

### 2.   *Determining Purposes*

The Supreme Court in *New Mexico* required a "careful examination" of the purposes for reserving land to determine the quantity of water reserved "because the reservation [of water] is implied, not expressed, and because of the history of congressional" deference to state water law. The

Court examined the language and legislative history of the Forest Service Organic Act and its predecessor bills to find that at the time of the Act Congress had two primary purposes (timber production and watershed) for authorizing establishment of national forests. They did not include fish and wildlife or stock watering. The Court contrasted the Organic Act with legislation expressing concern for wildlife (such as the National Park Service Act). Subsequent legislation such as the 1960 Multiple Use Sustained Yield Act broadened the administrative mandates for national forests to include wildlife, recreation and range but did not reserve any additional water for existing forests. United States v. City and County of Denver (1982). The Court, however, might reach a different result in a case concerning a forest reservation made after enactment of legislation expanding the national forest purposes.

The broad purposes of Indian reservations differ from the rather specific purposes of federal reservations. Typically documents establishing Indian reservations recite general goals such as encouraging "the habits of industry" or "advancing the civilization of the Indians." Nearly every Indian reservation was intended to be a homeland where Indians could remain self-governing and become economically self-sufficient. These purposes may justify numerous water uses including furnishing of municipal supplies, supporting a variety of economic endeavors such as agriculture, mining, and recreation and sustaining fish, wildlife and natural vegetation to support traditional pursuits. In a judicial proceeding to quantify such rights, however, courts need indicators of how water will be used. In Arizona v. California (1963), the Supreme Court found that "the only feasible and fair way" to measure the reserved rights of the five Colorado River tribes was based on the amount of water needed to irrigate all of the Indians' practicably irrigable acreage—a very substantial amount of water.

## B. Use for Other Than Original Purposes

Once reserved water rights have been quantified they may be put to uses other than those for which they were quantified. For example, the Indian reservations along the Colorado River are entitled to certain quantities of water based upon their irrigable acreage. But if the tribes want to apply water allocated to them to industrial purposes, they may do so. Arizona v. California (1979).

## IV.  WATERS RESERVED

Although courts have not specifically addressed all possible issues, it appears that reserved water rights are available to federal and Indian lands from every source now reasonably accessible to the reservation. Of course the source must have been unappropriated at the time the reservation was set aside.

## A.  Waters Bordering on or Traversing Reservations

In cases like *Winters* where a stream borders an Indian reservation or where streams run through reservations, selection of the particular land probably was influenced by proximity to water, implying a reservation of water from that source.

## B.  Waters Beyond Reservation Boundaries

A reservation is not necessarily deprived of the benefit of reserved water rights simply because there are no water sources within its boundaries or because those located there are inadequate for reservation purposes.  Thus, in Arizona v. California (1963) the Supreme Court upheld an allocation of water from the Colorado River to the Cocopah Reservation some two miles away; water from the river had been delivered to the reservation by an irrigation canal for several years before the decision.  Reservations of water-short tracts may have occurred for many reasons.  For example Indians may have chosen to retain an area where most of them lived, ceding lands between their residential community and the water sources they need to make the retained land productive and livable.  Or a national monument may be created on a small tract no larger than needed dependent on a water source elsewhere.

Almost all states (except the original thirteen, Texas and Hawaii) were created largely out of the public domain where the  government had control of virtually all waters. At the sufferance of the United States, private rights in those waters were created pursuant to state or territorial law. The reserved rights doctrine holds that the government impliedly withdrew its consent to creation of private rights each time it earmarked public lands for a specific federal purpose, to the extent necessary to fulfill that purpose. Thus the fact that a reservation was detached from water sources does not prove an absence of intent to reserve waters some distance away. Judicial references to such rights being "appurtenant" to reserved lands apparently refer not to some physical attachment of water to land but to the legal doctrine that attaches water rights to land to the extent necessary to fulfill reservation purposes.

The question whether a non-adjacent source may be used if on-reservation water is available may be influenced by practical considerations (such as ease of delivery or water quality) that demand that a more distant source be used first. If the government or a tribe elects one source from among several, a court is likely to defer to its exercise of discretion in making such a choice; but if the choice is unreasonable a court can be expected to intervene.

## C. Groundwater

In Cappaert v. United States (1976) the Supreme Court upheld an injunction against groundwater pumping by a private water user, who had perfected water rights after establishment of a nearby national monument. The purpose of the monument—preservation of the desert pupfish—would have been jeopardized by continued pumping. The habitat of the pupfish was threatened when the water level of a pool in a limestone cavern hydrologically connected with the source of the private user's well water dropped as the user pumped.

Many states apply different regimes of water law to closed aquifers than to those connected with surface waters (see Chapter Six), but they are not treated differently for the purpose of reserved rights. The Supreme Court in *Cappaert* said "we hold that the United States can protect its water from subsequent diversion, whether the diversion is of surface or groundwater." A district court has found that the "same implications which led the Supreme Court to hold that surface waters had been reserved would apply to underground waters as well." Tweedy v. Texas Co. (1968). The Department of the Interior has taken the position since at least 1953 that the doctrine applies to groundwater on Indian reservations.

It is probably immaterial to finding a reserved right that an aquifer was unknown at the time the reservation was set aside or that the water was not then practicably usable (e.g., technology was insufficient to pump from a deep aquifer). A reservation may not have been set aside because it was near a groundwater source unknown or inaccessible at the time, but that may not defeat future government attempts to tap the source if water is needed to fulfill reservation purposes. All available sources, not just specific ones, could be subjected to the reserved rights doctrine.

## V.  TRANSFERS OF RESERVED RIGHTS

By their nature, reserved water rights exist for the fulfillment of reservation purposes. In some situations this may dictate that waters be used by private parties on the reserved public lands or Indian lands; a concessionaire in a national park may use reserved water in operation of a lodge or campground and a lessee of tribal land may use Indian reserved water to irrigate the leased land. Contractual arrangements for use of reserved water rights on or off an Indian reservation may also fulfill the broad purposes of such reservations.

## A.  Users of Public and Indian Lands

Persons using the public lands for private purposes do not exercise reserved water rights and must perfect water rights in accordance with applicable state law. Reserved rights can arise only when public land is reserved—withdrawn from entry and dedicated to a specific federal purpose— and may be exercised by private individuals only while they are engaged in activity that fulfills the federal purpose. Consequently it is necessary to distinguish between those who use "open" public lands for their own purposes and those who function on reserved lands primarily to carry out the federal purposes of the reservation, but who also may profit from their role. Federal purposes that might be carried out by private entities include operation of a commissary at a military base, road building or other construction on any type of reservation, and operation of a concession in a national park.

Ordinarily lessees and permittees use public or Indian lands for their own purposes and must establish their own water rights under state (or tribal) law. But under some circumstances a lease of reserved water rights may be appropriate. Leasing of Indian lands for use or development by others itself fulfills the intent of the federal Indian lands leasing program and federal economic development goals for Indians. Indian water rights, like other real property interests of Indians, may not be conveyed without congressional consent. Leasing of Indian lands, including the right to use water, is allowed by statute, but no general consent has been given to leasing water rights apart from land.

## B.  Individual Indian Allotments

The General Allotment Act of 1887 fostered a policy of dividing up tribal lands into individual holdings. The purpose was to convert Indians from their nomadic ways to agricultural pursuits; it was thought that the most efficacious way to do this was to give each Indian a parcel to farm. Lands not allotted were "opened" to homesteading by non-Indians. Other allotment schemes embodied in treaties and legislation had similar approaches and objectives. Allotments were to be held in trust by the United States for twenty-five years during which they could not be taxed and could not be sold or otherwise alienated without consent of the Secretary of the Interior. The trust period was legislatively extended for fixed terms several times. Ultimately Congress realized the Act had been a failure and the trust period was extended for an indefinite duration. The Allotment Act was early amended to permit leasing of allotted land and land sales with the approval of the Secretary. These provisions have given many non-Indians access to Indian lands.

Nothing in the General Allotment Act purports to divide up a tribe's water rights along with the tribal lands conveyed in severalty to individual Indians. But section 7 of the Act empowered the Secretary to promulgate regulations to "secure a just and equal distribution" of irrigation water among reservation Indians. 25 U.S.C.A. § 381. The provision seems to assure allottees access to some share of tribal water rights.

In Colville Confederated Tribes v. Walton, *cert. denied* (1981), the Ninth Circuit Court of Appeals interpreted the Allotment Act as conveying a share of the tribe's reserved water rights to individual allottees. Because allotments are alienable, a non-Indian purchaser of an allotment takes the full share of the tribe's reserved water rights allocable to the allottee, whether the allottee had used any water or not, with a priority date as of the creation of the reservation. The result may be rationalized on the ground that Congress, in making allotments alienable, intended the Indian seller to derive full value from them, including the value of the full reserved water right.   If allotment purchasers have rights superior to most other private water users, however, they possess an advantage over their neighbors whose lands were homesteaded. The *Walton* approach can be criticized as disrupting state law water allocation schemes and divesting tribes of their reserved water rights in a piecemeal fashion, without congressional authorization.

## C.  Uses Outside Indian Reservations

The purposes of establishing Indian reservations include making Indian tribes economically self-sufficient.   This is reflected in the treaties and other laws setting aside the reservations.   Considerable federal legislation encourages economic development and resource use to the same ends. Many tribes develop reservation resources for profit but few have marketed water off the reservation. Recent reserved water rights dispute settlements anticipate off-reservation leasing and other arrangements for non-Indian use of water.

Absent federal legislative permission tribes probably cannot sell, lease or exchange their water rights because they are interests in real property subject to restraints on alienation established by federal Indian law.   Congress has not yet given any blanket approval to Indian water leasing or other marketing arrangements.   The idea has long been suggested as a way of removing some of the uncertainty created by the existence of reserved rights. The 1973 report of the National Water Commission recommended that leases of Indian reserved water rights be allowed to enable non-Indians to make efficient use of water resources not immediately needed by Indians.

One device for off-reservation marketing, a deferral or exchange agreement, secures a tribe's promise not to use its water for a period, allowing undisturbed use by non-Indian junior rights. As with a lease, this type of agreement probably is not valid without congressional authorization. It can benefit non-Indian users and, by letting the Indians become self-sufficient by encouraging profitable use of reservation resources, it can fulfill the purpose of the reservation. The deferral agreement is attractive from the standpoint of efficient water use, because it moves water to higher—more profitable—uses.

## VI.  QUANTIFICATION

In the prior appropriation system, ideally the priority dates and quantities of everyone's rights are known. This information, together with information on annual and seasonal flows, enables water rights holders to predict how much water may ordinarily be diverted. Incorporating reserved water rights into state water law schemes presents difficulties. First, the quantities of rights impliedly reserved are without an easily definable limit. Second, holders of reserved rights, the United States and Indian tribes, are immune from suit by virtue of their sovereign status, frustrating state efforts to adjudicate their rights or to regulate their water use. These difficulties have been partly resolved by a Congressional waiver of federal sovereign immunity and by negotiated settlements, legislation and litigation that set numeric quantities for reserved rights.

The courts have not resolved the problem of how to make the doctrine accommodate future uses as it was intended. Reservation purposes may demand varying amounts of water in the future. A military base may expand its population or functions; increased knowledge of impacts on fish and wildlife may expand the need for instream flows through a wildlife refuge; new types of recreational demands in a park may require deeper or faster water. The problem of varying water needs is especially great in the case of Indian reservations where the purposes are usually broad—ensuring a permanent homeland and livelihood for the tribe. Thus water requirements may change greatly.

Once a quantity has been set for tribal reserved rights, that amount together with the reservation's priority date can be integrated with the schedule of private water rights. Those whose water rights were perfected after the reservation was established, can discover the magnitude of potential water claims ahead of them. The government or an Indian tribe may not in fact use its entire entitlement, but knowledge of the full quantity of reserved rights that might be asserted allows others to make wiser decisions about their own uses.

## A. Adjudication

The most common method of quantification is by adjudication. A court applying the "practicably irrigable acreage" standard of Arizona v. California (1963), would hear evidence on soil characteristics, hydrology, engineering and economics. Land that is "irrigable," i.e., capable of supporting sustained agricultural activity without long-term deterioration in quality, is identified. The physical and financial feasibility of constructing necessary water delivery systems must be determined.

### 1. Suits by the United States

The United States can initiate a quantification of reserved rights by bringing suit against all other water users from the same source or against the relevant state or states in their parens patriae capacities. Several federal court cases seeking quantification of federal and Indian reserved rights have been initiated in western states. The most notable is Arizona v. California (1963), brought as an original action in the Supreme Court by Arizona under a prior understanding with the United States that it would intervene to assert federal and Indian rights. That case dealt with a congressional act allocating rights to Colorado River water among several states (see Chapter Ten, Section III).

The federal participation, however, resulted in adjudication of the quantities of reserved rights for Indian reservations and wildlife refuges to be deducted from the various state allocations.

The Supreme Court has indicated that once a quantification has been made it will not ordinarily be disturbed. Changing needs can be met by changing the type of use made of the quantity of water adjudicated for the reservation, but the quantity is fixed. In 1983, the Supreme Court said the allocation of water to the tribes in *Arizona* could be increased only if a court were to find that the irrigable acreage had changed because of a survey error or by a redetermination of reservation boundaries. The Court rejected claims that the tribes' share of the water should be increased because in the original proceeding the United States had not claimed water for all the lands now known to be irrigable. Arizona v. California (1983). The interest of non-Indians in certainty in water rights adjudications was found to be sufficiently great to preclude reopening the issue of how much practicably irrigable acreage is on the reservations.

The Court's concern with reliance of others on water rights adjudications was also the basis for the decision in Nevada v. United States (1983). The Pyramid Lake Paiute Tribe claimed the United States did not press a claim for water needed to maintain a fishery which was the reason their reservation was established. Instead, they said, the government secured most of the water for a reclamation project for irrigation of lands owned by non-Indians who competed with the Indians for water. The effect of the Court's decision is to bind Indians to determinations in stream adjudications in which they are represented by the United States government, even if the government's advocacy was weak, incomplete or compromised by a conflict of interest.

## 2. *Joinder of the United States in State Court Actions*

Because the United States may not be sued without its consent, Congress must waive governmental immunity for a particular action or a general class of cases. Immunity also can be waived to the extent the United States submits itself to suit by joining voluntarily as a party.

Indian tribes also enjoy sovereign immunity. Although tribes may be able to waive immunity from suit if the subject matter is a contract or other business transaction, a tribe's own enactment of a general waiver without congressional consent ordinarily would be invalid. This is because tribal property, including water rights, is held in trust by the federal government. But if a tribe exercises its right to initiate a federal lawsuit invoking the equitable jurisdiction of the courts to determine its rights, a court may find a valid waiver of sovereign immunity.

The United States has waived its sovereign immunity by a statute commonly known as the Mc-

Carran Amendment.  43 U.S.C.A. § 666.  The statute specifically consents to joinder of:

the United States as a defendant in any suit (1) for the adjudication of rights to the use of water of a river system or other source, or (2) for the administration of such rights, where it appears that the United States is the owner of or is in the process of acquiring water rights by appropriation under State law, by purchase, by exchange, or otherwise, and the United States is a necessary party to such suit.

Thus, when private parties go to court to adjudicate water rights throughout a stream system they may join the United States.  The inability to do so would leave uncertainty of outcome in a general stream adjudication in which the United States might have a substantial claim.

The McCarran Amendment does not authorize private suits to decide priorities between the United States and particular claimants, only suits to adjudicate the rights of all claimants on a stream. Dugan v. Rank (1963).  It applies to lawsuits, not proceedings before admininstrative agencies.  The Supreme Court has rejected a federal claim that the Amendment does not apply to reserved water rights but only to such water rights as the federal government may claim under state law.  United States v. District Court in and for the County of Eagle (1971).  The Amendment's language refers only to federal "rights by appropriation under State law, by purchase, by exchange, or otherwise

. . . ," but the Court found that the word "otherwise" includes reserved rights.

The McCarran Amendment's consent to joinder of the United States applies to suits in state or federal court, but as a practical matter, it is only used in state court proceedings because federal court jurisdiction would not encompass water rights claims of private parties against one another. Federal court jurisdiction does exist if the United States initiates suit, and the McCarran Amendment does not preclude adjudication of the government's water rights in that forum. Although there is concurrent jurisdiction, the Supreme Court has upheld district court dismissal of a federally initiated action filed even before the United States had been joined in a parallel state court proceeding. Colorado River Water Conservation District v. United States (1976) (*Akin* case). That case involved "exceptional circumstances," however. Although the federal suit was filed only six weeks before the United States was served in the state court action, the state proceedings concerning the stream system in question had been ongoing and some 1000 other parties, though not the United States, were already before the state court. In the short time involved nothing had occurred in federal court. The state court proceedings were comprehensive; the federal court action was piecemeal.

The water rights of Indian tribes are not federal property but are private rights held by the United

States as a fiduciary for the tribes. Consequently it has been argued that they do not come within the consent to be sued in the McCarran Amendment, which applies only to rights of which "the United States is the owner." But in the *Akin* case the Supreme Court ruled that Indian reserved rights are also covered by the Amendment because, "bearing in mind the ubiquitous nature of Indian water rights in the Southwest, it is clear that a construction of the Amendment excluding those rights from its coverage would enervate the Amendment's objective."

The Court has recognized that the McCarran Amendment does not waive the immunity of a tribe and that tribes may bring their own suits to adjudicate water rights. But it has held that concurrent federal court proceedings initiated by the tribe are subject to dismissal under *Akin* if the same rights are at stake in both proceedings. Arizona v. San Carlos Apache Tribe (1983). The San Carlos case involved the states of Montana and Arizona, both admitted to statehood under enabling acts that reserved jurisdiction and control over Indian lands to Congress. The states also were required to enact disclaimers of jurisdiction in their constitutions. The court held that the subsequent enactment of the McCarran Amendment removed the jurisdictional bar the federal enabling acts created for state court adjudications. But it left open the possibility that the disclaimers in state constitutions would bar state court adjudications of water rights. State courts have resolved this question of state law in favor of state court adjudication.

Once the government is joined, it must adhere to state procedural requirements. United States v. Bell (1986) (failure to claim water source specifically precludes later filing or priority dates as of date of reservation).

## B.  Other Methods of Quantification

Another means of quantifying reserved rights, particularly for Indian reservations, is by negotiated agreement. This approach has been used with the rights of the Fort Peck Indian Reservation in Montana. The Reserved Water Rights Compact Commission was formed for negotiation with the federal government and with Indian tribes to apportion water between them and persons who claim rights under state law. Negotiated settlements have also been reached with tribes in Colorado, Arizona, California and Utah. Negotiation avoids many of the tremendous costs involved in litigation and is more likely to reach a solution tailored to the needs of the parties.

Federal legislation has also been suggested as a means of quantifying reserved water rights. Although Congress has had numerous proposals before it for quantifying or modifying reserved rights, none has passed. The complex factual variables and the strength of political views involved in the process indicate that quantification may best be reached by negotiation or litigation. Of course

Congress must approve any negotiated settlement that limits or allows others to use Indian reserved rights.

## C.  Regulatory Authority

Although the federal government has abdicated most control of privately held water rights to the states, the doctrine of intergovernmental immunity prevents a state from regulating water rights held by the United States or Indian tribes absent consent or contrary congressional intent.  Further, a different test for determining whether state regulation is preempted applies to the rights held by anyone on an Indian reservation.  There is a presumption that state regulatory authority may not be exercised on Indian reservations.  On other federal lands the presumption is that state regulatory authority may be exercised to the extent that it does not interfere with specific congressional mandates or purposes.

### 1.  Preemptive Power of the Federal Government

Congress may exercise its constitutionally-based powers to preclude the operation of state law. Where such a power is found in the Constitution and is exercised the supremacy clause of the Constitution, art. VI, cl. 2, forces the states to defer to federal law.  But whether such preemption occurs in a particular case is usually a more difficult question because there is rarely specific legislative language relating to water rights revealing Congress's intent.  The Wild and Scenic Rivers Act, 16

U.S.C.A. §§ 1271–1287, and some recent wilderness designation acts define the extent of water rights the government is to claim for instream flows. This may become more typical in the future as a way of eliminating uncertainty.

Cases involving express preemption of state water laws are rare. Typically a court must determine whether Congress intended to preempt operation of state water law affecting the rights necessary to fulfill a reservation's purposes. It first finds the purpose of the reservation, then it asks whether application of state law may interfere with accomplishment of the purpose.

Under the law of reserved rights the state system of priorities is followed by fitting a federal reserved right into the ladder of appropriative rights according to the date of the reservation. But if the state attempts to impose its notion of beneficial uses to prevent a federal use, state law will be preempted. For example, if a state does not recognize that use of water for instream flows is a beneficial use, the government will nevertheless be able to use its water rights for instream flow because fulfillment of the purposes of the reservation otherwise would be frustrated. Requirements of filing reports with the state engineer, registering water rights, and other ministerial acts would not be prohibited. Whether the government can be required to release storage water to clear channels to control chemical concentrations or to divert water on a rotation schedule are essentially questions of what impact the requirements will have on the government's ability to carry out the reservation purposes. It would seem reasonable to apply to federal water rights the rule used to determine the extent to which state land use regulations govern public lands: state regulations apply to the extent they do not interfere with federal purposes or programs.

Courts have often cited an established federal policy of deferring to state water law. See California v. United States (1978). The policy, manifested in several federal statutes and in the practices of the Departments of Interior and Agriculture (Forest Service), does not depart from the principles discussed above. Rather, it is an aid in construing congressional intent in difficult cases. The Supreme Court has relied on the policy of deferring to state water law in defining the limits of the reserved rights doctrine (United States v. New Mexico (1978)) and in interpreting the meaning of provisions in the Reclamation Act regarding the role of state laws that could have an impact on a federal water project (California v. United States (1978), discussed in Chapter Nine, Section IV D). Similarly, the policy might influence a court to find that state regulation should prevail if it places a relatively insubstantial burden on federal programs or policies.

## 2.  Tribal Self-Government

The right of Indian tribes to govern tribal members and tribal territory stems from the tribes' aboriginal sovereignty, which has never been extinguished. Although Congress has the power necessary to terminate tribal governing powers it has generally not exercised these powers in ways that have affected tribal jurisdiction to regulate Indian water rights. In fact, most legislation that has submitted tribes to state jurisdiction has carefully excepted water rights. Further, recent federal policy and legislation has emphasized the importance of tribal self-determination and strengthening tribal governments. The only significant area of state jurisdiction with respect to Indian water rights allowed by Congress is the authority given by the McCarran Amendment to adjudicate Indian water rights in state as well as federal courts. See Section VI A 2 of this chapter.

The tradition of Indian self-government is embodied in numerous treaties between the federal government and tribes, as well as in statutes and policy. The existence of a tribal government within a reservation serves to reverse the presumption generally applicable to public lands in favor of applying state law unless a federal policy is frustrated. When non-Indians are involved, however, there are additional considerations, discussed below.

In 1953 (one year after the McCarran Amendment was passed) Congress enacted Public Law 280, giving certain states jurisdiction over criminal matters and civil causes of action on Indian reservations. Congress was careful to except from the grant any jurisdiction over alienation, encumbrance, or taxation of any real or personal property, including water rights, belonging to any Indian tribe . . . ; or . . . regulation of the use of such property in a manner inconsistent with any federal treaty, agreement, or statute made pursuant thereto; or . . . to adjudicate . . . the ownership . . . of such property or any interest therein.

28 U.S.C.A. § 1360(b); 25 U.S.C.A. § 1322(b). See also 18 U.S.C.A. § 1162(b); 25 U.S.C.A. § 1321(b). Public Law 280 thus restated the general proposition that there is no state jurisdiction over Indian water rights.

Regulation of Indian water use on reservation land is not subject to state jurisdiction. This authority is solely with the tribe unless Congress acts to allow federal or state jurisdiction. As stated above, Congress has not consented to state regulatory jurisdiction over Indian reserved water rights. One federal statute, § 7 of the General Allotment Act, allows the Secretary of the Interior to adopt rules "to secure a just and equal distribution" of water for agriculture among reservation Indians (25 U.S.C.A. § 381), but no regulations have been adopted under the statute. Section 7 does not limit a tribe's authority to regulate water use except that Secretarial regulations could prevent an inequitable allocation of agricultural waters.

Several Indian tribes have adopted their own water codes to regulate water allocation and use on their reservations. These codes and other tribal

regulatory actions are binding upon Indians using
reserved rights on an Indian reservation, both because Indian reserved rights are tribal property and
because of the tribe's sovereignty over its members
and territory. Tribal regulation would also govern
Indians exercising rights established by prior appropriation within the reservation. Although rights
existing under state law are not tribal property,
tribal sovereignty over all Indian activities on the
reservation is the basis for jurisdiction.

More difficult questions arise if an Indian tribe
or a state seeks to assert jurisdiction over non-
Indians using water on an Indian reservation.
One must distinguish between regulation of water
used pursuant to reserved rights and water in
excess of these rights—"surplus water." Use of
reserved rights in conjunction with a lease of tribal
or allotted land is subject to tribal regulatory authority and state regulatory authority is precluded
because of the tribe's sovereignty over Indian property within its boundaries.

Rights may be established pursuant to state law
in surplus water. Whether those rights may be
regulated by the state depends on whether exercise
of state authority has been preempted and whether
tribal self-government would be infringed. Unless
some special federal legislation is involved, the
answers turn on the respective interests of state
and tribal governments. A tribe has a clear interest in consistent, unified management of the resource throughout the reservation. Concurrent

state jurisdiction can conflict with tribal water management policy. But if the tribe lacks a system of water resources allocation and regulation, its interest in unified regulation may be diminished. The state, having an interest in seeing its water laws applied as widely as possible, might exercise jurisdiction over non-Indians using "surplus" waters on the reservation in so far as the tribe has not exercised its sovereignty over water rights because tribal self-government may not be infringed.

It is more likely that a court will find state regulatory jurisdiction of a stream that runs for most of its course through lands outside the reservations than one that is entirely or mostly within a reservation. Compare Colville Confederated Tribes v. Walton (1981) (state regulation preempted where stream within reservation), with United States v. Anderson (1984) (state regulation not preempted over stream that touched reservation for brief part of its course).

Other important factors are the relative extent of tribal and state regulation in the area, the degree to which the water source is relied upon for reservation uses and the existence of federal irrigation systems on the reservation.

## VII. "NON–RESERVED" FEDERAL WATER RIGHTS

State law is invalid to the extent that it restricts acquisition or use of water rights so as to hamper the federal program. Thus, in California v. United States (1978) the Supreme Court held that the state could condition use of state water rights acquired by the United States for a federal reclamation project but any conditions that conflicted with congressional directives on how the project was to operate would not be valid. Only when a federal program or congressional mandate is frustrated is state law preempted; state law must be complied with as far as possible. A careful examination of the relevant statutes is required, as it is in any preemption analysis, to determine Congressional intent to allow the land manager to appropriate and use water inconsistently with state law.

The federal government can hold rights under state law in addition to holding reserved rights. The United States may need to acquire rights pursuant to state law if, for example, the uses for the water go beyond the reservation purposes (i.e., stockwatering in a national forest), or available water rights are all held by private parties because the reservation was established after all available water was appropriated. Further, the federal government may acquire rights under state law because Congress directs it to or because of an executive decision to do so. So long as Congress has acted under constitutional authority there is no question about its power to acquire such rights.

# CHAPTER NINE

# FEDERAL POWER OVER WATER DEVELOPMENT

## I. FEDERAL ROLE IN WATER DEVELOPMENT

State law generally controls the use of water, but the federal government has assumed a significant role in water allocation because of its financial support of major water development projects, the need to carry out programs and policies for the public lands, the desirability of national regulation of pollution and the primacy of the federal government in matters concerning navigation and international treaty obligations. As the federal role in water resource development has grown, so have tensions between state and federal sovereignty. Conflicts tend to be more severe in the western states because of water scarcity and the concentration of federal lands there.

Waters within state boundaries, even on the public lands, are managed and allocated according to state and local laws absent some preemptive exercise of congressional power. The Supreme Court decided in California Oregon Power Co. v. Beaver Portland Cement (1935) that private persons taking title to public lands take only water rights perfected according to state law, because estates in land and water were severed by the 1877 Desert Land Act (if not by earlier manifestations of federal deference to state water law). Nevertheless, federal power over water is paramount when Congress chooses to exercise a constitutionally based power that requires water. The courts have recognized federal authority to deal with water resources under a variety of powers: commerce power (and its subsidiary, the navigation power), property power, war power and treaty power. The question is rarely whether power exists, but whether Congress intended to exercise its power to displace state law.

The preemptive federal power to reserve waters from appropriation pursuant to state law to carry out purposes designated for public lands is discussed in Chapter Eight. This chapter is concerned with other uses of federal power that may affect the ability of the states to deal with water resources.

## II. NAVIGATION

### A. The Navigation Power

Use of waterways has played an important part in the exploration, settlement and economic development of America. Lewis and Clark's exploration of the Louisiana Purchase lands relied partly on river transport, as did the early westward movement of settlers. Before advent of the railroads and modern motorized transport, waterways provided the most feasible means of shipping freight.

Large cities grew on the banks of the nation's rivers, nourished by these natural arteries of commerce. Accordingly, there is strong federal interest in assuring the free flow of commerce along navigable waterways.

In Gibbons v. Ogden (1824), the Supreme Court held that a grant to Robert Fulton by the State of New York of an exclusive right to operate steamships on New York waterways was repugnant to the commerce clause of the United States Constitution. Chief Justice Marshall declared, "All America understands, and has uniformly understood, the word 'commerce' to comprehend navigation." Congress' power over navigation, rooted in the commerce power, has since grown from a means to regulate traffic and prevent obstruction of navigable waterways into a far-reaching tool utilized for purposes only incidental to navigation (e.g., flood control).

## 1. Importance of the Navigation Power

The Supreme Court generally refuses to make an independent examination of whether the purpose of an act of Congress was in fact improvement of navigation. A congressional determination that it was necessary for navigation is usually conclusive. United States v. Chandler-Dunbar Water Power Co. (1913); United States v. Twin City Power Co. (1956). See also Greenleaf-Johnson Lumber Co. v. Garrison (1915) (congressional determination of an obstacle to navigation conclusive). Even projects that arguably interfere with navigability have been upheld as proper exercises of the navigation power. In Arizona v. California (I) (1931), the Court rejected Arizona's contention that the recital of navigation as the purpose of the Boulder Canyon Project Act was a subterfuge because it provided for extensive damming and consumption of the water of the Colorado River. The Court also has held that Congress may expressly invoke the navigation power to affect a non-navigable tributary of a navigable stream to protect the navigable capacity of the mainstream. United States v. Grand River Dam Auth. (1960).

In only one case has the Court not obediently followed Congress's invocation of a navigation purpose for a federal project. In United States v. Gerlach Live Stock Co. (1950), the Court did not accept Congress's declaration in the Flood Control Acts of 1937 and 1940 that the entire Central Valley Project was "for the purposes of improving navigation . . .." Instead the Court found authority for the project under the power to spend for the general welfare.

## 2. *Definition of Navigability*

Various definitions of "navigability" are applied for different purposes. The definition for determining title to streambeds is different from that used to invoke federal admiralty jurisdiction. Further, states may develop their own definitions of navigability for allowing public uses on certain streams. See Chapter Five. The discussion here concerns waters navigable under the federal test for determining when Congress may invoke its power to regulate navigation under the commerce clause. The definition of "navigability" is especially important, because it determines whether compensation is required.

The legal definition of navigability has varied with time and circumstances. Whether a waterway was navigable was held to turn on whether it was "navigable in fact." E.g., The Daniel Ball (1870). It was not necessary that the waterway was actually used for navigation at a given time. If the stream had once been navigable, navigability was not defeated by subsequent disuse. Eventually the definition of navigable waters was extended to include waters that can be made navigable with reasonable improvements. United States v. Appalachian Electric Power Co. (1940). Thus, under the current federal test for navigability, a stream is navigable if it: (1) is navigable in fact; (2) could be navigable with reasonable improvements; or (3) was once navigable.

## 3. *Extension of Navigation Power to Non-Navigable Tributaries*

In an early case, the United States sought to enjoin a private irrigation project from diverting water from a non-navigable tributary because the diversions threatened navigability of the mainstream. The Supreme Court held that the navigation power extended to tributaries of navigable streams, upholding a federal statute prohibiting obstructions to the "navigable capacity" of United

States waters.  This established that depletions as well as conventional obstructions to navigation are subject to congressional control.  United States v. Rio Grande Dam & Irrigation Co. (1899).  Flood control projects on non-navigable tributaries have also been sustained as protecting navigable waters. Oklahoma *ex rel.* Phillips v. Guy F. Atkinson Co. (1941) (flood control was one of several stated purposes).

## B.  The Navigation Servitude

The navigation power should be distinguished from the navigation servitude.  The navigation power is the source of congressional authority to legislate on matters relating to navigation under the commerce clause;  the "navigation servitude," or rule of no compensation, is a much narrower concept that allows the federal government in special circumstances to regulate waterways and to adversely affect private rights without compensation.  Such circumstances may arise when the federal government destroys or removes privately-owned structures in or near waterways, or when federal dams flood land adjoining a waterway or destroy the water power value of a private power plant by raising the water level.  If the navigation servitude applies, the affected private rights may be taken without compensating the owners.

The Fifth Amendment to the Constitution prohibits taking of private property rights for a public use without just compensation, but regulatory interference with use of private property is allowed without compensation. Of course the regulation must be a proper exercise of a congressional power enumerated in the Constitution. Only when interference with property is severe enough to render it useless will the action be classified as a "taking." A notable exception to the compensation requirement arises when certain property rights in or on navigable waters are damaged or destroyed by the government in exercise of the navigation power.

## 1. Basis of the Navigation Servitude

Historically navigation has been an important public right. In England, the Crown held and could grant certain property rights in the beds of navigable waters. The rights granted were subordinate to the public right of free and unhindered passage of vessels for navigation, which was protected by the Crown; interference with the public right created a nuisance subject to abatement. The American colonies assumed the Crown's interests in waterways. The power to regulate commerce was then yielded to the United States government by the colonies in agreeing to the commerce clause of the Constitution, but ownership of the beds was not ceded. The federal government thus controls the navigable capacity of waterways, while states own the beds.

Some decisions have attempted to justify the navigation servitude on a "notice" theory. E.g., Union Bridge Co. v. United States (1907). Since investments in navigable waterways are made with knowledge of the paramount historical importance of navigation, it is argued that investors can have no reasonable expectation of compensation. The notice theory has some appeal in situations in which compensation is denied for removal or destruction of a structure that obstructs travel on a navigable waterway. But the cases go well beyond the rationale. Denial of compensation based on notice is less appropriate in the case of streams that have become "navigable" by broadening the definition of navigability or when land or other property is seized for use in a massive multipurpose federal project having only a nominal connection with navigation. The no compensation rule as now applied was criticized by the 1973 Report of the National Water Commission, which recommended legislation to provide for compensation in many navigation servitude cases.

## 2. *Extent of the Navigation Servitude*

Application of the navigation servitude depends on the location of the affected property and type of property rights involved. Ordinarily, the navigation servitude applies only to property located on (and property rights in) navigable streams. Takings of property on non-navigable tributaries must be compensated. United States v. Kansas City Life Insurance Co. (1950). The right of compensation can be defeated if the affected property is located on a non-navigable stream, however, only if Congress expressly states that its purpose is the improvement of navigation (and there is a reasonable relation to a navigation purpose). On a waterway subject to the navigation servitude the rule of no compensation extends only to the ordinary high water mark of the stream. Noncompensable property includes title to the streambed (including all land under the stream up to the ordinary high water mark) and structures within the stream. The servitude also limits the amount of compensation for certain types of property.

### a. Obstructions to Navigation

The earliest cases applying the navigation servitude concerned removal of obstructions to navigation, to which the public right of navigation most clearly applies. Obstructions typically were located in the stream itself or spanned the stream blocking passage of vessels.

The first navigation servitude case to reach the Supreme Court involved condemnation of a toll-collecting franchise on the Monongahela River. *Monongahela Navigation Co. v. United States* (1893). The taking was found compensable because the Court found the locks and dam had been constructed at the "implied invitation" of Congress. *Monongahela* has been repeatedly distinguished in later decisions as an estoppel case. It is uncertain what type of congressional "invitation" is sufficient to invoke estoppel, but more is required than, for example, issuance of a federal dredge and fill permit.

Subsequent cases dealing with obstructions to navigation held that obstructions are subject to the servitude. For instance, in Union Bridge Co. v. United States (1907) the government successfully utilized the 1899 Rivers and Harbors Act to force modifications of an obstructing bridge on the Allegheny River. Finding the loss noncompensable, the Court justified the servitude on a notice theory: the bridge company had built with the knowledge that the federal government might someday use its navigation power.

### b.  *Damage to Property in Navigable Waterway*

An early case, United States v. Lynah (1903), held that flood damage to land between a stream's low and high water marks caused by a federal dam was compensable. The decision, had it stood, might have given landowners on navigable streams a right to have the water level maintained in its natural condition. *Lynah* was overruled, however, by United States v. Chicago, Milwaukee, St. Paul & Pacific Railway (1941). That case held that the navigation servitude extends to lands on a navigable stream up to the ordinary high water mark— an average of the high water marks over all seasons.

Everything within the navigable waterway is subject to the navigation servitude; thus compensation has been denied for privately owned oyster beds destroyed by dredging Great South Bay in New York. Lewis Blue Point Oyster Cultivation Co. v. Briggs (1913).

## c. Project on Navigable Stream Causing Damage to Property Rights on Non-Navigable Tributaries

When water backs up behind a dam on a navigable stream, causing flooding or other damage to property on a non-navigable tributary, the damage is compensable, unless Congress expressly invokes the navigation power to protect the navigable capacity of the mainstream. In United States v. Cress (1917) a government dam on a navigable mainstream raised the water level in tributaries, flooded lands along the tributaries and destroyed the water power potential of a mill located on a tributary. The Supreme Court held the injuries compensable.

The *Cress* rule gives a landowner the right to maintain the tributary's stream level in its natural condition. The rule has been criticized because it makes the compensability of property turn upon its location: taking of property on a non-navigable tributary is compensable, yet an identical injury on a navigable stream is noncompensable under *Chicago*. The Court reaffirmed the *Cress* rule, however, by awarding compensation for destruction of a farm when the soil became saturated by flooding of an adjacent non-navigable tributary caused by a dam on the Mississippi River. United States v. Kansas City Life Insurance Co. (1950).

In United States v. Willow River Power Co. (1945), a dam on a navigable river raised water levels in both the mainstream and a tributary. This destroyed the water power value of a diversion through an artificial channel from a tributary into the mainstream. The Court denied compensation, finding that the affected property right was in the mainstream, not in the tributary as in *Cress*.

Flooding on a tributary, caused by a dam on the tributary, may be noncompensable if Congress has expressly applied the navigation power to the tributaries to protect the navigable capacity of the mainstream. United States v. Grand River Dam Auth. (1960).

### d. Waters Rendered Navigable by Private Effort

If waters formerly non-navigable are rendered navigable by private activity, the government must pay compensation to assure public access to the newly navigable waterway. In Kaiser Aetna v. United States (1979), a developer deepened a pond and converted it into a marina by opening a channel to the ocean. The pond was both "navigable in fact" after improvements, and navigable before improvements under the earlier "ebb and flow" test. The Army Corps of Engineers sought to obtain a public right of access to the pond as a navigable waterway. The Supreme Court held the navigation servitude inapplicable. Although present navigability was sufficient to invoke federal regulatory power (i.e., to prevent activities interfering with navigation), condemnation of private property was required to obtain public access. A companion case, Vaughn v. Vermilion Corp. (1979), applied the *Kaiser Aetna* reasoning to deny applicability of the servitude to a system of manmade canals in Louisiana that connect the Gulf of Mexico with an inland waterway.

## 3. Measure of Damages for Condemnation

The taking of uplands (lands above the ordinary high-water mark) is compensable even if they are located on a navigable stream. However, private rights that depend on the flow of a navigable stream are subject to the servitude and are noncompensable. Rights in the flow include water power value, rights to consumptive use and site value (i.e., value added to the land by proximity to the waterway).

### a. Value of Water Power

In United States v. Chandler-Dunbar Water Power Co. (1913), the United States condemned both a power plant located in the river and the adjacent uplands to preserve the navigability of the St. Mary's River in upper Michigan. The Court found the water power value attributable to rapids in the stream noncompensable, not only because the servitude allowed removal of structures from the river, but because the claimed water power right is a form of right to the streamflow. The Court dismissed as "inconceivable" the idea that rights to the flow of running water in a navigable stream are capable of private ownership subject to compensation.

## b. Site Value

Land adjacent to a waterway may be more valuable because of its usefulness as a hydroelectric power site, a recreational area, or a port or marina. When riparian lands above the ordinary high-water mark are condemned as part of a federal project the question arises whether the condemnation award should include the site value. United States v. Twin City Power Co. (1956) involved land along the navigable Savannah River acquired by a power company as a possible reservoir site. The power site value was approximately seven times the agricultural value of the land. The owner argued that the lands did not fall within the navigation servitude since they were located above the high-water mark. The Court rejected the argument, observing that the increment of value attributable to location on the stream is inherent in the flow of the stream, and is thus noncompensable under the rule of *Chandler-Dunbar*.

The decision in *Twin City Power Co.* does not modify the physical reach of the servitude, defined in *Kansas City Life Ins.*, as including only that part of the streambed bounded by the high-water mark. *Twin City* does, however, exclude from compensability the portion of the value of uplands attributable to the streamflow. Although uplands are clearly compensable, their value may only include suitability for non-riparian purposes such as agriculture or mining.

In United States v. Rands (1967), Rands owned land along the Columbia River in Oregon, which the state had an option to buy for use as a port site. The land, which was about five times as valuable as a port site than for the next most valuable uses (sand, gravel and agriculture), was taken by the United States as part of a comprehensive plan for development of the Columbia River. The Court held that special values such as port site value arising from access to a navigable waterway are subject to the navigation servitude, thus denying any compensation attributable to such values. In addition, it held that the increase in value of lands remaining in Rands' ownership because of its new riparian location was a benefit to be deducted from the amount of any compensable harm.

The rule of *Rands* could have very harsh results, as illustrated in an example provided by the late Dean Trelease. Suppose a tract of land is worth $10,000 regardless of proximity to the water, but location on the waterfront adds a value of $5,000 to the portion of land on the water. If the half of the tract on the water is taken and flooded, the condemnation award should be only the nonriparian value ($5,000), since port site value is not considered. But value is added to the remaining land because it is now on the waterfront ($5,000), which is to be deducted from the award. Consequently the owner receives no compensation for the flooding of the lost land.

Because of the absurd effect of the *Rands* rule,
pressure was brought to bear on Congress to expand compensability for condemned lands. In
1970, Congress passed § 111 of the Rivers and
Harbors Act, 33 U.S.C.A. § 595(a), providing that
compensation to be paid for real property taken for
a navigation improvement project is the fair market value of the property in its highest and best
use; the highest use may be based upon access to
or utilization of navigable waters. Thus an owner
can recover waterfront value of land taken. The
amount of actual recovery still must be reduced by
the enhanced value of uplands now located on the
water. In Trelease's hypothetical above, § 111
would give the landowner $10,000 for the flooded
land (port site value included), but $5,000 would be
deducted for appreciation of the remaining land for
a net compensation of $5,000. Section 111 also
limits compensability for depreciation of remaining
(uncondemned) land that results from loss of access
to navigable waters.

The rule that the value added to uplands by
proximity to a navigable stream is noncompensable
has also been judicially limited by allowing compensation if flowage easements are taken. A flowage easement is an interest in land that allows the
holder to flood the land of another. In United
States v. Virginia Elec. & Power Co. (1961), a
power company planned to construct a reservoir
for hydroelectric power purposes and bought a
flowage easement to allow it to flood the land of

another. The United States then decided to build a federal project on the same site. The power company conceded that potential hydropower value was noncompensable, but argued, and the Supreme Court agreed, that the flowage easement had other value not dependent upon streamflow. The Court's rationale was that the holder of a flowage easement has the right to destroy, by flooding, the value of the subservient fee. The fee owner, before sacrificing the use of the land for agriculture, timber or grazing, would charge the easement holder the value of those uses. Thus, the easement has ". . . a marketability roughly commensurate with the marketability of the subservient fee." The Court limited the award of damages by discounting the easement's value to reflect the possibility of its non-exercise, since a fee owner would sell a flowage easement for less if the holder of the easement were unable or unlikely to flood the land. The fact that the federal government had decided to build the project, however, was not to be included in the calculation of the "probability of the easement's exercise."

### c. Water Rights Created Under State Law

Federal power may come into conflict with state-created water rights in a number of ways. If water use is regulated by a proper exercise of congressional power, there is no right to compensation. If a water right is taken or totally destroyed, the right to compensation will depend on whether the water right was subject to the navigation servitude.

The United States may regulate water use to carry out federal legislative purposes. In United States v. Rio Grande Dam & Irrigation Co. (1899), the Supreme Court sustained the government's right to prevent exercise of state-created water rights in order to carry out federal legislation protecting the navigable capacity of streams, an exercise of regulatory authority and not a compensable taking. Congress may also authorize federal officials to distribute water from a federal project without regard to water rights priorities established under state law. See Arizona v. California (1963). The only question for a court is whether Congress intended to override, or preempt, state law.

When a federal project makes it necessary to take or destroy a state-created water right, compensation must be paid unless the purpose of the project is for navigation, in which case the rights are subject to the navigation servitude. In United States v. Gerlach Live Stock Co. (1950) farmers in California's Central Valley irrigated their grasslands with the seasonal overflow of the Sacramento River. As part of the massive Central Valley Project the government constructed Friant Dam, which eliminated the river's seasonal flooding thus depriving downstream landowners of the overflow. The government contended that the loss was noncompensable, since Congress had authorized the

Central Valley Project for the control of navigation. The Court said the project was in fact a reclamation project, not a navigation project, despite a general congressional declaration that the entire project was to improve navigation. Because the 1902 Reclamation Act expressed an intention that the federal government conform with state law in acquiring property for such projects, the water rights taken were held to be compensable.

## III.  FEDERAL WATER POWER PROJECTS

### A.  Congressional Power

#### 1.  *Federal Power Act and the Commerce Power*

The Federal Power Act of 1920 established a comprehensive national policy for hydroelectric power (hydropower) development. The Federal Power Commission, now the Federal Energy Regulatory Commission (FERC), was created as in independent agency to administer the Act. FERC has authority to license private hydropower facilities and to regulate interstate sale and transmission of electricity.

The Federal Power Act was the result of years of effort by conservationists, who had sought federal legislation to insure comprehensive nationwide water power planning. One objective was to reconcile conflicting uses (e.g., navigation, irrigation, recreation, wildlife preservation, hydropower and flood control) within the planning scheme.

The Act requires (in the absence of an existing, pre-1920 right-of-way) that a license be obtained from FERC for hydroelectric power facilities, including "dams, water conduits, reservoirs, powerhouses or other works incidental thereto," that cross, adjoin or are located in navigable waters, public lands or federal reservations. It also requires that permits be obtained for use of surplus water or water power from a government dam.

Facilities on non-navigable waters require licenses if the Commission finds the "interests of interstate or foreign commerce would be affected" by the proposed project. This language has led the courts to uphold broad extensions of the Commission's licensing jurisdiction. In Federal Power Commission v. Union Electric Co. (1965), a power company proposed to build a "pumped-storage" facility, in which water is pumped to a high reservoir, stored and then released to generate power during periods of peak demand. The Supreme Court sustained a Commission decision to require a license of the project because the power generated would be transmitted across state lines. The Court added that if the project was not properly operated timing of the flows of the downstream navigable portion of the river could be affected.

The Commission has declined to exercise jurisdiction in other situations in which electric power generation has a substantial effect on navigable waters and interstate commerce. Only if the project produces power by hydroelectric generation will the Commission require a license. The Supreme Court upheld the Commission's refusal to assert jurisdiction over several huge coal-fired power plants that would use large quantities of cooling water from the navigable Colorado River and would transmit power in interstate commerce throughout the Southwest. Chemehuevi Tribe v. Federal Power Comm'n (1975). The Court held that the plants were not "project works" requiring a license under the Act. Nor did they use "surplus water" from a federal dam. The Court held that Congress only intended to license hydroelectric power plants, not plants that burn fossil fuels to make steam for power generation.

## 2. The Defense Power

The Supreme Court has held that the defense power also gives Congress constitutional authority to construct a hydroelectric dam. Ashwander v. Tennessee Valley Auth. (1936). The dam in question was authorized under the 1916 National Defense Act to provide power to munitions plants. The defense power, said the Court, continued to apply to the peacetime operation of the plant, since the dam needed to be kept available for possible future defense uses.

## B. Conflict With State Law

Federal dams can dramatically affect the flow of streams, causing disruption of the normal allocative schemes of state law. Although conflicts usually involve water laws, other state laws for protection of fish habitat and the environment may also be affected. This is especially evident in states such as Oregon and Washington where anadromous fish (e.g., salmon) spawning migration patterns are obstructed by large federal dams.

The Federal Power Act has two provisions that appear to protect state law from federal encroachment. Section 9(b) requires license applicants to submit satisfactory evidence of compliance with state laws concerning hydropower development. Section 27 of the Act provides:

Nothing contained in this chapter shall be construed as affecting or intending to affect or in any way to interfere with the laws of the respective states relating to the control, appropriation, use, or distribution of water used in irrigation or for municipal or other uses, or any vested right acquired therein.

Both sections seem to preserve state law, but judicial interpretation has limited their effectiveness.

It has been held that § 9(b) does not give state governments a veto power over federal projects. First Iowa Hydro-Electric Coop. v. Federal Power Comm'n (1946). In *First Iowa*, a hydropower cooperative applied for a license to construct a dam on a tributary of the Iowa River. Although the dam would significantly reduce the flow of the river, the Commission granted the license. Iowa law required an additional permit, but compliance with both state and federal permit requirements appeared impossible. The Supreme Court held that to give the state a veto power over a project that may violate state law would frustrate the Act's purpose of comprehensive nationwide planning. The Court stated that § 9(b) is merely informational; if the Commission is itself satisfied with state law compliance, its decision is binding.

The *First Iowa* rule applies to situations involving exercises of the property power as well as the navigation power. In Federal Power Commission v. Oregon (the *Pelton Dam* case) (1955), the Supreme Court found Commission jurisdiction under the property power because a dam was to be located on federal reserved lands. It upheld granting a license to a private hydropower project on a non-navigable stream over objections of the State of Oregon that the fish population would be harmed.

Section 27 has been held merely a general provision that cannot override the specific provisions or overall purpose of the Act. It does require compensation to be paid if state-created rights are taken by eminent domain. Portland General Electric Co. v. Federal Power Comm'n (1964); Scenic Hudson Preservation Conference v. Federal Power Comm'n (1971), *cert. denied* (1972).

A hydropower license endows the licensee with certain preemptive powers of the federal government. In City of Tacoma v. Taxpayers (1958), the city applied for a license to build a dam on a tributary of the Columbia River. The State of Washington opposed the project because the reservoir behind the dam would flood a state fish hatchery and state law forbids municipalities from condemning state property, but the Commission granted the license. The Supreme Court held that the license delegated to the city federal eminent domain power necessary to condemn state property.

## C. Protection for Fish and Wildlife

Hydroelectric power generating facilities are especially disruptive to fish habitat and interrupt migration patterns. Columbia River harvests of salmon are now only about 8% of their size 100 years ago. The primary reason for destruction of anadromous fisheries has been construction of hydropower facilities on major rivers which obstruct upstream spawning migration.

Fluctuating flows also alter water temperatures and change the chemical composition of the water, endangering the migrating fish.

Several federal laws require considerations of fish and wildlife in planning water projects. The Federal Power Act requires the Federal Energy Regulatory Commission to find that a proposed project is "best adapted to a comprehensive plan" for water development for navigation, water power, "and for other beneficial public uses, including recreational purposes." 16 U.S.C.A. § 803(a). This includes consideration of the effects on anadromous fish. Udall v. Federal Power Comm'n (1967). A court will examine FERC's refusal to develop such a plan to determine if it can be supported by the record or is arbitrary and capricious. National Wildlife Fed'n v. Federal Energy Regulatory Comm'n (1986).

A number of federal environmental statutes require consideration of fish and wildlife values in projects constructed or licensed by the federal government. First, the National Environmental Policy Act (NEPA), 42 U.S.C.A. §§ 4331–44, requires preparation of an environmental impact statement identifying the environmental consequences of any proposal for a major federal action. Other sections of the Act require the government to use "all practicable means" to achieve environmental protection goals by planning, interdepartmental coordination and full consideration of environmental values in decisionmaking. Yet the courts have been reluctant to enforce any provision of NEPA except the environmental impact statement requirement. That provision at least provides some assurance that decisionmakers are aware of the environmental effects of their actions.

Second, the Fish and Wildlife Coordination Act, 16 U.S.C.A. §§ 661–666c, demands "equal consideration" for wildlife conservation in water resource development programs. The mandate appears to require parity between the values of the multiple purposes of water projects on one hand and fish and wildlife values on the other, although it is extremely difficult in practice to give meaning to such a requirement. The Act also requires coordination among the agency undertaking or permitting a project, the Fish and Wildlife Service, and relevant state fish and wildlife agencies before construction of a project to help assure protection of state interests in fish and wildlife.

A third federal act, the Pacific Northwest Electric Power Planning and Conservation Act, 16 U.S.C.A. § 839, is not really an "environmental" statute, but a comprehensive act for planning allocation of existing supplies of federally produced hydropower. The Act contains significant requirements for preserving and restoring anadromous fish resources in the region of the country hardest hit by the impacts of hydropower facilities. A regional council develops a plan for protection, mitigation and enhancement of fish and wildlife, and managers of federal power facilities are required to afford "equitable treatment" to fish and wildlife, insuring that their operations do not subordinate fish and wildlife to other project objectives. The Council's plans must be "tak[en] into account at each relevant stage" of FERC proceedings. See National Wildlife Fed'n v. Federal Energy Regulatory Comm'n (1986).

Another means of preventing federal (or private) water projects from adversely affecting fish and wildlife exists when Indian tribes have treaty fishing rights on the river in question. Interference with river flows by diversion, impounding or pollution of waters that damages fish habitat may reduce the ability of tribes to take a meaningful share of fish as guaranteed in their treaties. If the federal government is responsible for such actions (directly or by licensing) it may be liable in damages for violating federal treaty obligations. States similarly are obligated to consider the effects on Indian treaty rights of projects undertaken or authorized by them.

## IV. FEDERAL RECLAMATION PROJECTS

### A. Purposes

Congress sought to encourage settlement of the public domain by enacting legislation such as the Homestead Act to provide free or low cost land to settlers. Much western public land was too arid to be used without irrigation. Settlers seldom had the capital required to construct dams and diversion works, so support grew for an increased federal role in financing and construction of irrigation projects.

Originally "reclamation" referred to the process of draining swamps and marshes to make them useful for agriculture. The same word was later used for the process of converting desert lands to agriculture, typically by use of irrigation water supplied by a federal project. In 1902, Congress passed the Reclamation Act, which is still the basis of reclamation law. The Act established the Bureau of Reclamation as the agency to administer the reclamation program.

The original purpose of the 1902 Act was to provide water for irrigation, but legislation has expanded the purposes of reclamation projects to include hydropower, industrial and municipal uses. In 1911, the Secretary of the Interior was authorized to sell surplus waters for use outside project lands. Recreation, fish and wildlife protection, flood control and navigation benefits are often provided by reclamation projects. Early proposals for a reclamation program suggested it would be self-sustaining. But a changed political conception of the program, in light of the meager repayment abilities of project beneficiaries and a belief that the nation generally would be benefited, led to a program of substantial subsidies. In recent years, however, greater concern for economic efficiency of reclamation projects has given impetus to requirements for detailed feasibility studies involving cost-benefit analysis and for repayment of project costs.

Enactments subsequent to the Reclamation Act provided funding for specific projects. For instance, the Boulder Canyon Project Act, 43 U.S.C.A. § 617, passed in 1929, authorized construction of a series of dams (including Hoover Dam) on the Colorado River as part of a comprehensive development plan. The Small Projects Act, 43 U.S.C.A. §§ 422 et seq., provides for expedited approval and partial federal funding of small projects, provided that a local government entity secures necessary water rights, easements and land.

## B. Congressional Powers

Several constitutional bases exist for congressional involvement in reclamation projects. Early cases based congressional authority on the property power, under which Congress may pass laws for the management of federal property. Kansas v. Colorado (1907). The power to tax and spend to promote the general welfare is another basis. United States v. Gerlach Live Stock Co. (1950).

Once Congress has decided to proceed with a project by proper exercise of a constitutional power, it may use the federal eminent domain power for acquisition of lands for projects.

## C.  Limitations on Beneficiaries of Projects

### 1.  Background and Policy

Congress's purpose in allowing settlement on the public lands was to create a class of independent family farmers. It was frustrated by abuses that occurred during early disposition of the public domain. Wealthy speculators (e.g., railroads and timber interests) were able to aggregate vast tracts of public lands under their ownership or control, making extravagant profits.

The 1902 Reclamation Act included provisions to prevent speculation. Reclamation water was not to be used on more than 160 acres in single ownership and the user of the water had to be a bona fide resident on or near the land to prevent absentee owners from reaping the benefits of the reclamation subsidy. In addition, the reclamation program subsidy was limited by requiring recipients of project waters to pay back a portion of construction costs. Payment terms, however, were very lenient, including provisions for delaying or forgiving payment obligations.

## 2. *Acreage Limitation*

Section 5 of the 1902 Act prohibited the sale of reclamation water for lands in excess of 160 acres. The acreage limitation (or "excess land" provisions) gave rise to more controversy and evasion than any other part of the reclamation law. Abuses led to an attempt at reform in the Omnibus Adjustment Act of 1926. Section 46 of that Act provided that excess lands could not receive project water unless owners entered into a "recordable contract" with the Secretary agreeing to sell their land. Contracts typically gave the Secretary a power of attorney to sell the lands if the owner failed to sell them within ten years.

Acreage limitations were evaded by use of elaborate multiple ownership devices. Congress also provided a variety of exemptions for specific projects. The acreage ceiling was raised beyond 160 acres (480 acres, San Luis Valley Project), or the limitation removed altogether (Colorado-Big Thompson Project) on the rationale that since the lands were already irrigated, reclamation water is merely "supplemental" and the risk of speculation therefore diminished. Another type of exemption allows landowners to avoid the recordable contract (limitation of resale price) provisions by agreeing to pay interest charges for water delivered to excess lands (Washoe Project). Hardship for large landowners in the Imperial Irrigation District was avoided by a judicial interpretation. The Court held the district was effectively exempted by the Boulder Canyon Project Act. Bryant v. Yellen (1980).

The acreage limitation is less important since the 1982 Reclamation Reform Act increased the acreage that may be benefited from 160 to 960 acres, with an overall limit on ownership and leasing of 2080 acres. Excess lands are now subject to higher water charges.

### 3. Residency Requirement

Section 5 of the 1902 Act limited sales of reclamation water to bona fide residents on the land or in the neighborhood of the land (determined in 1910 regulations as a 50-mile radius). The Bureau maintained for a time that this residency requirement was abolished and superseded by the recordable-contract provisions of the 1926 Act. After a federal court ruled that the residency requirement was applicable, the Department of Interior proposed regulations in 1977 to enforce the requirement. The Interior regulations were never enforced. Finally in 1982 Congress removed the residency requirement.

## D.  Conflicts With State Water Law

Federal reclamation projects may come into conflict with a variety of state water laws (e.g., area-of-origin protection statutes or preference statutes). Like the Federal Power Act, the 1902 Reclamation Act contains state law savings provisions that appear to require federal compliance with state law. Section 8 provides that the Act is not to be construed as interfering with state laws "relating to the control, appropriation, use or distribution of water used in irrigation . . ., and the Secretary of the Interior, in carrying out the provisions of this Act, shall proceed in conformity with such laws . . ." Despite its broad language, the provision does not allow state law to override specific conflicting provisions of the reclamation law or legislation authorizing a particular project.

Until 1978 the Supreme Court interpreted § 8 to require observance of state law only to the extent of defining the property interest, if any, for which compensation must be made when a project is constructed. Still, no state law could prevent acquisition of rights for authorized purposes of a federal project or require distribution of water in conflict with those purposes. But in 1978 the Court announced a new and stricter standard for determining whether state law must be observed. In acquisition of water rights, the Secretary must decide whether state law permits appropriation or condemnation of water rights needed for the project. If state law would not allow acquisition of the rights, the Secretary should refuse to initiate the project absent further congressional directives. If the Secretary decides to proceed, state law must be followed. Once rights are acquired, water from the federal project must be distributed by the United States according to state law, except to the extent state law is directly in conflict with a provision of the federal reclamation law. California v. United States (1978). The Court disapproved statements in its earlier decisions that had read § 8 as requiring state water law to be observed in acquisition of water rights only to the extent that it defined water rights for which compensation must be paid, and denying that states could impose conditions on water delivery.

On remand the district court closely examined a variety of state permit conditions. Ultimately, they all were upheld, including a prohibition on consumptive uses designed to benefit fish and wildlife. United States v. California (1982).

The decision in *California* did not overrule earlier Supreme Court decisions recognizing extensive federal preemptive authority over state water laws in the operation of reclamation projects but it did narrow the interpretation of those decisions. The most important precedents were City of Fresno v. California (1963); Ivanhoe Irrigation Dist. v. Mc-Cracken (1958); and Arizona v. California (1963). In *Fresno* the city attempted to enforce state law preferences for domestic uses and uses in the watershed of origin. The Court said that § 8 did not require the Secretary to observe state law in direct conflict with § 9(c) of the Reclamation Act (giving preference to irrigation uses). *California* disapproved the Court's alternate ground—that under § 8 state law could not prevent the United States from exercising the power of eminent domain to acquire water rights.

In *Ivanhoe*, the Court held the 160-acre limitation in § 5 of the 1902 Act applicable to the Central Valley Project in spite of a state law doctrine imposing a public trust in favor of project water beneficiaries and requiring that adequate water be furnished to each regardless of the acreage they owned. The Supreme Court held that § 8 of the Reclamation Act did not override the express acreage limitation in § 5.

In Arizona v. California (1963) the Supreme Court held that provisions of the Boulder Canyon Project Act delegating discretion to the Secretary of the Interior to apportion project waters from the Colorado River were sufficient to override state water allocation laws. Although the Secretary might have been able to follow state law as prescribed by § 8, the Court found that Congress had not intended that he be so bridled in administration of project waters. It cited *Fresno* and *Ivanhoe* as standing for the proposition that the United States is not bound by § 8 of the Reclamation Act to follow state law priorities in the delivery of project water. In California v. United States (1982) the Court disavowed its Arizona v. California (1963) interpretation of *Fresno* and *Ivanhoe*, suggesting that the decision could have rested on a direct conflict between state priorities and the operation of the federal project, although in *Arizona* no actual conflicts were cited.

## V. ENVIRONMENTAL LEGISLATION

### A. The Clean Water Act

The Clean Water Act was passed in 1972 to replace ineffective state regulation of polluters with a comprehensive national system involving federal-state cooperation. 33 U.S.C.A. §§ 1251–1376 (Section numbers later in this section refer to the original legislation, not the code.) The goal of the Act was to eliminate discharge of pollutants by 1985 and to "restore and maintain the chemical, physical and biological integrity of the Nation's waters . . .," with an interim goal of swimmable, fishable waters by 1983. The Act allows enforcement by citizen suits, provides for monitoring and record-keeping, and subjects violations to criminal penalties and loss of government funding.

Pollution control standards under the Act are of two general types. Effluent standards limit the concentration of pollutants at the source; ambient water quality standards limit the concentration of pollutants in the stream. Because it is often difficult to identify the exact source of pollution in applying water quality standards, the Clean Water Act utilizes effluent standards based on available control technology.

### 1. NPDES Permitting System

Section 402 of the Act establishes an effluent permit system known as the National Pollutant Discharge Elimination System (NPDES). NPDES permits are required for discharge of pollutants from a point source into navigable waters. A "point source" is a pipe, ditch, tunnel, floating vessel, well, container, concentrated feedlot operation or other concentrated source of effluent, as distinguished from diffused sources such as runoff. The Act specifies that return flows from irrigated agriculture are not point sources.

To obtain an NPDES permit, the applicant must comply with EPA effluent standards. The effluent standards of § 301 originally required use of the best practicable technology currently available (BPT) by July 1, 1977, and use of the best available technology economically achievable (BAT) by July 1, 1983. The 1977 amendments to the Clean Water Act authorized extensions of the 1977 BPT deadline to as late as July 1, 1983, and of the 1983 BAT deadline to July 1, 1984. The amendments also created a new class of "conventional pollutants" (suspended solids, coliform bacteria, B.O.D. and acidity), for which best conventional control technology (BCT) must be used. 1987 amendments again extended deadlines for meeting certain standards. Special effluent standards are addressed to different types of sources (e.g., existing point sources (§§ 301 and 304) or new sources (§ 306)). Section 307 contains toxic effluent standards.

Effluent standards can be so stringent that they require new treatment techniques that are highly consumptive. For example, the least-cost method of meeting the standards may be to halt all discharges into the stream, allowing the effluent to run onto land and evaporate. In that case, downstream users would object to loss of return flows.

Dam construction may also require § 402 NPDES permits. Water discharged from dams is typically colder than the stream water, with a lower dissolved oxygen content and a higher concentration of sediment and dissolved metals. An EPA policy of not treating dams as point sources was unsuccessfully challenged in National Wildlife Fed'n v. Gorsuch (1982). It could be argued that § 402 requires permits for certain transbasin diversions; the terminus of the pipeline may be construed as a "point source" and the imported water may contain "pollutants" (material foreign to the region into which the water is imported).

## 2. Water Quality Standards

Administration of water quality standards is left to the states, which are free to impose stricter controls than are required by federal effluent limitations. Many states had adopted some form of ambient water quality standards before passage of the Clean Water Act. Congress authorized the states to continue to promulgate water quality standards, but if they are inadequate in light of conditions and uses of the waterway, the Environmental Protection Agency (EPA) may impose its own.

Section 303 requires states to identify "water quality-limited" segments of streams (those receiving such heavy discharges that effluent standards are inadequate to preserve water quality) and to establish "total maximum daily loads" for each, allocating among users the total allowable waste load. The Environmental Protection Agency may establish stricter effluent limits on point sources (as described below) if existing effluent limitations are inadequate to maintain ambient water quality (e.g., where streamflows are insufficient to dilute the effluent).

Because the § 402 NPDES permit process also requires compliance with water quality standards, new water uses that degrade water quality (either by adding pollutants or reducing dilutive capacity of the stream by depleting flows) must comply with § 303 of the Act providing for establishment of numerical water quality criteria (e.g., maximum dissolved solids concentrations). Ordinarily these criteria are set for each state. On the Colorado River, however, criteria limiting the river's salinity have been set by the states acting jointly to be measured at three dam sites. In Environmental Defense Fund v. Costle (1981), the court refused to force the EPA to adopt state-line standards for salinity when the states failed to do so.

### 3. Planning Requirements

Section 208 of the Clean Water Act provides for development of area-wide waste treatment management plans. Areas with waste treatment problems are designated and local agencies formed to develop and implement waste treatment plans to be enforced by local ordinances. Plans must identify necessary treatment facilities and include siting recommendations. The EPA has combined plan requirements of §§ 208 and 303 into single requirement for "water quality management plans." If a § 208 plan requires limits on siting, noncompliance may result in withholding of federal construction funds or § 402 NPDES permits. Downstream water users may be affected by enforcement of § 208 siting requirements if effluent from the treatment facility enters the stream at a lower point, depriving the water users of the effluent.

### 4. Non-point Source Controls

The largest cause of uncontrolled water pollution is from so-called "non-point" sources. These include diffused sources such as urban and irrigation runoff, surface mining and construction sites. They also include sources, like agricultural irrigation return flows, that are statutorily exempted from the definition of a point source. These sources have been left out of Clean Water Act controls because they are difficult to control or regulate. They are numerous and controls often are not cost-effective. In some cases such as agricultural sources control efforts encounter serious political opposition.

The § 208 management plans are required to include an identification of procedures for controlling diffuse sources by use of "best management practices." This requirement has been largely unsuccessful in motivating effective control on non-point sources. Absent more substantial directives states were reluctant to impose controls that might be costly to irrigators and could lead to limitations on water diversions. For instance, some water quality problems are caused by the amount and timing of diversions as well as the manner of use. Salts and other chemicals may pollute a stream because too much water is diverted and spread on the fields; diverting too much water may also cause pollutants in the stream to be concentrated. Limitations on diversions or use, however, are seen as contrary to property rights in water by some.

The 1987 Amendments to the Act required each state to develop a non-point source management program. If the program is not implemented there is no sanction except ineligibility for a sparsely funded program of related grants. Thus, control efforts remain essentially in the states.

## 5. Dredge and Fill Permits

Section 404 of the Clean Water Act requires dredge and fill permits from the Army Corps of Engineers for discharge of dredge and fill materials into waters of the United States. Section 404 has enormous reach because of the territory and types of activities that are encompassed and the federal requirements that can be imposed.

Jurisdiction extends not only to navigable waters but to tributaries and to any waterway involved in interstate commerce, including intrastate water-

ways used by interstate travellers for recreation.
United States v. Byrd (1979). The Corps' definition
of "wetlands" includes almost all waters and the
wetlands adjacent to them; it was upheld in United States v. Riverside Bayview Homes, Inc. (1985).
Thus, the areas regulated include thousands of
acres of public and private lands often far from
any river, that support plant growth typical of
wetlands (e.g., willow trees).

The scope of activities covered by the section is
far broader than dredging and filling and the controls imposed go beyond wetlands protection. Regulated activities include, for example, bridges,
dams, buildings, roads, flood control activities and
shellfish operations. There are exemptions for
"normal farming, silviculture and ranching" and
for irrigation and drainage ditches. But a new
dike and drainage system to enable bringing more
land into agriculture has been held to require a
§ 404 permit. United States v. Akers (1986).

Once an activity falls under the section the
Corps' considerations include "all relevant factors." Agency regulations list economics, cultural
concerns, energy needs, water supply and conservation and the needs and welfare of the people as
well as a variety of environmental factors. These
factors can lead the Corps to deny or condition a
permit. Once the Corps issues a permit it can be
reviewed and vetoed by the EPA. There does not
appear to be another environmental statute that

has such an extensive coverage and vests such far-reaching discretionary powers in federal officials.

Section 404 incorporates the full panoply of federal environmental law by requiring imposition of conditions to assure compliance with these laws in a permit for a project. Private permit applicants who otherwise would not be subject to many such laws thus must comply with the Fish and Wildlife Coordination Act, Endangered Species Act, Wild and Scenic Rivers Act, Coastal Zone Management Act, National Environmental Policy Act and other laws whose provisions were designed to regulate federal projects.

The Endangered Species Act (ESA) is one of the farthest-reaching environmental laws implicated by § 404. Section 7 of the ESA mandates preservation of endangered species habitat. The Corps typically relies on the biological opinion of the U.S. Fish and Wildlife Service to determine effects on habitat. Section 7 was invoked to deny a § 404 permit for Tellico Dam because the dam would affect the critical habitat of a tiny fish, the snail darter. Tennessee Valley Auth. v. Hill (1978). The snail darter case raised such controversy that amendments were passed exempting certain agency actions from Endangered Species Act requirements, provided that: 1) no reasonable and prudent alternatives to the agency action exist; 2) benefits of the action clearly outweigh benefits of actions consistent with preserving the endangered species; and 3) the action is of regional or national significance. If exemptions apply, however, applicants must use reasonable mitigation and enhancement measures (e.g., transplantation and habitat acquisition and improvement) necessary to minimize adverse effects.

The Corps of Engineers may use § 7 of the ESA as a basis for imposing conditions on § 404 permits. Thus, the court upheld a condition requiring releases of water from a proposed dam in Colorado to protect critical whooping crane habitat downstream in Nebraska in Riverside Irrigation Dist. v. Andrews (1985).

## 6. Wallop Amendment

Concern with the potential effect of the Clean Water Act upon water uses led to the inclusion of language assuring that established water rights were not to be defeated. The Wallop Amendment, § 101(g), is a statement of congressional policy that the Clean Water Act should not be construed to abrogate, supersede or impair state authority over water allocation or rights of states to water (e.g., under interstate compacts). The amendment's purpose, however, is not to prohibit "legitimate water quality measures" that affect individual water rights only "incidentally." See National Wildlife Fed'n v. Gorsuch (1982). Where necessary, this can result in curtailing depletions and consumptive use of water permitted under state water rights. Riverside Irrigation Dist. v. Andrews (1985).

## 7. *Effects on Common Law Remedies*

Section 505(e) of the Act says that it shall not restrict any statutory or common law rights to enforce effluent limitations "or to seek any other relief." Thus, remedies in nuisance and trespass may still be sought in state courts. Biddix v. Henredon Furniture Indus., Inc. (1985). Such actions may be brought by an affected party against a polluter in another state, but the suit must be judged by the law of the polluter's state. The Supreme Court has held that a contrary result would undermine the Act. It construed section 505 as allowing enforcement of additional state remedies only with respect to pollution occurring in the remedying state. International Paper Co. v. Ouellette (1987).

## B. Fish and Wildlife Coordination Act

The Fish and Wildlife Coordination Act requires federal agencies sponsoring or issuing permits for water projects to consult with the U.S. Fish and Wildlife Service "with a view to the conservation of wildlife resources," and requires mitigation measures to minimize adverse impacts. See Section III C of this chapter.

## C. Wild and Scenic Rivers Act

The purpose of the Wild and Scenic Rivers Act is to preserve in a free-flowing condition certain rivers possessing outstanding "scenic, recreational, geologic, fish and wildlife, historic, cultural, and other similar values . . . ." Congress may designate rivers, and states may recommend rivers for inclusion in the Wild and Scenic Rivers system subject to approval by the Secretary of the Interior. The Act provides for study of rivers by the Secretary of the Interior (or the Secretary of Agriculture if national forest lands are involved), who submits recommendations to Congress, along with recommendations of state and federal officials. As of October 1989, 112 rivers were included and 105 rivers were under study.

The Act prohibits the Federal Energy Regulatory Commission from licensing of water projects "on, or directly affecting" rivers included in the system and provides interim protection for rivers under study for inclusion by temporarily prohibiting project licensing on such rivers. There has been disagreement as to whether interim protections extend only to secretary-recommended rivers or to state-recommended rivers as well. In North Carolina v. Federal Power Commission, *cert. granted, vacated and remanded* (1976), the court held that state recommendation for study does not require a halt in the licensing process.

## VI. INTERNATIONAL TREATIES

Water from waterways or aquifers accessible to more than one country usually is of vital importance to all affected countries. Historically, upstream nations, including the United States, have insisted upon absolute control over waters originating in their territory. The doctrine of "absolute territorial sovereignty," however, has given way to the practical necessity of dealing amicably with neighboring nations. Today, the more flexible doctrines of limited territorial sovereignty and equitable apportionment generally govern the resolution of international water disputes, most often by means of treaties.

The United States is party to several water treaties with Canada including the 1909 Boundary Waters Treaty, the Lake of the Woods Treaty, the Saint Lawrence Treaty, and the Columbia River Treaty, and treaties with Mexico including the 1906 Irrigation Convention and the 1944 Colorado River Treaty. Once the federal government enters into a treaty with another nation it is the "Supreme Law of the Land;" under the Constitution any inconsistent state laws are preempted. Thus treaties affect the manner and extent to which state-defined rights may be exercised.

## A. Examples of International Treaties

### 1. *Mexico*

The Mexican Treaty of 1944 was an effort to end years of disagreement between the United States and Mexico over the waters of the Lower Colorado River. The United States as the upstream nation initially relied on the "Harmon Doctrine," based on a theory of absolute territorial sovereignty. However, pressures for Mexico to receive a share of water from the river grew as uses in Mexico increased. The 1922 Colorado River Compact had provided that the upper and lower basin states must contribute equally to supplying any future obligation to deliver water to Mexico. The United States finally decided to enter treaty negotiations, which involved not only Mexico and the U.S. but representatives of the Colorado River Basin states as well.

The treaty allocates to Mexico a guaranteed annual flow of 1.5 million acre feet a year of Colorado River water, to be reduced in the event of a serious drought in the U.S. The treaty is administered by an international commission.

The treaty with Mexico, signed in 1944, was concluded in haste and several troublesome ambiguities were glossed over by the negotiations. Most notably the treaty mentioned nothing about water quality. In 1944 there were sufficient excess flows in the river to minimize salinity and upstream development was comparatively sparse. The river's salinity increased, however, as more water was consumed and large dams and storage reservoirs were created; less water in the river meant greater evaporation from storage reservoirs and greater concentrations of salinity. In addition, irrigators added to the problem by returning waters with high concentrations of dissolved solids.

The salinity problem lay dormant until 1961. In that year the Wellton-Mohawk Irrigation District in Arizona began drainage pumping of extremely saline waters from beneath its lands, pouring those saline waters into the Colorado just north of Mexico. Mexico protested to the U.S. The U.S. and Mexico reached a series of interim agreements under which the U.S. consented to undertake salinity abatement measures. The final agreement, Minute 242 of the International Boundary Waters Commission, places a ceiling on the increase in the river's salinity once the waters pass Imperial Dam.

The federal government has to assume responsibility for meeting the salinity obligations of Minute 242. It is to be accomplished by federal salinity abatement projects such as bypassing the Wellton-Mohawk flows, a desalination plant and construction projects that reduce salt loading by physically isolating the river from various sources of salt. These federal projects are in effect an "insurance policy" against development constraints being imposed on the Colorado River basin states by the salinity obligation.

Many water problems with Mexico remain unsettled. For instance, there is currently no system for dividing transboundary groundwater. As unregulated pumping continues, border cities such as El Paso and Juarez find themselves competing for dwindling supplies. In addition, disposal of hazardous wastes may seriously affect groundwater quality. The problem was addressed in a recent agreement, Minute 261, which gave the International Boundary Waters Commission increased authority over water quality in the border region.

## 2. Canada

Canada is both an upstream and a downstream nation because the river system meanders in and out of the two countries. Canada threatened to divert Columbia River waters if the U.S. dammed its part of the river and invoked the doctrine of absolute territorial sovereignty.

Another issue concerned storage responsibilities of the two nations and Canada's right to share the benefits obtained by the U.S. from storage in Canada. Large-scale storage was most feasible in Canada, but Canada had no incentive to build storage facilities. Initially the U.S. simply offered to pay Canada compensation for any damages caused by flooding of Canadian lands behind storage dams. Canada instead sought a share of the far more valuable downstream benefits to the U.S. from storage, including increased hydroelectric power and protection from flood losses. After much debate over downstream benefit sharing, the two nations provided for an equal sharing of economic benefits in the Columbia River Treaty. The treaty specifies that Canada will provide 15.5 million acre feet of storage; the U.S. will operate dams to obtain maximum benefits from the Canadian storage; the U.S. may (for a price of $1.875 million per call plus hydropower losses) demand storage in emergencies despite Canadian hydropower needs; and Canada will not divert the Columbia River away from the U.S. into the Fraser River.

# B.  Supremacy of Treaties Over State Water Law

The U.S. Constitution, art. I, §§ 8 and 9, gives the President power to enter into treaties with the advice and consent of the Senate.  State water law is thus subservient to international treaties.  In Sanitary Dist. of Chicago v. United States (1925), the Court enjoined the City of Chicago from diverting water out of Lake Michigan because the diversions lowered the water level of the lake, and were in excess of amounts allowed under the 1909 Boundary Waters Treaty with Canada.

# CHAPTER TEN

# INTERSTATE ALLOCATION

Because state political boundaries generally do not correspond to the boundaries of river basins or aquifers, exercises of state police power often are inadequate to resolve disputes or to undertake desirable planning concerning water from a single source. Today there is a growing interdependence of regional interests as the national economy becomes more integrated and as technology and new uses (e.g., slurry pipelines) increase. Long-range planning for water development demands a reliable method of allocating interstate waters. Interstate disputes have been resolved by means of three mechanisms:

1. Judicial allocation (interstate litigation);

2. Compacts (agreement of parties); and

3. Legislative allocation (congressional apportionment).

## I. ADJUDICATION

### A. Litigation Between Private Parties

A typical interstate suit between private parties involves a downstream plaintiff alleging harm from diversions of an upstream defendant in another state. The court in which the suit is brought must have jurisdiction over both parties and subject matter.

## 1. Personal Jurisdiction

Personal jurisdiction is usually obtained by personal service upon the defendant within the defendant's state of residence. Long-arm statutes, however, have removed the necessity of bringing suit in the defendant's state.

## 2. Subject Matter Jurisdiction

Private parties generally bring suit in the state courts of defendant's or plaintiff's jurisdiction. Action may be brought in federal court if the suit meets the requirements of subject matter jurisdiction (i.e., diversity of citizenship and amount in controversy, or a federal question).

The ability of courts in one state to adjudicate water use in another state has been disputed. An early view of the problem was that, since a water right is a form of real property, an action to establish water rights is in the nature of a quiet title action; the suit must therefore be brought in the state where the real property is situated. Conant v. Deep Creek & Curlew Valley Irrigation Co. (1901). Other courts have adopted the more liberal view of jurisdiction that once a court obtains personal jurisdiction over a nonresident party, the decree need not operate directly upon the property; the court can enforce its decree by using the coercive effect of its contempt power. The Ninth Circuit used this personal-jurisdiction/coercion theory

in Brooks v. United States, *cert. denied* (1941).
*Brooks* involved water rights of Arizona and New
Mexico users on the Gila River. Defendants had
submitted to jurisdiction in Arizona and the court
was held to have exclusive jurisdiction to adjudicate the matter, although rights of water users in
the adjoining state had to be considered. Problems
of jurisdiction are magnified by the requirement
that in a general stream adjudication all affected
users on a stream must be joined. If the United
States has water rights on the stream, it too must
be joined; a federal statute waives sovereign immunity for this purpose. 43 U.S.C.A. § 666.

### 3. *Justiciability*

Article III, § 2 of the Constitution confines federal court jurisdiction to "cases and controversies."
Even if a court has both personal and subject
matter jurisdiction, it may decline to adjudicate
cases that are not "justiciable," that is, in a form
suited to judicial resolution. A suit may be rendered non-justiciable if it is moot, collusive, not
ripe or if the matter is a "political question" (i.e.,
would usurp executive or legislative authority).
The issue of justiciability usually arises in water
cases as a ripeness problem: e.g., there is no present "harm" to a downstream state claiming excessive use upstream, causing courts to find no "case
or controversy." Thus water rights for future development cannot be adjudicated. Further, the
Supreme Court has said it will issue no declaratory
decrees in interstate suits. The practical effect is

often to deny plaintiffs relief and to perpetuate unbalanced development on an interstate stream, since secure water rights are needed for investment financing and congressional authorization of water development projects.

## 4.  *Parens Patriae Suits*

A state may sue in its role of *parens patriae* to prevent harm to its citizens from actions of private parties in another state.  In civil actions by a state against citizens of another state, the Supreme Court has original, but not exclusive, jurisdiction; there is concurrent district court jurisdiction. States have standing to sue in their *parens patriae* capacity under certain limited conditions:  the state must have an interest independent of its individual citizens, so the suit is not merely an attempt to act on behalf of individuals; and a substantial portion of the state's inhabitants must be adversely affected.  This rule, expressed in Kansas v. Colorado (1907), usually requires that a substantial area of the downstream state must be affected by actions in an upstream state.  A state suing in *parens patriae* is deemed to represent all its citizens, and each citizen is bound by the decree. Thus, private suits are often foreclosed once the state's rights are adjudicated.  *Parens patriae* actions are further limited by the eleventh amendment, which states that "the judicial power of the United States shall not be construed to extend to any suit brought by citizens of one state against a state."  As interpreted by the Supreme Court, the amendment prevents a state from invoking the Court's original jurisdiction in a suit against another state seeking a remedy for an individual citizen (e.g., money damages) that would be prohibited in a suit brought directly by individuals.

## 5. *Enforcement*

Decrees in private interstate suits raise serious enforcement problems since continuing supervision and modification of decrees is often required. For instance, in Lindsey v. McClure (1943), the New Mexico State Engineer's attempt to forbid use of water from a New Mexico dam by users in Colorado was held invalid. The court stated that the proper enforcement remedy was by judicial procedure, not orders of the state engineer. In one case the United States Supreme Court upheld a federal court's enforcement of appropriation priorities across state lines. Bean v. Morris (1911).

## B. Litigation Between States

## 1. *Original Jurisdiction of Supreme Court*

The Supreme Court has original jurisdiction in all cases in which a state is a party. As with private interstate suits, the "case and controversy" requirement limits jurisdiction to "justiciable" controversies. In suits between states the Supreme Court serves as a trial court. Procedurally, the action begins with filing a complaint and hearings on motions (e.g., to dismiss). If the complaint survives the motions, the respondent state files an answer. Typically the Court appoints a special master to hear and evaluate evidence, prepare findings of fact and conclusions of law, and recommend a decree, which the Court is free to follow or disregard.

The decree in an adjudication between states is binding on all claimants to the water in question, whether or not they were parties to the suit. Private users have no rights in excess of the state's share of the stream because under the doctrine of *parens patriae* the state is deemed to represent all its citizens and each is bound by the decree. No private intervenors are permitted, unless the intervenor can show a compelling interest apart from that of a citizen of the state.

The Court has been reluctant to take jurisdiction in water allocation disputes, for a number of reasons, among them:

(1) The vagueness of standards of apportionment;

(2) The need for continuing supervision and the Court's disinclination to take on the role of "continuing referee;"

(3) The unmanageable mass of technical data introduced and the Court's lack of special expertise;

(4) The expense of litigation and of paying a special master (in the early 1960's litigation expense in Arizona v. California (1963) exceeded

fifty million dollars; special master's compensation was $185,000).

Even when it has taken jurisdiction, the Court suggested that interstate compacts can lead to superior solutions.

## 2.  Sources of Law:  The Doctrine of Equitable Apportionment

Federal common law is applied in a narrow class of cases where there is a significant federal policy or interest that will not be effectuated by the application of state law.  As such the courts have a unique role in fashioning the rules of decision in cases involving state boundaries or shared resources like interstate rivers.  The courts have developed considerable common law to resolve disputes over allocation and pollution of interstate rivers.  If Congress speaks to such matters the courts then decline to assert common law and defer to statutory law.  The Supreme Court had taken jurisdiction over a nuisance suit by two states charging Milwaukee with polluting Lake Michigan with sewer discharges.  Later, the Court found that federal common law had been displaced by the intervening enactment of amendments to the Clean Water Act by Congress.  Milwaukee v. Illinois (1981).  Thus, courts are cautious in applying federal common law so as not to invade prerogatives of Congress.  In only one instance has Congress entered the realm of interstate allocation of water sufficiently to displace the courts.  See Ari-

zona v. California (1963), discussed in section III of
this chapter.

The Supreme Court has developed a comprehensive federal common law doctrine for interstate
allocation of water by "equitable apportionment."
It was announced in 1907 in Kansas v. Colorado
(1907). A basic tenet of the doctrine is that "equality of right," not equality of amounts apportioned,
should govern. "Equality of right" simply means
that the states stand "on the same level," or "on
an equal plane, . . . in point of power and right,
under our constitutional system." The purpose of
the Court is to "achieve an equitable apportionment, without quibbling over formulas." Thus, the
Court will balance equities.

In a dispute between two appropriation states,
the Court has applied the appropriation doctrine as
the method of equitable apportionment. Wyoming
v. Colorado (1922). Application of the appropriation doctrine is, however, qualified in two ways.
First, the pure appropriation doctrine will not be
applied between states if protection of established
uses may be more equitable than strict priority.
Factors that might justify deviation from strict
priority include:

(1) Physical and climatic conditions;

(2) Consumptive use of water in the several
sections of the river;

(3) Character and rate of return flows;

(4) Extent of established uses and economies built on them;

(5) Availability of storage water;

(6) Practical effect of wasteful uses on downstream areas;

(7) Damage to upstream areas compared to the benefits to downstream areas of the limitation imposed on the former.

See Nebraska v. Wyoming (1945), *modified* (1953).

In Colorado v. New Mexico (1982), the Court refused to apply strict priorities between two appropriation states since the effect would have been to protect wasteful and inefficient downstream uses in New Mexico at the expense of newer, efficient uses in Colorado. The Court refused to allocate waters in this case to junior users in Colorado against the interests of the inefficient appropriators in New Mexico because Colorado lacked a concrete, long-term plan for future water use.

A second deviation from strict priority between appropriation states in an equitable apportionment may occur by use of the "mass allocation" approach. Since the Supreme Court is reluctant to interject itself into intrastate allocations, it awards to each state a quantity of water to be distributed by the state's appropriation system. The Court may hold that certain specific diversions are within one state's share of the allocation, that a state may have a stated quantity of water, or that a state may have a given percentage of the flow, regardless of the mix of individual priorities within the state.

## II.  FORMATION OF COMPACT

Interstate compacts are used to effectuate a variety of objectives by mutual agreement of two or more states. They have been used to allocate interstate waters twenty-two times, reaching agreement on an "equitable apportionment" that otherwise might have required Supreme Court adjudication. See State *ex rel.* Dyer v. Sims (1951) (Eight state compact to control pollution in the Ohio River.)

The availability of a judicial remedy encourages settlement of interstate disputes by compact. One great virtue of compacts over adjudication is that compacts avoid the justiciability problem when the stream system in question is not yet over-appropriated. The compact allows parties to allocate unappropriated water, thus making a "present appropriation for future use." Ability to make these determinations in advance is crucial to long range water project planning. Compacts relating to interstate waters are formed for a variety of purposes besides allocation of water, including storage, flood control, pollution control and comprehensive basin planning (principally by joint federal-state compacts).

## A. Constitutional Authority

The basis for negotiating interstate compacts is found in article I, § 10, clause 3 of the Constitution, which states:

No state shall, without the consent of Congress . . . enter into any agreement or compact with another state, or with a foreign power . . . ..

The compact clause impliedly recognizes state power to negotiate and enter into agreements subject to congressional consent. In Hinderlider v. La Plata River & Cherry Creek Ditch Co. (1938), the Supreme Court stated: "The compact . . . adapts to our Union of sovereign States the age-old treatymaking power of independent sovereign nations."

Typically, compact formation involves three steps. First, Congress authorizes negotiation of the compact, usually providing for a federal representative at the negotiations. Second, the compact is negotiated. Third, Congress consents to the compact.

Congress's consent determines whether the compact is a permissible agreement or a constitutionally prohibited "treaty, alliance, or confederation." Whether all interstate agreements require congressional consent is the subject of considerable debate. One view is that consent is required only for agreements that increase the political power of states, potentially upsetting the political balance of the union. Virginia v. Tennessee (1893). Others contend that consent is required for all interstate compacts, based on an implication in State *ex rel.* Dyer v. Sims (1951). There is general agreement that compacts allocating interstate waters require congressional consent.

## B. Administration and Enforcement of Compacts

Recent compacts uniformly call for creation of an administrative agency, typically a "compact commission," to make rules to carry out the compact and to collect information on physical circumstances (e.g., rate of river flow) for determining whether and to what extent the compact is applicable. The commission is usually comprised of members appointed by the governors of the party states and a federal member with no vote or only a tie-breaking vote. Generally states hesitate to vest substantial powers or prerogatives in a compact agency.

## C. Legal Effect of Compacts

### 1. Limitations on Private Water Users

Apportionments of water by compact are binding upon the citizens of the compacting states, whether or not individual citizens were parties to the negotiations. In Hinderlider v. La Plata River & Cherry Creek Ditch Co. (1938), New Mexico and Colorado had agreed to divide the flow of the La Plata River equally so each state would get the full flow of the river every other day. Plaintiff, a senior appropriator, sought to enjoin the rotation scheme as a violation of rights established under state law, but relief was denied.

The Court's rationale was that a water rights decree under state law cannot confer water rights in excess of the state's share of the waters. Although the state may choose to pay compensation, the Court found that no compensable taking of vested property rights had occurred under the compact terms. The Court in *Hinderlider* implied that, without evidence of some defect in the compact's formation, or of inequity or bad faith in the negotiations, no taking of a vested right had occurred, especially since plaintiff had ample opportunity to object during the negotiations.

## 2.  *Effect of Congressional Ratification*

State legislation that conflicts with terms of an interstate compact cannot prevent enforcement of the compact. State *ex rel.* Dyer v. Sims (1951). But there is some uncertainty over the extent to which Congress is bound by its ratification of compact terms. Congress retains power to override a compact provision by explicit legislation. Although it cannot modify the terms of an agreement between states, Congress might condition its ratification upon agreement of the states to modify the compact. Congress has power to authorize states to regulate and impose burdens on commerce that would otherwise be unconstitutional. State actions that interfere with interstate commerce are regularly held repugnant to the constitutional delegation to Congress of all power over commerce. Congressional consent to a compact has the effect of immunizing state legislation from attack as an interference with interstate commerce. Intake Water Co. v. Yellowstone River Compact Comm'n (1983), *aff'd* (1985), *cert. denied* (1986).

## D. Interpretation of Compacts

Whether federal courts have jurisdiction to interpret compacts depends upon whether the dispute "arises under the Constitution, laws, or treaties of the United States." Six federal district court cases have held that interstate compacts are not federal law, but the Ninth Circuit has found federal question jurisdiction to interpret interstate compact provisions. League to Save Lake Tahoe v. Tahoe Regional Planning Agency (1974), *cert. denied* (1975). The Court appeared to rest its conclusion on two bases: (1) that an interstate compact is a form of federal law, and (2) that the Supreme Court had twice granted certiorari to review state court decisions interpreting interstate compacts. The *Tahoe* decision is questionable because compacts are creatures of states and their interpretation is not a matter "arising under" federal law, although their validity may give rise to a federal question. The fact that state court decisions interpreting compacts qualify for Supreme Court review under the statute governing grants of certiorari is irrelevant to a determination of federal question jurisdiction. Under logic and the law the Supreme Court is the final arbiter of the meaning of compacts. It is, after all, the Supreme Court that has set the standard of equitable apportionment that most water allocation compacts pursue.

The Supreme Court made it clear in *Hinderlider* that to the extent compact provisions are based on equitable apportionment principles they will preempt contrary state laws. This raises the question of whether, in interpreting an interstate water compact, the Court will feel bound by the intentions of the parties. In one case, the Court refused to follow a Master's recommendation on how to resolve a compact commission deadlock over whether to follow an allocation procedure that was based on erroneous factual assumptions. The Court added that no court could interfere with the terms of a compact unless it is unconstitutional. Texas v. New Mexico (1983).

A particular problem of compact construction may arise when two compacts overlap in coverage of a particular basin. If the same parties are involved in both compacts, it may be reasonable for the later compact to control if there are inconsistencies. A more serious question is raised if different states are involved. Only a new compact with federal approval or a Supreme Court interpretation specifically addressing the problem of coverage can resolve the matter. Absent agreement among all relevant parties, the Court might appropriately employ its notions of equitable apportionment to the overlap problem.

## III.  LEGISLATIVE ALLOCATION

The lone example of legislative allocation of interstate waters concerns the Colorado River. The Supreme Court in Arizona v. California (1963) held that Congress, in passing the Boulder Canyon Project Act of 1928, intended to divide the waters of the river among the lower basin states. In so holding the Court recognized that Congress may act when the other apportionment mechanisms of compacts and judicial allocation have failed, are unavailable or are not used.

Southern California early experienced rapid economic growth and a large population influx. Extensive irrigation water uses (especially in the Imperial Valley) were also established. Arizona had experienced more gradual expansion, although the state anticipated future growth. Most Arizona uses were satisfied by pumping groundwater because geographical obstacles and lack of diversion facilities limited use of Colorado River water. Decline of Arizona water tables as a result of groundwater mining, however, made it clear that preserving the economy would eventually require resort to the waters of the Colorado. To do so, an elaborate diversion and transportation project was necessary. Later the Central Arizona Project was planned to bring Colorado River water to the more populated parts of the state.

A compact commission formed in 1921 allocated the Colorado's annual flow (assumed to be well over fifteen million acre feet (MAF)) equally between the upper basin states (Colorado, New Mexico, Utah and Wyoming) and the lower basin states (Arizona, California and Nevada). Ratification of the compact was stalled by a long-standing dispute between Arizona and California over their respective shares in the 7.5 MAF allocated to the lower basin. Arizona feared the compact would solidify California's claim to most of the water and refused to ratify it. Weary of the impasse, Congress enacted the Boulder Canyon Project Act in 1928, authorizing construction of Hoover Dam and a series of other storage reservoirs on the Colorado. It was opposed by Arizona. In return for Arizona's support of the project California had to agree to limit its allocation to 4.4 MAF plus half of any lower-basin surplus. The Act was conditioned on acceptance of the compact arrangement by at least six of the seven states; accordingly the compact was ratified without Arizona's agreement.

Arizona brought suit for an equitable apportionment of the waters of the lower Colorado, but the suit was dismissed in 1936 because the United States, an indispensable party, refused to be joined. Arizona v. California (1936). The U.S. later consented to suit, however, and after a three-year trial before a special master, 25,000 pages of testimony and 22 hours of argument before the Supreme Court, the decision was rendered. The Court held that:

(1) Congress may, under its navigation and general welfare powers, apportion interstate streams by legislation.

(2) By enacting the Boulder Canyon Project Act, Congress exercised its power in two ways:

   (a) Directly, by "apportioning" 4.4 MAF to California in the limitation provision;

   (b) Indirectly, by delegating to the Secretary of the Interior the power to contract for storage and delivery of project waters.

(3) Federal law controls both the interstate and intrastate distribution of project waters; preempting state water law. (Note the contrast to the mass allocation approach, which leaves intrastate allocation to state law.)

(4) The Secretary's water delivery contracts determined apportionment of lower basin waters. The contracts were for 4.4 MAF to California, 2.8 MAF to Arizona, and 300,000 acre feet to Nevada.

(5) The Secretary is empowered to allocate waters in times of shortage by any reasonable method, although "present perfected rights" must be satisfied.

(6) Water from Arizona's tributaries (1.75 MAF) is not part of the allocation to be shared with California, but is available to Arizona in addition to its allocation of 2.8 MAF.

*Arizona* raises several important issues concerning the scope of federal power over water resources allocation. See Chapter Nine. The opinion demonstrates that the Court prefers congressional allocations of interstate waters to playing the role of a trial court in complex litigation. The Court strained to find that federal power exists to allocate water among states and that the power had been exercised, even departing from its traditional insistence on equitable apportionment in deference to Congress's determination.

## IV.  STATE RESTRICTIONS ON WATER EXPORT

Until a 1982 Supreme Court decision, several states had statutes forbidding or limiting diversion or appropriation of water for out-of-state uses. The ostensible purpose of such statutes was to conserve scarce water resources by limiting nonresident access to local supplies. Since embargo statutes effectively block uses such as coal slurry and development of new municipal supplies, they may be challenged as unconstitutional burdens on interstate commerce. However, there were two apparently conflicting court decisions on the issue. Hudson County Water Co. v. McCarter (1908) (water is not an article of commerce); and City of Altus v. Carr (1966) (Texas law could not prohibit export of groundwater which, under other Texas law, is an article of commerce).

The commerce clause of the United States Constitution, art. I, sec. 8, cl. 3, empowers Congress to regulate commerce among the states. The Constitution does not explicitly limit the ability of states to burden commerce, but courts have found "negative implications" from the grant of commerce power to Congress. This doctrine forbids states from discriminating against or unreasonably burdening interstate commerce even if Congress has not legislated in the affected area. The doctrine is aimed at promoting free trade and preventing protectionism.

In evaluating state legislation for repugnance to the commerce clause courts consider whether:

(1) the statute discriminates against nonresidents;

(2) a legitimate state interest is present;

(3) the state interest outweighs any competing national interest;

(4) less burdensome alternatives are available to accomplish the state's purpose.

The test is essentially one of reasonableness of the state regulation in light of competing state and federal interests.

In Sporhase v. Nebraska *ex rel.* Douglas (1982), the Supreme Court held that Nebraska groundwater is an article of commerce and that a Nebraska statute restricting lawful water exports to states that allowed the reciprocal privilege of export to Nebraska was unconstitutional on its face.

Whether state statutes violate the commerce clause depends partly on whether the state has a strong interest in protecting its water resources. Arid western states, where water is scarce, have a strong conservation interest. The federal interest in free trade, along with other federal interests, will be weighed against such state interests. Only even-handed state restrictions that are equivalent to the state's efforts to protect water resources within the state will be upheld. In order for the court to find that there is no alternative less burdensome upon commerce than an embargo, a state would have to prove water scarcity and maximum efforts to deal with the problem by in-state conservation measures.

New Mexico has had difficulties preventing El Paso, Texas, from developing and using waters from an aquifer in New Mexico. The New Mexico statute banning interstate export of groundwater was unconstitutional. A revised statute was held constitutional insofar as it subjected exports to review under "conservation" and "public welfare" standards because public interest review applied to instate uses as well. But other provisions giving priority in the State Engineer's considerations to the interests of New Mexico citizens discriminated against interstate commerce. El Paso v. Reynolds (1984).

Colorado requires that any waters diverted into another state must be credited to the state's obligation to deliver water to the importing state under any applicable compact or other allocation. To the extent that this is seen as carrying out a congressionally approved allocation it should be upheld. Other devices to protect state interests may also be tried, such as comprehensive statewide water planning, economic pricing of water and innovative taxation schemes.

# CHAPTER ELEVEN

# WATER SERVICE AND SUPPLY ORGANIZATIONS

The water company or city water agency that provides water for domestic, municipal and industrial uses is the most widely known entity involved in supplying water. Most private water companies are investor owned; a few are "mutuals" owned by the water users. Water companies usually are public utilities regulated by a state agency. They, and not their customers, are holders of water rights. In the eastern states where riparian rights prevail it was necessary to pass special laws granting authority to companies and even to municipalities selling water to their residents to take water for use on non-riparian lands.

Although nearly everyone is served by a domestic water service utility, the most important organizations and agencies in terms of quantity of water distributed are those that supply agricultural irrigation water in the West. Many of them also supply water for municipal and industrial purposes.

The scarcity of available water was a barrier to settlement of the arid West. The first public lands utilized were near streams where water was readily accessible for mining and agriculture. The 1866

Mining Act validated the use of public land for building facilities to transport water to more distant lands, but construction and maintenance costs were a substantial obstacle. Crude, inefficient ditches were built to distribute irrigation water to river bottom lands, but the growing numbers of farmers soon exhausted the easily irrigable lands. For those unable to pay the cost of building their own ditches over considerable distances, the only feasible solution to bringing water to benchlands was cooperative effort. A main canal could be constructed with lateral ditches to distribute water to several farmers, and storage facilities assured availability of water during times of limited supply and high demand.

The Pueblo Indians and the Spanish speaking people of the Southwest provided early models for cooperative irrigation efforts, having used communal ditches to irrigate their lands for many years. Some of these ancient community ditches, known as *acequias*, still operate today in New Mexico. At first individualistic settlers were resistant to such cooperative efforts and many who were unwilling to organize sufficiently to build large facilities failed. The earliest settlers to accept and use cooperative methods were the Mormon pioneers in Utah; their strong social organization facilitated successful irrigated agriculture in the dry, inhospitable Utah Territory.

The early settlers' enterprises evolved into a variety of present organizations that deliver needed water. Water users' organizations can be divided into public and private entities. Private water distribution companies are for-profit ("carrier ditch companies" and water utilities) or non-profit ("mutual companies"). Private companies are usually organized as corporations, but may take other business forms. Few irrigation water supply organizations are totally private, for-profit companies today; most enjoy the benefits of tax exemption or other public subsidy. Public organizations can be roughly divided into regulatory bodies and water supply organizations. Regulatory bodies, such as groundwater management districts, engage in administration of water laws and conservation planning. Water supply organizations, such as irrigation and conservancy districts, are formed primarily to raise revenue for irrigation projects (by property taxation and bond sales) and to contract with the federal government to administer government-financed reclamation projects.

# I.  PRIVATE ORGANIZATIONS

## A.  Water Utilities

Water utilities are private companies having rights to take water and divert, store and distribute it to customers by means of owned facilities. They may be corporations, partnerships or sole proprietorships. The water is usually sold as a commodity, the company having reduced it to possession. Some western states (e.g., Colorado) consider the water to be property of the state and the company's charges to be for the service of water delivery. Water companies are made public utilities by statute in nearly every state. In exchange for an exclusive franchise or monopoly to serve an area, they are subjected to public regulation by a state commission, board or municipal government. Typical regulations require delivery of water to all within a defined service area, non-discrimination among users, and submission of major transactions (e.g., sale of assets, mergers, dissolutions, acquisitions) for approval. The most significant form of control is rate regulation. As with other types of utilities (e.g., electric, telephone, gas) rates are fixed to allow a reasonable profit. A consumer owns no water right as such, but has rights under state public utility law.

## B.  Mutual Water Companies

Mutual water companies exist to serve their shareholders. Some states regulate them as public utilities but most do not because as non-profit corporations or associations owned by the water users themselves regulation is less necessary. Mutuals are not usually permitted to sell water to other than their own shareholders, nor may they be compelled to do so. Water rights of a mutual company are generally owned by the shareholders themselves, the quantity of rights being evidenced by shares of stock. Much of the discussion below of mutual ditch companies applies to mutual water companies.

## C.  Carrier Ditch Companies

Private for-profit companies, known as carrier ditch companies, achieved an early popularity during settlement of the West.  Carrier ditch companies backed by profit-seeking investors financed construction of irrigation works to deliver water to which individual users held rights.  Nearly all such companies failed, either because of infeasibility or because projected uses did not materialize as farmers opted for "free" rainwater or groundwater or chose to do dry land farming rather than pay for water delivery.  Many of these companies were subsequently reorganized as irrigation districts or non-profit mutual ditch companies; investors recouped some of their money by selling out to these entities.  A few carrier ditch companies still operate in Arizona, Texas and elsewhere.

## D.  Mutual Ditch Companies

Formation of mutual ditch companies was authorized by special state laws as early as the 1860's.  Mutuals were formed in several ways, including: by holders of water rights who transferred their rights to the newly formed companies in exchange for stock; by joint owners of a ditch who traded their interests for stock, expanded the facilities and sold stock to others; by land developers who conveyed a share of stock along with each acre sold; and by local water users after bankruptcy of for-profit companies serving the area.  Because of the usual origin of the water rights of such companies, each shareholder remains the beneficial owner of a ratable portion of the company's rights. The greatest growth of mutual ditch companies occurred after western state constitutions (Colorado, Arizona, New Mexico, Utah and Wyoming) exempted ditches, canals and the associated works owned by mutuals from state property taxation.

Some mutual ditch companies were formed to contract with the federal government for reclamation project water, and are still in operation for that purpose. Now, however, this purpose is most often served by irrigation districts, as described below.

### E.  Irrigation Companies

Irrigation companies provided a means for organizing water users, usually as corporations, to finance and maintain facilities to transport, store and distribute water to shareholders. Irrigation companies that are non-profit organizations may be exempt from both state and federal income taxes but they are subject to the Fair Labor Standards Act and to unemployment compensation laws.

A number of private irrigation corporations were formed under the 1894 Carey Act, 43 U.S.C.A. § 641, which awarded one million acres of arid federal lands to any western state that would cause the land to be irrigated and settled. Often this was done by encouraging formation of companies to build irrigation works. The lands were then sold by the state to individuals who bought shares

in a mutual ditch or irrigation company created by
the contractor to operate the irrigation works.
Like carrier companies, many Carey Act corporations failed because they could not repay capital
costs; some reorganized as irrigation districts.

## 1. *Financing*

Irrigation companies secure revenue almost ex-
clusively from water users (i.e., by user fees and
stock assessments), but some issue bonds secured
by irrigation works or shareholders' lands. Assessments of stock (to pay operating costs and bond
amortization) may be enforced by withholding
water for nonpayment. Henderson v. Kirby Ditch
Co. (1962).

## 2. *Ownership of Rights*

Irrigation companies typically issue shares of
stock that represent the quantum of the shareholder's right to receive water. The company holds
legal title to the water rights and represents its
users against other appropriators, such as in conflicts with other ditch companies. But each shareholder is beneficial owner of the individual water
rights in the appropriation evidenced by the shares
(contra, Texas). Jacobucci v. District Court (1975)
(shareholders in a mutual ditch company are real
parties in interest and should be joined in an
action to condemn water rights of the company,
although company holds legal title). Courts will
protect private water rights of shareholders
against abuses by the company.

### 3. Transfers

Holding water rights as shares of ditch company stock facilitates transfers. Stock issuance must comply with federal securities laws and state blue-sky laws. Stock is commonly considered appurtenant to (and thus passes with) land which is described on the face of the stock certificate. The Uniform Stock Transfer Act provides that transfer of title to shares requires either personal delivery by the owner or a written power of attorney, but in fact no paper shares exist in some small companies because "shares" simply pass with the land. Presumptions may be imposed by statute. For example, a Utah statute provides that water company stock does not pass with the land without an express declaration by the transferor that the stock is appurtenant. To protect the company against having to make uneconomical water deliveries to distant users, shares may be made inseverably appurtenant to land by provisions in the articles of incorporation or by-laws.

State laws relating to transfers of water rights may also apply. And the company itself may restrict transferability (e.g., by requiring the company's consent, Riverside Land Co. v. Jarvis (1917)). California has recognized the right of companies to prohibit transfers to another ditch, Consolidated People's Ditch Co. v. Foothill Ditch Co. (1928), but Colorado has allowed transfers if the transferor continues to bear a proper share of maintenance costs. Wadsworth Ditch Co. v. Brown

(1907). If a change in the place or type of use results in harm to others, however, the transfer may be restricted. See City of Boulder v. Boulder and Left Hand Ditch Co. (1976); Chapter Three, Section IX.

### 4. Priorities

As a rule no priorities exist among shareholders with a proportionate interest in the same water supply even when supply is insufficient for all users. But if users conveyed rights to a mutual company with different priority dates the company can issue different classes of stock related to the priorities. The different classes of shareholders may be subject to different burdens and privileges. Thus, a holder of shares evidencing a high priority may be assessed at a higher rate because the high priority confers greater benefits.

### 5. Regulation

A company may be treated as a public utility subject to regulation. This usually results if water service is provided to other than shareholders. E.g., Yucaipa Water Co. No. 1 v. Public Utilities Comm'n (1960) (company delivered water to lessees of shares of stock).

## II.  PUBLIC ORGANIZATIONS

### A.  Regulatory and Planning Bodies

Some public entities regulate present water uses while others plan for future uses. For example, the Colorado Water Quality Control Commission promulgates water quality standards under the Colorado Water Pollution Control Act, and administers water pollution control assisted by the state Attorney General's office. The Water Conservation Board engages in joint federal-state water project and water use planning, and is involved in the financing of public and private irrigation projects. The Groundwater Commission determines rights and regulates water use in designated groundwater basins. Within designated basins, groundwater management districts may be formed (having both use-regulation and taxing powers) to assist the Groundwater Commission in regulating groundwater use. Types and activities of such regulatory bodies vary from state to state.

## B. Municipalities

Laws of most states recognize the authority of cities to distribute water to their residents. State statutes or constitutions often authorize municipalities to avoid certain restraints in water law in carrying out their water service responsibilities. For example, they may allow municipalities (which are not riparians) to obtain and use rights to water on non-riparian lands. And in appropriation jurisdictions municipalities may be able to appropriate water in ways and for purposes not available to other users. Thorton v. Farmers Reservoir & Irrigation Co. (1978) (even state legislation could not limit city's constitutional powers by restricting condemnation of water rights to those needed for 15 years in the future).

A municipality that serves its citizens generally may be considered a public utility subject to regulation.   Under most state laws, however, they may serve consumers, including those beyond municipal boundaries, without becoming subject to regulation as public utilities.   Board of County Comm'rs of Arapahoe County v. Denver Bd. of Water Comm'rs (1986) (city is a public utility but is statutorily exempt from Public Utilities Commission regulation).   Municipalities do not have a duty to serve consumers outside their boundaries, however. Fulghum v. Town of Selma (1953).   But if they regularly do so, they probably will be required to provide service in a non-discriminatory manner. See Robinson v. City of Boulder (1976) (city held itself out as ready to serve all members of the public in the area to the extent of its capacity). This does not mean the same rates must be charged.

## C.  Irrigation Districts

Irrigation districts exist under several names, including conservancy district, conservation district, reclamation district, water control district and fresh water supply district.   Although they have many different organizational forms and powers, the distribution of irrigation water is common to each.   Some perform functions such as electric power generation, drainage and flood control.   Irrigation districts are formed under special provisions of state law and enjoy a governmental or quasi-governmental status; yet most have a certain degree of autonomy exempting them from much public accountability. Irrigation districts distribute about half of all water used in the West, giving them economic power. Many also have lobbying organizations and political influence.

## 1. Formation of Districts

Beginning with California's Wright Act in 1887 all western states passed laws authorizing formation of irrigation districts. The statutes define the organizational form, powers and purposes of the districts. Typically they provide for formation upon petition of local landowners or electors. The petition sometimes can be acted upon by a state court after hearing; often an election is required. Some types of districts in some states may be formed by act of the legislature without voter or landowner consent. Reluctant property owners can be forced to participate in projects for the benefit of an area that are feasible only with full participation. Objecting landowners have been uniformly unsuccessful in challenging formation of districts. E.g., People *ex rel.* Rogers v. Letford (1938) (inclusion and taxation of nonirrigable lands within incorporated cities, with an adequate water supply, did not violate due process clause); *In re* Reno Press Brick Co. (1937).

## 2.  Benefits of Districts

Possessing power to levy assessments against all property within their boundaries, irrigation districts provided an effective way to finance irrigation works.  They helped solve problems of capital formation that had beset agriculture in much of the arid West.  A significant motive for forming irrigation districts was to take advantage of benefits such as tax exemption and the ability to raise capital by selling tax exempt bonds.

The most powerful motive behind creation of most irrigation districts was to provide a vehicle for participation in federal reclamation projects.  The federal reclamation program began around the turn of the century and has subsidized water projects benefiting much of the irrigated agriculture of the western United States.  See Chapter Nine, Section IV.  At first the government intended to operate the projects directly, but since 1922 it has been authorized to contract with irrigation districts to manage, operate and maintain federal projects upon their completion and to distribute the water from them.  The districts usually must agree to repay project costs directly attributable to irrigation benefits, which is accomplished by use of their assessment authority and user charges.

## 3.  Ownership of Water Rights

Irrigation districts, not their constituents, own the water rights they exercise.  The users' rights are essentially contractual.  The Supreme Court, however, has construed a quirk in California law to vest the water right in the individual users. Bryant v. Yellen (1980). The California Supreme Court stated that users within a district are actually beneficial owners of the district's water rights and the district, as legal owner of the rights, holds them in trust for the users. The Supreme Court found that a provision in the Boulder Canyon Project Act requiring satisfaction of "present perfected rights" meant that the Reclamation Act's 160 acre limitation could not apply to individuals who had been served with water before the Act. Thus it assumed that the users, not the district, owned the rights.

## 4. Election of Boards

Board members of irrigation districts are usually elected. Some types of districts in some states (e.g., "conservancy districts" in Colorado) provide for their appointment. The right to vote in a district election may be in each elector, each landowner, or weighted according to the amount of acreage owned. Irrigation district voting has been held not subject to the one-person, one-vote principle established under the equal protection clause of the fourteenth amendment to the Constitution. Ball v. James (1981). In *Ball*, a multipurpose district limited voting privileges to landowners and allowed one vote per acre of owned land. Plaintiffs, each owning less than an acre of land, alleged that the district's broad powers (to condemn property and sell tax-exempt bonds) and its nonirrigation purposes (providing hydroelectric power to metropolitan Phoenix) affected non-landowning voters sufficiently to require that they be given voting rights. The Court disagreed, following the rule of Salyer Land Co. v. Tulare Lake Basin Water Storage District (1973) that certain districts may limit the voting franchise to landowners. If a district has a limited purpose and its activities disproportionately affect landowners, the Court in *Ball* said, the voting limitation bears the required "reasonable relationship" to statutory objectives. As a result, a few large landowners control all decisionmaking in many districts.

## 5. *Financial Aspects*

Irrigation districts may be empowered to raise revenues by assessing property, imposing taxes, charging users for water and furnishing other services. Revenue raising powers of districts depend on the state laws that authorize their creation. For instance, in Colorado "conservancy districts" may tax all lands in their boundaries, but "irrigation districts" are limited to taxing irrigable lands. It is not necessary that taxes be in proportion to the benefits received. Millis v. Board of County Comm'rs of Larimer County (1981). State laws may allow assessments to be levied upon all land in a district based upon the value of the land or upon land classifications (e.g., tract size or type of soil). Some districts impose a flat assessment for each acre of land. Others assess different classes of stock at different rates. Robinson v. Booth-

Orchard Grove Ditch Co. (1934). Bonds may be issued by virtually all irrigation districts; it is this governmental authority that led to formation of most early districts. Sullivan v. Blakesley (1926).

User fees are sometimes charged for water actually used. These charges may be in addition to taxes and assessments.

## 6.  *Functions*

Irrigation districts began as rather simple organizations whose sole purpose was to deliver irrigation water, but today many districts are involved in other activities such as hydroelectric power generation, operation of recreation facilities, drainage, flood control, sanitation, and municipal and industrial water supply. An example is the Salt River Project Agricultural Improvement and Power District, serving metropolitan Phoenix, Arizona, which derives ninety-eight percent of its total revenue from power sales. Multiple purposes complicate administration of irrigation districts and may lead to conflicts among different constituencies, however. Irrigation users may feel with some justification that their interests are subordinated in disregard of the original legislative purpose of creating irrigation districts.

Although irrigation districts are commonly spoken of as "political subdivisions of state government," they have both public and private attributes, enjoying many benefits of both. Their public character gives them tax-exempt status, the power

to tax and freedom from regulatory agency interference, yet their private character allows retention of centralized control. The Supreme Court in
*Ball*, supra, recognized that the Salt River Project
Agricultural Improvement and Power District was
a "governmental entity," but also was a "business
enterprise" in its dealings with power consumers.
As the federal government's willingness to finance
costly reclamation projects declines and the functions of irrigation districts move farther from their
original purposes, many state legislatures may
reappraise the place of the districts in political and
economic life.

### D.  Municipal Water Districts

Some states authorize creation of several special
types of districts that deal with problems of procur-
ing water supply not necessarily related to irrigation. They are akin to "irrigation districts" that
develop and transport water and then distribute it
to a number of water companies, municipalities
and large consumers. California has passed enabling legislation for the creation of special districts
known as municipal water districts and replenish-
ment districts to manage imported surface waters
and local groundwater resources by administering
rights determined in basin-wide adjudications, controlling pumping to safe annual yield rates, importing supplies and preventing salt water intrusion.
See Chapter Six, Section III B.

*

# INDEX

### References are to Pages

437

**CLEAN WATER ACT—Cont'd**
Purpose, 381
Wallop Amendment, 389

**CLOUD–SEEDING**
Rights in precipitation, 112, 305

**COLORADO DOCTRINE**
See Prior Appropriation

**COLORADO RIVER**
Boulder Canyon Project Act, 350, 374, 380, 412–415
Compact of 1922, pp. 412–413
Legislative apportionment, 412–415
Mexican Treaty of 1944, pp. 392–394
Reserved rights,
    Federal, 311–315, 322–323, 332–333
    Indian, 311, 322–323
Salinity, 384, 392–394
Transbasin diversions, 162

**COMMERCE CLAUSE**
    See also Marketing Water
Federal Power Act, 365
Interstate exports, 416–418
Navigation, 219, 349–352
Reserved rights, 314
Water as article of Commerce, 83–84

**DAMS**
See Federal Power Act; Reclamation Act; Storage

**DESERT LAND ACT OF 1877**
Prior appropriation recognized, 20–21, 80, 194–197, 315
Text, 196

**DIFFUSED SURFACE WATER**
    Generally, 9–10, 291
Capture of, 303–304
Damage from surface flows, 293–295
Defined, 293
Drainage projects, 300–302

**PRIOR APPROPRIATION**—Cont'd
  Impediments, 102
  Interstate, 415–418
  Severed from land, 159–160
  Stock in ditch or irrigation companies, 426–427
  Transbasin diversion, 111–114, 160–163, 383
Waste,
  See Beneficial Use; Efficiency, Inefficiencies, this topic
Waters subject to,
            See also, Public "ownership" and state police pow-
              er, this topic
  Generally, 106–107
  Foreign waters, 111–114
  Groundwater, 240, 247–251, 252–254, 267–273, 278–285
  Instream flows, 116–119
  Lakes and ponds, 110–111
  Reserved rights, 117–119, 316–317, 322–324
     See also, Reserved Rights
  Salvaged water, 114–115, 134
  Springs, 111
  Streams, 108–110
  Tributary water,
     See Groundwater, this topic
  Watercourses, 107–111
  Waters withdrawn from appropriation, 115–120


**PUBLIC LANDS**
  See also, Reserved Rights
Acquisition of water rights, 311–313, 315–319, 345–346
Appropriation doctrine, 19–21, 77–80, 181–182, 194–202
Rights of way, 181–182


**PUBLIC RIGHTS**
            See also, Prior Appropriation, Permits, Public "owner-
              ship" and state police power, and Surface Use
  Generally, 10
Groundwater, 251–252
Navigable waters, 45–46, 223–224
Non-navigable waters, 225–228, 232–234
State laws, 84–85

†